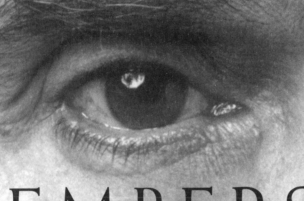

ERIC ABRAHAM & ROBERT HAGGIAG
present

JEREMY IRONS
PATRICK MALAHIDE

EMBERS
by CHRISTOPHER HAMPTON

with
JEAN BOHT

Based on the novel by
SÁNDOR MÁRAI

Directed by
MICHAEL BLAKEMORE

STRICTLY LIMITED SEASON

DUKE OF YORK'S THEATRE
St Martin's Lane, London WC2

0870 060 6623 bkg fee applies
www.emberstheplay.com

GRANTA

GRANTA 93, SPRING 2006
www.granta.com

EDITOR   *Ian Jack*
DEPUTY EDITOR   *Matt Weiland*
MANAGING EDITOR   *Fatema Ahmed*
ASSOCIATE EDITOR   *Liz Jobey*
EDITORIAL ASSISTANT   *Helen Gordon*

CONTRIBUTING EDITORS   *Diana Athill, Sophie Harrison, Gail Lynch, Blake Morrison, John Ryle, Sukhdev Sandhu, Lucretia Stewart*

ASSOCIATE PUBLISHER   *Sally Lewis*
FINANCE   *Geoffrey Gordon, Morgan Graver*
SALES DIRECTOR   *Frances Hollingdale*
PUBLICITY   *Louise Campbell*
SUBSCRIPTIONS   *John Kirkby, Julie Codling*
PUBLISHING ASSISTANT   *Mark Williams*
TO ADVERTISE CONTACT   *Kate Rochester*
PRODUCTION ASSOCIATE   *Sarah Wasley*

PUBLISHER   *Sigrid Rausing*

GRANTA PUBLICATIONS, 2-3 Hanover Yard, Noel Road, London N1 8BE
Tel +44 (0)20 7704 9776 Fax +44 (0)20 7704 0474
e-mail for editorial: editorial@granta.com

Granta, 2–3 Hanover Yard, Noel Road, London N1 8BE
Tel 020 7704 9776 Fax 020 7704 0474
email for editorial: editorial@granta.com

In the United States, Granta is published in association with Grove/Atlantic Inc, 4th Floor, 841 Broadway, New York, NY 1003

TO SUBSCRIBE call 020 7704 0470 or e-mail subs@granta.com
A one-year subscription (four issues) costs £27.95 (UK), £35.95 (rest of Europe) and £42.95 (rest of the world).

Granta is printed and bound in Italy by Legoprint. The paper used in this publication meets the minimum requirements of American National Standard for Information Sciences—Permanence of Paper for Printed Library Materials, ANSI Z39.48-1984.

Design: Slab Media
Front cover photograph: Photonica/Getty
Back cover photographs: David Graham

ISBN 0-903141-84-1

A NIGHT AT THE MAJESTIC

JOYCE

PICASSO

PROUST

PROUST AND THE
GREAT MODERNIST
DINNER PARTY
OF 1922

DIAGHILEV

STRAVINSKY

RICHARD DAVENPORT-HINES

THE EXTRAORDINARY TRUE STORY, OUT NOW FROM FABER

GOD'S OWN COUNTRIES

National Portrait Gallery

1856·2006

2 March –
29 May 2006

Open 10.00-18.00
Thursdays & Fridays
until 21.00

Tickets £8
£5.25 concessions

Advance booking
recommended
0870 013 0703
(transaction fee applie

St Martin's Place
⊖ Leicester Square
www.npg.org.uk

150 Years
Collecting for the Future

Anniversary Partner
Herbert Smith

Anniversary Media Partners

THE SUNDAY TIMES

THE TIMES

Searching for
Shakespeare

Exhibition sponsor
CREDIT SUISSE

William Shakespeare?, known as the Chandos portrait (detail)
attributed to John Taylor, c.1600-10
© National Portrait Gallery, London

CONTRIBUTORS

Nadeem Aslam was born in Pakistan and now lives in England. He is the author of the novels *Season of the Rainbirds* (Faber/Abacus) and *Maps for Lost Lovers* (Faber/Vintage).

Diana Athill's books include the memoirs *Yesterday Morning* (Granta Books) and *Stet: An Editor's Life* (Granta/Grove Atlantic). For fifty years she was the editorial directer of André Deutsch, where her authors included Jean Rhys, Gitta Sereny and V. S. Naipaul. She lives in London.

Kees Beekmans worked for ten years as a teacher in Amsterdam. 'Tales out of School' is a translation from his recent book *Een Hand Kan Niet Klapt* (One Hand Can't Clap) which is published by Het Spectrum in the Netherlands.

John Borneman works on political anthropology in Europe, the United States, and the Middle East. 'Kiss Daddy!' is taken from his book, *Syrian Encounters*, to be published later this year by Princeton University Press.

Andrew Brown writes for the London *Guardian*. He lived in Sweden as a child in the late Sixties, and as an adult from 1977 until 1984. His most recent book is *In the Beginning Was the Worm* (Pocket Books/Columbia University Press). He is working on a book about Sweden and the future that disappeared.

Geoff Dyer's most recent book is *The Ongoing Moment* (Abacus/Pantheon), a sort of history of photography. His story, 'White Sands', appeared in *Granta* 91.

Maureen Freely was born in New Jersey and grew up in Istanbul. She is the author of five novels and three works of non-fiction. Her translations of Orhan Pamuk's novels *Snow* and *The Black Book,* and of his memoir, *Istanbul,* are published by Faber. She lectures at the University of Warwick and lives in Bath.

Nell Freudenberger's short-story collection is entitled *Lucky Girls* (Picador/Ecco Press). Her story, 'The Tutor', appeared in *Granta* 82. Her first novel, *Dissidents*, is to be published by Ecco Press. She lives in New York.

David Graham is based in London. He is a former businessman who became a professional documentary photographer following a spinal accident to his son.

Simon Gray is a playwright, diarist and smoker. Two volumes of his memoirs, *The Smoking Diaries* and *The Year of the Jouncer*, are published by Granta Books.

Jackie Kay's 'The Lord in His Wisdom' is taken from her memoir-in-progress. Her new collection of short stories, *Wish I Was Here,* will be published by Picador in June 2006. She was brought up in Glasgow and lives in Manchester.

A. L. Kennedy was born in north-east Scotland. Her most recent novel is *Paradise* (Vintage/Vintage US). She was one of *Granta*'s Best of Young British Novelists in 1993 and 2003.

Richard Mabey lives in Norfolk. His memoir, *Nature Cure,* (Pimlico) was shortlisted for the 2005 Whitbread Biography Award.

Andrew Martin's latest novel, *The Lost Luggage Porter*, is published by Faber and completes a fictional trilogy set among Britain's Edwardian railways.

John McGahern's most recent book is *Memoir* (Faber/Knopf). His novels include *The Barracks* and *Amongst Women* (Faber/Penguin). He lives on a farm in County Leitrim.

Pankaj Mishra is, most recently, the author of *Temptations of the West: How to be Modern in India, Pakistan, Tibet, and Beyond* which will be published this spring by Picador in the UK and by Farrar, Straus, and Giroux in the US.

Blake Morrison's books include the memoirs *And When Did You Last See Your Father* (Granta/Picador) and *Things My Mother Never Told Me* (Vintage/Granta). He is a professor of creative and life writing at Goldsmiths University, London.

Kamran Nazeer is an editor at *Prospect*. Born of Pakistani parents, he has lived in New York, Jeddah, Islamabad and Glasgow. His first book is *Send In The Idiots: Or How We Grew To Understand The World* (Bloomsbury).

Karen Russell was born in Miami in 1981 and now lives in New York. 'St Lucy's Home for Girls Raised by Wolves' is the title story from her first collection, to be published by Knopf in September 2006. Her stories have appeared in *Conjunctions* and *The New Yorker,* and she is working on a novel.

Gary Shteyngart was born in Leningrad in 1972 and now lives in New York. His first novel is *The Russian Debutante's Handbook* (Bloomsbury/Riverhead) and his second, *Absurdistan*, will be published later this year by Random House. His story, 'Several Anecdotes about My Wife', appeared in *Granta* 78.

Alison Smith is the author of the memoir *Name All the Animals* (Scribner). She has written for *McSweeney's* and *The Believer*. She lives in Brooklyn, New York.

Wendell Steavenson has written about Georgia in *Stories I Stole* (Atlantic/Grove) and is working on a book about Iraqis. She has travelled extensively in the Middle East. Her piece, 'Osama's War', appeared in *Granta* 87.

Lucretia Stewart is, most recently, the author of *Making Love: A Romance* (Vintage/University of Wisconsin). She lives on the Greek island of Naxos.

CAST INCLUDES
JEROME FLYNN
ROBERT GLENISTER
SALLY HAWKINS
ROGER LLOYD-PACK
DANIEL MAYS

DIRECTION **IAN RICKSON**
DESIGN **ULTZ**
LIGHTING **JOHANNA TOWN**
SOUND **IAN DICKINSON**

THE WINTERLING
BY JEZ BUTTERWORTH

2 MARCH - 8 APRIL
JERWOOD THEATRE DOWNSTAIRS
BOX OFFICE 020 7565 5000
TICKETS £7.50-£25
BEST SEATS AVAILABLE £15 ONLINE
ROYALCOURTTHEATRE.COM
SLOANE SQUARE, LONDON SW1

ROYAL
COURT
THEATRE
50
SPONSORED BY COUTTS & CO

South Bank Centre London
Queen Elizabeth Hall
Purcell Room

London's year-round literature festival

14 Mar	**Helen Dunmore, Anna Enquist + Michel Faber** (Stop the Clock: Writers and the Perception of Time)
21 Mar	**Douwe Draaisma, Ekow Eshun + Hilary Mantel** (Stop the Clock: Writers and the Perception of Time)
28 Mar	**Ismail Kadare + Harry Mulisch** (Stop the Clock: Writers and the Perception of Time)
1 Apr	**Henning Mankell**
20 Apr	**Annie Kirby, Helen Simpson, Marina Warner** with **Kate Pullinger** celebrate 10 years of the Asham Award, the short story prize for women
22 Apr	**Seamus Heaney**
25 Apr	**Snake Bites: Serpent's Tail is 20.** Devised by **Neil Bartlett**. A collage of the spiciest and spikiest writing from Serpent's Tail, where actors will impersonate writers and writers will be even stranger!
4 May	**Chuck Palahniuk**

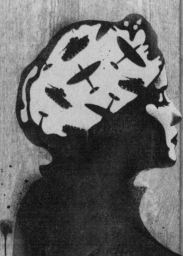

Illustration by Jimmy Turrell.
Interpretation of 'Spitfire headscarf'
from Sarah Waters' latest book
The Night Watch

Box Office:
08703 800 400

**More information
& online booking:**
www.rfh.org.uk/literature

INTRODUCTION

And God saw everything that he had made, and, behold, it was
very good.
—Genesis chapter 1, verse 31

For most of the twentieth century, and not only in the West,
organized belief in the supernatural was held to be in decline. All
of us know the story. Science, rationalism and materialism—usually
personified by the Europeans Darwin and Lyell, Marx and Freud—
had given religious belief such a bashing that its explanations of how
the world came to be, how we came to be in it, how we should best
live in it, and what would happen to us after our death—these
explanations and the strictures that went with them became, quite
simply, unbelievable and disagreeable. The idea of God as creator
and custodian died, and many words in the old vocabulary were
robbed of their potency, even their meaning: heaven, hell, salvation,
sacrilege, blasphemy.

Or so the secularists thought, forgetting the great psychologist
William James's judgement that beliefs do not work because they are
true, but true because they work. Today the godly, if not God, have
bounced back. As I write, I can see them at work in today's news. In
Washington, President Bush in his State of the Union address is
advising the people of Iran to rise against their repression by the
'clerical elite'—one department of the godly advising another
department to get rid of a third department, the biblical instruction
regarding motes and beams apparently forgotten in the White House,
if it were ever known there. In London, Tony Blair's government has
very narrowly failed in a parliamentary vote to pass legislation which
would make it a criminal offence to 'criticize, express antipathy
towards, abuse, insult or ridicule any religion, religious belief or
religious practice' if the result fomented religious hatred. In
Copenhagen, Denmark's largest-selling broadsheet newspaper has just
issued an apology to the 'honourable citizens of the Muslim world'
after publishing a series of cartoons of the Prophet Muhammad, one
of which depicted him wearing a bomb-shaped turban, which in
Muslim eyes was insult added to injury (most branches of Islam regard
any depiction of the Prophet as sacrilege). According to the report in
the *Guardian*, 'Danish businesses started to take fright after religious
leaders in Saudi Arabia, which last week recalled its ambassador to

Copenhagen, called for a boycott of Danish goods. The dairy group Arla Foods reported that two of its staff in Saudi Arabia had been beaten by angry customers.' A few other European newspapers have reproduced the cartoons—the managing editor of *France Soir* was consequently fired—and there have been bomb warnings to newspaper offices and threats to Danish troops in Iraq. Most of the European media is happy enough to publicize art or literature sacrilegious to Christians—for example, the recent *Son of a God* exhibition by the artists Gilbert and George—or which would have been sacrilegious if clerical doubt and public apathy hadn't gnawed away at so much Christian power and dogma. On the other hand, England still has a blasphemy law. There is confusion and argument.

Is it that we notice the godly more only because of the politicization of Islam? Certainly there is a widespread belief that the British government's proposal to outlaw acts leading to 'religious hatred' was no more than a sop to the Muslim electorate, to keep Labour MPs in their parliamentary seats. The phrase 'Muslim electorate' is significant in itself: a redescription of various populations who had usually described themselves by their countries of ancestral origin— Bangladesh, Pakistan, India, the nations of the Middle East. Religious belief and its traditions have become for them a superior badge of identity. But it isn't just Muslims. Christians (Christian fundamentalists, if you prefer) have become a powerful force in the United States; Israel's religious parties are no longer an eccentric sideshow; a party founded to uphold the Hindu cause until very recently ran India and could easily do so again. Religion is the way all of them choose to see themselves socially and politically, though whether it is pure faith alone that binds them together in groups, rather than a mutual struggle against perceived injustice or the need to preserve economic advantage, is a different question.

How many people, after all, have ever come to God as Tolstoy did rather than sucking Him up from the cradle? William James in his book *The Varieties of Religious Experience*, first published in 1902, describes Tolstoy as a man of fifty whose 'sense that life had any meaning whatever was for a time totally withdrawn... the questions "Why?" and "What next" began to beset him more and more frequently... as they became ever more urgent, he perceived that it was like those first discomforts of a sick man, to which he pays but little attention till they run into one continuous suffering, and then he realizes that what he took for a passing disorder means the most momentous thing in the world for him, means his death.' Tolstoy at the time had everything going for him; he had no obvious need to be born again. He wasn't a drunk like George Bush or crippled by professional failure or divorce. As he wrote of himself, he had a good wife whom he loved and who loved him; good children; a large and increasing amount of property; the respect of his friends and relations. He was 'loaded with praise by strangers' and 'without exaggeration I could believe my name already famous'. Neither was he mad, or ill. 'I could mow as well as the peasants, I could work my brain for eight hours uninterruptedly and feel no bad effects.'

Tolstoy eventually diagnosed his craving for meaning, this 'pining emotion', as a thirst for God. Slaking it led him to the ascetic life and a denunciation of his earlier self, as well as some trouble with his wife. But during his struggle, that earlier self had doubted 'that this condition of despair should be natural to mankind'. Or, he might have added, that even if it were more common, God didn't always step forward as the cure for the afflicted, even in the late nineteenth century. Professor John Carey was persuasive when in his introduction to the *Faber Book of Reportage* he warned against the assumption that our ancestors, in the main, were any more deeply religious than we are. Religion was just the permanent backdrop to daily life, as the media is today. (Carey wrote: 'Reportage provides modern man, too, with a release from his trivial routines, and a habitual daily illusion of communication with a reality greater than himself.')

In January 1892, when Tolstoy was living the redeemed life in Russia, my grandfather in Glasgow got a book; his name and the month and year are inscribed inside. Whether he bought it, whether he was given it by a well-meaning Christian, whether he read it: these questions have no answers now. But it's an attractive little book with a seductive title, so he may well have bought it and read some or all of it. The cloth cover is engraved with a drawing of a Victorian soccer game—the boy players in knickerbockers, jackets and caps—while a setting sun sinks in gold above them, its gilded rays spreading into the title: *A Bright Sunset: The Last Days of a Young Scottish Football Player*. According to the title page, this was the seventh edition; more than 30,000 copies were already in print.

Ian Jack

As a child I used to dip into this book to savour its overwhelming sadness. There is very little football in it. On page three, the sixteen-year-old hero hurts his knee playing the game at school; the injury becomes cancerous; the rest of the book is devoted to his dying. It isn't a novel. A Church of Scotland minister writes in his introduction that the text has been edited from letters the boy's mother wrote to her sister in America: 'The following papers were never intended to meet the public eye...' Today it might be categorized as a 'misery memoir'—except that each painful step towards the grave is lightened by the certain knowledge of what lies on the other side of it. 'We were all wrong about death,' says the suffering boy to his younger brother. 'We don't die at all... This body of mine has been going on for seventeen and a half years, and it's tired, very tired, and it must be laid in the grave for a very long rest; but my spirit is not the least tired, and it will go straight to Jesus. Then you know, *there*, a thousand years are like one day; so I'll not be weary.'

How many people were convinced of the truth of this idea in Victorian, Christian Scotland is impossible to say, but probably far fewer than had Bibles in their homes and not, I think, my grandfather. Today it seems to come from a vanished world, until you remember how firmly suicide bombers believe in paradise, or you read the letter favourably quoted by President Bush in February's State of the Union address. All US troops in Iraq are encouraged to write farewell letters in case they die there. The late Sergeant Daniel Clay of the Marines wrote one to his family before he was killed near Fallujah in December, 2005. He said: 'This letter being read means that I have been deemed worthy of being with Christ... The secret is out. He lives and His promises are real... What we have done in Iraq is worth any sacrifice.'

This is the first issue of *Granta* under new ownership. Rea Hederman, the New York publisher, sold it in December, 2005, to Sigrid Rausing, the London-based publisher and philanthropist. *Granta* owes a great deal to Rea Hederman's generosity and commitment to new writing over the past two decades, as it will also to Sigrid Rausing's in the years to come. Publishing a literary quarterly is never a way to find earthly fortune. Forgive the phrase, but the rewards are more likely to be found in heaven.   *Ian Jack*

GRANTA

A PRISONER OF THE HOLY WAR

Wendell Steavenson

A Prisoner of the Holy War

In Baghdad, in 2003, I went looking for former Iraqi POWs from the Iran–Iraq War. In the eight years of the war there were as many as a million casualties, and tens of thousands of captured soldiers on both sides, many of them held captive long after the war ended in 1988. I suppose I was looking for a story of a Martin Guerre or a Rip Van Winkle.

I met several. One, a Sunni from Diala, had come home to find his family impoverished and his brother a rich man. 'My wife got old while I was away. She has no teeth left in her mouth! My brothers tell me I should take another wife.' His wife shrugged at this.

Another was a Kurd who had spent twenty years in prison thinking that the tales the Iranians told him—of violently razed Kurdish villages during the Anfal campaign, of 5,000 Kurds gassed in Halabja in 1988—were propaganda told to reduce his will and spirit. When he got home he found that they were true.

Another had been repatriated in the mid-1990s and was very happy to be given 40,000 dinars by the government. A fortune! He went to a restaurant in Baghdad on his first day to eat his fill before hiring a taxi to take him all the way home to Ramadi. But when the bill came he realized he could only just pay it—inflation had made the dinar almost worthless—and he could barely afford a bus ride.

Some of the returning prisoners came home to find their wives had remarried, having long presumed their husbands dead. Some found their families gone abroad. One man I met said that he had walked up his street on the day he came home and stopped outside his house and saw his mother bent over, sweeping leaves in the garden. He called out to her and she turned and tried to shoo him away; he was thought long dead and she did not recognize him.

One former POW refused to talk to me. He had been home for only a few months and there were American tanks in his neighbourhood and everyone was saying disrespectful things against Saddam. He had been held in Iran for twenty-three years. He came to the door of his house, dishevelled, disoriented, bitter, confused. He shook his head at my translator. 'My tragedy is so large, it can be understood only by one person. By Saddam. I wanted to meet him, but this hope became impossible. Everything changed, even my family, everyone has become an enemy to me. None of them can help me in any way. It is no use to me to meet any journalist—no one can understand my suffering.'

There were many stories, apocryphal, melodramatic, true. The one I remember most is Thayr's. He came to my hotel because he had heard a journalist was interested in POWs. I remember him standing in the reception, tall, handsome, ramrod straight. His hair was clipped neatly, he had a trimmed, thick moustache. On that first occasion he wore a perfectly pressed dark formal suit; later he dressed more casually, but he was always impeccable, a proud Sunni officer. His trousers had stiff pleats, his shirts were ironed, his jackets hung straight from his wide shoulders. He was always freshly shaved.

We talked almost every week for six months. His brother sold cars in Baghdad—after years of sanctions, second-hand cars were pouring over the border from Jordan. It was a good business, and Thayr came down from Samarra often to help him. We would sit by the pool at the Hamra Hotel and I would write everything down. Thayr would pause and look up at the eighteen-foot-high concrete blast walls around us. 'I always look at a wall and wonder: how high is that? How can I get over that?' Or at the foil triangle of cheese I was spreading on my croissant. 'It was that much cheese—very small.' Or at the sun and sky above, now buzzing with Blackhawk helicopter flies near the Green Zone. 'It used to blind us when we went outside, it was dazzling.'

Thayr was born in a village on the outskirts of Samarra in 1960. The village was a collection of low mud-and-straw plastered huts, tethered cows, chickens, a standpipe, ragged children. There was no electricity. When it rained the huts leaked and the mud dripped in between warped door jambs. Thayr's hut had two rooms, one for living in, with bedding rolled in the corner and a plastic tablecloth to spread on rush mats for meals, and a second room reserved for guests, with a clean cement floor and bolsters and cushions arranged around the edges. It was strictly off limits to the children. Thayr had one older brother—four other sons had died in infancy—and several sisters. Thayr's father worked on the railway. He was an intelligent man, but illiterate; he wore the traditional long dishdasha and sandals and a red-and-white-checked keffiyeh wrapped around his head; he kept an old British rifle for hunting and 'tribal problems'.

In 1968, when Thayr was eight, revolution came. He heard the neighbours shooting their guns in the air with the excitement. His father muttered and did not join in the celebrations; he did not like the

Ba'athists much. He remembered the violence from their last revolution, in 1963, and they were socialists, which meant they were not good Muslims. But at least they were not atheist foreign Communists who had no God at all. 'When it rains in Moscow,' he used to say, 'all the members of the Iraqi Communist Party have to put up umbrellas!' Perhaps the Ba'athists would not be so bad: their leader, Ahmed Hassan al-Bakr, seemed old and wise enough, an officer who talked of Arab pride and nationalism, like Gamal Abdel Nasser in Egypt.

Thayr went to the village school and learned to read. His father used to bring him magazines from the town and he devoured them; everyone could see he had a talent for learning. His older brother went to work with his father on the trains when he was twelve, but it was decided that Thayr should continue his education, so the family sold a small plot of land and moved to Samarra, where Thayr could go to a secondary school.

Samarra was a bustling town on the Tigris, a regional capital (a few years later, that honour was taken away and awarded to nearby Tikrit) that was dominated by a gold-domed shrine, visited by Iranian pilgrims, and a spiral minaret, so famous it was printed on the money. After the quiet, closed life of the village, Samarra was a profusion. In Samarra many people wore trousers and shirts and closed-toe leather shoes, and so did Thayr. After school in the village there were always chores to do, but in the town, he liked to stop in teashops and listen to the politics and the arguments, Communists, Islamists, Ba'athists, Nasser and Brezhnev and Palestine. Thayr's father did not like him hanging around these places and would set him a curfew. The politics of the time, however, were impossible to ignore. There were demonstrations in the streets and fights in the playground at school. One time the whole town joined together to embargo the Communists: no one bought from their shops or rented property to them or visited their homes. When Thayr asked his father why, his father told him it was because they were unbelievers.

The vice president, Saddam Hussein, drove around the country in a gleaming black convoy that became longer every year, dispensing colour televisions and electricity to villages that pleased him, gold watches to doctors and teachers, and speeches to the students, 'the future of Iraq'. He was tall and handsome, a pin-up for girls and a pillar of admiration for the boys. In 1978 he visited Samarra and the schoolchildren lined his route with flowers and flags. Up close they could see his broad smile under his thick moustache, his vigour, his outstretched hand leading them forward. He said that the government would build new hospitals and schools and technical colleges, that students must catch up with the West, that there would be grants to study abroad and pensions for the old and sick. Oil money flowed after the Iraq Petroleum Company was nationalized in 1972, and all these promises seemed to be coming true.

Thayr looked up to the Ba'ath Party. When he was thirteen he joined Student Youth for Iraq's Security, one of its junior rungs. He filled out the form with his name, age, father's name and tribe, and attached a photograph and a report from his sponsor. He knew his father would be angry so he didn't tell him. The membership was fifty *fils*—a very small amount—a month and the meetings were conducted semi-clandestinely in classrooms after school. They were given lectures and pamphlets on Arab unity and social justice, sound principles that Thayr, growing up in a village of poverty and hearing the stories of landowners shooting poor farmers to quell their grumbling, respected. He had the opinions of his age. The party was a ladder to the future: status and employment.

Thayr rose through the ranks of the Ba'athist Student Union, drilled with rifles after school, lifted weights, formed a radio club that broadcast to sick people in hospitals. He read history books about strong men—Saladin, Hitler—and the glories of the Mesopotamian past, wrote to pen pals in other countries (especially if they were girls) and composed reports on party members as was required. He was vain and his confidence shone and everything, even Iraq around him, seemed poised for a prosperous future. He bought himself a gold digital watch and spent hours in front of the mirror in the hall outside the bathroom, carefully combing his hair into a thick coif and lacquering it with hairspray. His father, watching him, would 'pah!' at his vanity.

'Is your hair gold, that you would take such care of it?'

With Bakr increasingly frail, Saddam Hussein consolidated power in 1979 and the names of the executed, those purged, were read out every afternoon on the television. The evening news was full of denunciations of the Iranians and Ayatollah Khomeini. Khomeini called for Saddam to be overthrown. Old Arab–Persian enmity led to a border dispute along the Shatt al Arab waterway. The rhetoric fuelled cross-border artillery attacks. Then Iraq invaded on September 22, 1979.

Persians living in Iraq, many of whom had been there for generations, many of them merely of Persian descent, were deported. Among them was Zakia, a girl Thayr was in love with (one of them, anyway). Her family were among the fifty Shi'a Persian families who lived in Samarra and had businesses connected with the pilgrim trade at the shrine. Thayr pleaded with the authorities. 'Why is she being sent away, she was born in Iraq! She doesn't want to go!'

The official raised an eyebrow. 'Would you like to join her?' he warned. The official told him not to question such decisions, that it was government law. Thayr was very unhappy about her leaving, but the war was a much larger thing. Zakia was said to have kissed the Samarran earth before they put her family on the bus.

The war was initially exciting and victorious. The Iraqis seized the city of Mohammerah (known as Khorramshahr in Iran), and shot down the Iranian jets that strafed Baghdad. Thayr went to the military college in Hilla and trained to be an artillery officer. For him it was a clear matter of principle: Khomeini was threatening a Shi'a revolution in Iraq, and he would fight for his country. He wore a new, clean-edged dark green uniform with the insignia of a lieutenant on his shoulder, a gold star, embroidered in yellow thread instead of a clinking brass badge that would catch the sun and give away his position to the enemy. On his head was a blue cap that indicated he was with a mortar company, on his hip an Austrian pistol known as a 'Tariq' in a leather holster and on his feet well-polished black American army boots. His greatest fear was that the war would end before he could get to the front.

In the meantime there was weekend leave in Baghdad, picnics with girls who could be persuaded to go on picnics, cafes, restaurants and a craze for buying keychains on which young soldiers engraved the names of their beloveds. At night officers were welcomed into bars and nightclubs—some of Thayr's friends were crazy about Western throbbing music and imported Filipino girls and whisky. Thayr drank beer, but he never drank whisky and he couldn't fathom the alien rhythms of rock music.

Some of his friends did not want to join the army and fight. They talked about quitting Iraq until it was all over. He saw them on the edges of the funerals for Iraqi acquaintances or relatives killed in action. They looked frightened. On television Saddam railed at those who did not want to fight: they were cowards, no better than their wives, and if they talked like cowards he would cut them into four pieces. Thayr was disappointed he knew such cowards. He tried to argue with them about their lack of patriotism.

In January 1982 Thayr was sent to the front. The Iranians had been positioning to retake Mohammerah for some time and by the spring it seemed they would attack at any moment. The Iraqis readied themselves for the assault, night followed tense night, and the adrenalin of anticipation dissipated into exhaustion, lassitude and fatalism. Worn nerves, shot sleep. When the attack finally came in May, it was a rout. There was confusion and terrible casualties; tens of thousands of Iraqis surrendered. There was a sense in the Iraqi newspapers, on the radio, that the battle of Mohammerah would mean the end of the war. Saddam had the general in charge shot.

Thayr spent several weeks in retreat, skirmishing, falling back, standing, fighting. Whatever he was asked to do, he did. There were many in the ranks who fought with shallow hearts; it was enough for them to fire shots in the direction of the enemy to cover their escape towards the safety of Basra. Thayr fought with faith. His father had told him to keep his head high. After all, a soldier's job was death: what else could you expect from it?

Sometimes he slept in his boots, sometimes he didn't sleep at all. One morning his company took a band of Iranians prisoner. They were volunteers; frightened and either too young or too old to be regular soldiers. They wore black-and-green headbands and thin fatigues; their boots were full of holes and their feet were blistered. They were very tired and thirsty. They cried 'Ab! Ab!' but it was not until much later that Thayr understood they had been asking for water.

Saddam announced that the army would retreat to the Iraqi border. Perhaps he hoped Khomeini would be satisfied with this. Khomeini was not. Still, for the time being the Iraqis dug themselves into trenches in the desert and settled for a fractious stalemate. It was summer, and blazing hot. The Iraqis scratched holes and trenches in the grey yellow desert. Mortars came over; shells fell behind them. The dust storms were so bad they had to wear goggles.

Sand scratched pimples, skin erupted and itched, rashes spread, foot rot festered in those who didn't take their boots off to sleep. Washing meant buckets of brown salty water.

Thayr was stationed east of Basra at a place called Makhfar al-Basra. The land was an empty, scarred place, flattened mounds of desert rutted with trenches, overlaid with cables and tracks and piled with berms. It undulated so that it was impossible to ever see over the next bump or mound. There was only the hot sky above, and random inaccurate shelling and rumours of an impending Iranian attack.

A friend of Thayr's, Abdullah Raza Mane, a more senior artillery lieutenant, lived in Basra. Life went on there as usual, despite the influx of soldiers—the government had forbidden civilians to evacuate. Once a week Thayr would take his car, drive to the town, go shopping, stay with Abdullah's family or at the Officers' Club, wash, shower. Abdullah and he became close friends. They had a brother-soldier-comrade routine, before battle, of exchanging shirts so that each could be martyred in the other's clothing. It was Ramadan and most of the men were fasting. Thayr was not fasting and he did not get up for *sohor*, the meal before the dawn prayer. He slept until his servant, a man from a poor family, came with his breakfast: rice and gravy and fruit and tea. Thayr wrote a letter home, saying that he hoped to have leave over Eid. He pretended to his parents that he was stationed in Basra, as he did not want his mother to worry about him being at the front. He also wrote to a Moroccan girl called Fatih Masawi whom he had met when she was on a youth delegation to visit the holy places in Iraq. He wrote to her often, telling her his hopes and about his daily life and sending her pictures of himself in his uniform. She sent back messages of strength and patriotism, and magazines and books.

On July 13 Thayr received a typed order warning that an Iranian attack was expected on the Ninth Unit, which was located adjacent to Thayr's Fifth. Thayr countersigned the paper to show he had received it. The warning order had specified an Iranian attack near Fish Lake, a stretch of filthy waterlogged desert, at 22.00. The troops were put on Alert G, the maximum level. Later, after dusk, he addressed his company. He told them they were about to be in a battle. He reminded them of old Arab leaders and heroes and battles, he reminded them of Kaakaa, who had destroyed the Persian Empire.

'Our women are behind us. They expect us to protect them. Our enemy is coming to take them and to kidnap our children. You have to fight to protect the land you were born in and will die in.'

He hugged Abdullah and they swapped shirts. Abdullah was smaller than he was and his shirt was tight across Thayr's chest. Thayr felt differently this time, a pang of fate, but he shrugged it off and stretched his arms through the constricting sleeves. In the dark he and Abdullah each took a jeep with a driver, a messenger and a sergeant to go ahead and pick out targets and correct the fire of their mortar companies. They met up with their direct superior, Naqib. He gave them a pep talk and reminded them that if they retreated there would be execution units stationed behind them.

Thayr was on a forward observation ridge in the early morning, the sky pink and serene. He stood with his binoculars, scanning distant puffs of explosions to his left. To the north, deep booming artillery rumbled.

At about ten o'clock a platoon of Iranians came over the ridge and captured them. There were simply too many Iranians: they were close and then suddenly next to them and then his hands were in the air. There was no way to escape.

The Iranians made Thayr strip off his uniform. One of them hit him a couple of times across the back of his head. They took his money and his gold digital watch. They shot bullets at the dirt near his feet. He stood, bruised and aching with an empty pale band of skin on his wrist where his watch had been, Abdullah's undershirt black with sweat.

He was pushed into the back of a truck and taken to the nearest Iranian divisional headquarters, where he was interrogated about Iraqi troop positions. He gave them only his name and unit number. He tried to stand up straight, but they beat him again and then they blindfolded him and put him in the back of a car.

He felt the car moving and it drove for a while, and then it stopped and his blindfold was removed; his eyes opened to bright, blinking sun. He found he was facing a building and all around him a quiet crowd of Iraqi prisoners, some reduced to shorts and vests, some bare-chested and still in their combat trousers, milled about. An Iranian propaganda officer told him to broadcast denunciations of Iraqi aggression on the radio. He refused and was beaten again.

The sun went down on the desert. It was July 14, 1982. Thayr was twenty-two years old.

Sometimes in the retelling Thayr would find himself transported back to his youth and remember the opinions and tenets of those times. Shaking his head, he looked again at those months of battle and casualties and executions before his capture. 'Now I consider these deaths a great loss. We lost everything.' The whole war, in fact, was ultimately for nothing. 'Everything was lost. Much blood was shed and our sacrifices had no effect.'

After two or three days the prisoners were loaded on to a train for transportation. They could see the flat parched desert and the brown towns go past the windows. The train moved slowly, lurched, stopped and went forward again. Another prisoner, a captain called Selim, suggested they try to escape. 'They aren't paying any attention. We could go to the toilet and jump out of the window when the train is moving slowly. They couldn't stop us.'

Thayr was unconvinced. 'And jump where? In the middle of the Persian desert? How is your Farsi?'

'We could try,' said Selim.

'Ah, leave it,' said Thayr. 'We'd break our legs, and the war will be over in a couple of weeks anyway. They'll negotiate a peace and then we'll all be sent home.'

The first weeks of captivity were prison-barrack routine, men crammed in triple bunks, barbed wire and lectures. Sometimes twice-a-day lectures. The Iranians, full of revolution and righteousness and carrying batons, seemed resolute in wanting their prisoners to denounce their government. They hung pictures of Khomeini and the Iraqi Shi'a ayatollah Sadr on the walls. They brought in Iraqi Shi'a opposition leaders to regale the prisoners, in their own Arabic, with tales of the crimes of Saddam, his tortures and repressions. They had slides and blackboards. They played on the sympathies of the poor downtrodden southern Shi'a and the conscripted Kurds. They led them in cursing and chanting: 'God is great! God is great! Death to America! Death to Israel! Death to Russia! Death to Saddam!'

Thayr and other officers dismissed it all as enemy propaganda. Some Iraqi prisoners went along, some of the Shi'a, some who wanted to get better food or to curry favour. Informers were rewarded, privileges given. Divisions cracked: once Thayr saw a collaborator hung by his fellow cellmates. He felt sick about it, but he understood.

There were several thousand men held in the prison. They were not released after a few weeks. The war went on. Iran attacked and Iraq counter-attacked, and the prisoners were still held. After about a year, many began a hunger strike to demand access to the Red Cross. The Iranians were angry. A group of prisoners were gathered, their heads shaved, and they were made to sit on the ground in a row in the exercise yard, so the prisoners in their barracks could watch from the windows. The guards swung thick black electrical cables and cracked them against their heads.

'The Red Cross is an inhuman organization which works with the Americans! You people will eat! Or we will finish you!'

A large metal tray of food was brought, rice with gravy. The unfortunate men were handed aluminium bowls and spoons and beaten again. Some of them bent their heads and picked up the spoons and ate.

The prisoners watching this began to chant. 'Death to Iran! Long live Iraq! *Nam, nam, nam Saddam!*' They turned on their guards and beat them out of the prison. The Iranians brought up reinforcements and stood outside the walls with guns.

The standoff lasted two days.

On the morning of the third day, the prison was surrounded by Iranian Special Forces wearing helmets with visors. Fifteen simple pine-wood slat beds were lined up in the dust. A list of names was read through a megaphone, fifty-four officers and fifty-four soldiers. An uneasy ripple went through the crowd of prisoners. They were told that further movement would be answered with shooting. Those whose names were listed, Thayr among them, walked forward. They were ordered to strip to their underwear and arranged in groups.

The megaphone said, 'A hundred lashes.'

Two big Iranians stood on either side of the beds with black cables in their hands. Two more guards held each prisoner down, one held the two arms outstretched, the other held the feet to keep the legs taut. Still the bodies rucked and arched against each assault, until they became unconscious and inert, just bodies.

Thayr was in the second group. They were ordered eighty lashes. The blows came fast; the two men worked in tandem, beating body, neck, back and leg. They wrapped the cable around their hands and raised their arms high up, to gather the strength of their whole body into the descending thwack. Thayr felt the pain split his body in two. He wrenched himself upright, kicking and flailing, and was dragged back. The cables made a slapping sound against his skin; the agony was sudden and tremendous. His ribs cracked against the pine slats under him, while the pine slats themselves cracked. Thayr blacked out after fifty; one man never walked again.

Afterwards, the prone bodies were thrown in a cell with a tiled floor. The men were left there for a day, pissing blood, moaning at each other, trying to keep very still to lessen the pain. Thayr felt the suffering all around him. He felt there was no other power to turn to but God.

After a few days they were moved to a room with beds and they began to recover. In their new prison wing were a group of badly injured prisoners who were being repatriated to Iraq. Among them was a nephew of Tariq Aziz, then deputy prime minister, who had been left blinded on the battlefield for three days until the Iranians found him. Tariq Aziz's nephew had the gift of an incredible memory and he memorized the names of more than 250 POWs so that he could take news back to their families in Iraq. Thayr told him to please remember his name but never to tell his family about the conditions he endured.

Some time after that they were mysteriously moved to a different prison, a less brutal one. They did not know why. They were allowed to write one letter every two weeks, and to receive them. After three months, on June 15, 1983, Thayr received a letter with his brother's handwriting on the envelope. He was so happy he literally jumped for joy and tears came into his eyes. He put the letter away, close to his heart, deciding not to tear it open and read it immediately, but to save it. Thayr wept and thanked God that he had been whipped and ended up in that place. His brother wrote that he had a son. The letters continued for almost a year. Then Thayr was moved to another prison and they stopped.

A second year went by, and a third; different prisons with different routines: exercise half an hour a day, or locked up all the time, or let out once a week. A hundred men in a barrack cell, or 300, or forty; hot water to wash, or cold showers weekly. Soap small, vanishing, rare;

thin straw mattresses, or wooden slats, or sometimes only the floor. Tea—there was always tea—sometimes sugar, sometimes not, thin soup, half a boiled black rotten potato, no potato, small pieces of cheese, then for several years no cheese at all. Sixty cigarettes per month per prisoner and then none for seven years, and then after seven years they were each given seven cigarettes a week and they were so happy to have something new to do that they all took up smoking immediately. They cut the cigarettes into quarters with a piece of wire and two people would share each quarter, shaving the ash off carefully. They each had one blanket, which they sewed up along one side to make a more comfortable sleeping-bag arrangement. Thayr was tall and his feet always stuck out. They made their own needles by sharpening bits of wire between rocks and then piercing the end with a nail, they darned their clothes with thread pulled from rags and old vests. They became experts in all manner of domestic improvisation.

They taught each other languages: Farsi, French, German, English. They scratched alphabets in soap, or they took a length of dark material and rubbed it with soap to make a white filmy wax surface on which they incised words. They made ink from soot they wiped off the inside of the glass hoods of the kerosene lamps and mixed with shampoo. At first they dipped sticks in it to write with, but this was laborious. Then they made a pen from a syringe by cutting the needle to make a nib. It worked well.

Many of the men died from hunger or from bloody diarrhoea or from giving up. They used to say it was like fuel in a car: when one of them became too exhausted to live any more, his fuel had run out.

Many times Thayr held friends in his arms until they died. Once, one among them was very ill when there was little food. They persuaded the guards to let them trap small birds in the exercise yard for him. The prisoners got good at making catapults with the elastic taken from undershorts, and they killed sparrows easily. They were allowed to catch three a day, but the sick prisoner soon died and their trapping privileges were stopped.

'These are Iranian birds!' they were told. 'You cannot kill so many of them!'

When a prisoner died the Iranians handcuffed his corpse and blindfolded his dead eyes and took the body away, as if to tell them that there was no freedom, even in death.

The war ended in August 1988. Many POWs had been sent home, but as Iraq held on to prisoners after the ceasefire, so did Iran. Thayr found himself grouped with a few hundred other diehard loyalists.

They learned of Iraq's invasion of Kuwait in 1990 by overhearing the guards talking about it. Another war! Against the Americans! Thayr and the other remaining prisoners hung their heads and knew that they were forgotten, lost. Few thought this new war would end well for Iraq. Where there had been negotiations for their release and repatriation before, now there were none.

The Iranians still tried to convince them to denounce their regime. Thayr held out. He would not betray his country, he would not betray his leader. For what, a toilet break? For extra food while his brothers went hungry? Sharing his bread with a hungry brother, holding someone's head as they wept or vomited—Thayr found that however bad his misery, there was always someone worse. He discovered tiny moments of humanity, he remained cheerful, he could laugh. Patriotism and Ba'athism were the same; no amount of Iranian temptation could separate them.

There were discussions, of course, there were arguments. Some men insisted on the might of Saddam and the inferiority of Kuwait, while others thought this was a mistake. But the prisoners remained the party members and soldiers they had been the year of their capture. They were officers in Saddam's army and they owed a debt of honour and service to that position and to that person, and when they got home—God, hope and His Excellency the President willing—they would be rewarded as heroes, given handsome pensions for their sacrifice, cars, houses, positions. They also knew, being good party men, that if they criticized their president in prison in Iran, they would be informed upon. They didn't want to get home only to find another prison cell waiting.

Not long after this, the prisoners were sent to Kashan, an ancient fort then used as a training ground for Iran's Revolutionary Guards. It was a dank dungeon of crumbling brick built half underground. There were always 598 prisoners kept at Kashan; when one died another was transferred to take his place. Thayr never knew why, though 598 was the number of the UN resolution that had called for a ceasefire between Iran and Iraq. Perhaps the Iranians were having their little joke. In any case, at Kashan they never got tired of beating the prisoners. They wanted to erase any Ba'athist will, numb the spirit into submission. Beating was normal, like eating. They beat them at night so their screams would keep the other prisoners awake. They made the prisoners curse Saddam. '*Marg bar Amrika! Marg bar Saddam!*' Death to America! Death to Saddam! As common as 'Good morning' in revolutionary Iran.

One morning, blinking yellow, bruised, hungry as always, Thayr and his cellmates were rounded up and taken down stone steps into a corridor none of them had ever seen before. Seven of them were pushed into a cell which measured eight feet by five feet. It was windowless and had a low domed ceiling that Thayr hit his head against. The walls were brick, yellow-dust-coloured and cracked, and they smelled like a stifling tomb. Some said there were corpses buried there.

It was pitch dark. Thayr could not see his hand in front of his face. After a few hours they began to feel faint and realized they were running out of oxygen. One of them had a match and they decided to light it and try to find a draught, but there was so little oxygen the match wouldn't light. They fell to banging on the door, but no one heard, no one arrived. By chance, when they had all collapsed, a guard came to check on them and found them unconscious. He shouted for other guards and they were taken out and given oxygen. Other prisoners in adjacent cells were dead. Two of Thayr's cellmates had heart attacks and carbon monoxide poisoning; their bodies gave off fumes of rotting gas. One became completely paralysed: the only thing he could do was breathe.

The Iranians knocked through a chimney for ventilation and piled four of them back in the cell. There was just enough space for them to lie down and sleep wedged together. They were left there for a very long time.

They took a needle they used for sewing repairs and broke off the eye. They tied a piece of wood to the point and used it like a handle to turn the broken needle like a drill. It took them a week to make a tiny hole in the door through which they could look into the corridor. When they were not using it they blocked the hole with soap and rubbed some dirt into it so that it could not be seen.

One day when they were tired of repeating old rumours about negotiations for their release, Thayr told each of them to make up a story, and to make up something with a little exaggeration.

Anad stood up. His parents were rural landowners, he had studied to be a film-maker. 'My mother has a rooster,' he began. His mother had trained the rooster specially. She would walk out from her farm and go to the palm grove where she cut firewood. But she was an old woman, and it was a distance back to the house, so after she chopped the wood she would load it on to the back of the rooster and he would totter home, carrying it for her.

They laughed at that for days. They would wake up and ask, 'How is the rooster of Um Anad?' It became their morning joke.

Majid had been a policeman in Kut and he told a story about a date palm.

'One day we planted a date palm.' The date palm was very small, but when Majid bought it he had been told it had some kind of special properties. So he took it home and planted it in his yard. It was hardly as tall as his own legs, but almost immediately it began to grow bunches of fat yellow dates. His son, a little boy of two called Ahmed, would stand under the diminutive date palm and reach up easily and pick the dates and eat them.

Khalid, a fighter pilot from Baghdad, told them how he had gone hunting one day and seen a bird in the sky. As the bird came closer, he saw that it was an eagle. The eagle swooped low over a herd of sheep and right under the shepherd's nose, carried off a sheep in its claws. It flew high and then low, and it came towards Khalid and deposited the sheep right at his feet. Seeing this gift, he killed the sheep and feasted on its meat.

Thayr laughed so hard at Khalid's tale he gasped and cried, 'Enough! We cannot laugh so much—we will run out of oxygen!'

When the conversation ran dry the four prisoners spent their time playing with the ants. Each had their own colony of ants they called their units. The ant units lived in different cracks in the wall. It was possible after some time to recognize individual ants in a unit and they gave them names of girls they had once loved. They would trap flies and leave them wriggling in their death throes on the floor and watch as a single ant, the scout, would walk out of the crack. He would circle around the mangled fly wing or the crumb of offered bread and then go back to a second ant, a halfway ant. The scout and the halfway ant would touch face to face, as if they were talking about it, and then the halfway ant would turn around and go back into the colony. Seconds later, a procession of ants, just like an army, would march out and gather around the carcass prize.

There were different ants with different jobs: cutters, pullers and carriers. Sometimes the prisoners would tease the ants and remove the dead fly or the morsel in between the scout seeing it and the unit coming out to claim it. Then, when the column arrived, the ants would see that there was nothing there and attack the messenger. They would pull him into pieces and leave his body behind.

If the fly was half alive there would be a tremendous battle between the fly and the ants. The ants would crawl on to it. The only thing the fly could do was try to fly, but the ants would cling to it airborne. They knew to bite it around the neck. The ants were very small, but they had the power of intelligent organization.

When the ants bothered them they would block up the cracks so they could not get out. But when they were bored and missed the ants they would move a few ants to a new crack, give them a little food to get started and begin a new colony. When an ant from one colony was put in among the ants from another, they did not welcome him; the strange ant would turn around and try to get away from them. So when Thayr and his friends found an ant that had got lost, they gave him a new place to live, provided a crumb of bread and watched as other ants came to establish a new colony in the crack with him. You could see them digging inside and showering fine dust down the wall with their excavations.

Khalid, the Baghdad fighter pilot, was mad. He would wake up with nightmares, screaming so badly that the guards came in and shook him. He would hit out at the guards and curse Khomeini; he didn't care what he was saying. His tongue was fluent with swearing and he knew all the old Baghdad curses. He had been tortured into madness and the Iranians beat him through his outbursts. When they were tired of beating him they gave him tranquillizing shots and he would glaze over or sleep.

But when he was lucid, Khalid was wonderful company. He had travelled to Pakistan, spoke English very well and was an educated man. His father had died a drunk and Khalid had looked after his family with gifts from Saddam of land, money, cars—fighter pilots were well rewarded. In sorrowful moments Khalid would remind himself that at least his family had a house, they would be all right. Even if he had to suffer in prison for it, they would keep their status because he was holding out in Iran.

But then he would stop talking and go quiet and sit staring, and they knew that a fit was coming. He became angry and delusional. He would gabble about his plane and clutch at the hallucinations of lever and dial and knob and instrument; his hands would flash and swoop as if he was piloting again, as if he was flying, as if he was the plane itself. At other times he would pick up imaginary telephones and call his mother in Baghdad, he would have long discussions with Saddam. 'Yes, Mr President; I am here with Thayr and Anad and Majid. We are all here, loyal to you, Mr President.'

After three years underground at Kashan, Thayr and the other prisoners were allowed back into the dormitories. On August 24, 2000 they were moved to another prison. Thayr felt good about it. He knew it was a prison from which prisoners had been released; they had taken a step forward instead of backwards.

Rations were better: there was chicken, tins of sardines, rice and gravy. They could make their own tea and there was enough sugar. There were some second-hand clothes laid out for them. They were able to go outside whenever they felt like it and play volleyball on a court marked out on the cracked asphalt. And, most extraordinarily of all after eighteen years cut off from the outside world, there was a television.

It was black and white and the reception was fuzzy and often the picture was trapped between horizontal black bars. The only stations it showed were Iranian, but most of the prisoners had picked up Farsi by then and they gathered and watched and were amazed. For several weeks all they did was watch television.

The Soviet Union had collapsed! The great strong Soviet Union was all small countries, Georgia and Azerbaijan and Uzbekistan, and some of them were Muslim! Yugoslavia had split up! There was a war: Muslims against Serbs. Arafat was in Palestine! Last they had known, he was still in exile in Tunis. There were telephones that could be used anywhere like radios, cars that were curvy and small, there were heart transplants and something called the Internet that somehow went down phone lines. They saw pictures of the American stealth bomber, sleek like a bat wing, and they were incredulous.

The first Iraqi they saw on television was Taha Yassin Ramadan, a government minister who was taking a foreign tour. When they had last seen him in the early 1980s he had been a fat man; now he looked thin, wrinkled, with hair dyed black to disguise his age. A heated discussion blew up over whether it was really him: it was him, it wasn't him, it was a fake clip, the Iranians had manufactured it, all Iranians were liars. The same minister appeared on subsequent bulletins and they saw that it was him. Finally they saw Saddam: even he had aged!

A whole world flickered on the screen. They looked at it all and at each other, and Thayr realized that he had not noticed, until then, that they had become old. He had grey hairs now when he looked in the mirror to shave, flecks of silver shot through his black hair. His friends had wrinkled jowls and pouchy eyes, they were bald or missing teeth. The pictures from Iraq looked like another country. Carts pulling wheat, donkeys, naked boys swimming in irrigation ditches, rubbled Baghdad, cracked sewers. The Iranian news camera lingered on these details of subjugation. The newsreader (wearing a tight scarf and no lipstick, but still the first woman they had seen for almost two decades) intoned statistics of stillborn babies, cases of tuberculosis, death rates. The prisoners looked and could not believe what they were seeing, did not want to believe it and said it was Iranian propaganda. It couldn't be true.

One evening Iranian TV showed the movie *Papillon*, in which Steve McQueen plays a man sentenced to life in a French penal colony in Guiana. It's a battle of hope and freedom against tropical misery— three times Papillon tries to escape—and it seemed to the prisoners, each watching with the pain of autobiography, that the penal colony in French Guiana was not so bad; it seemed quite colourful, in fact. They had known only khaki and dust, wood and nails and concrete. By the end of the movie, when Steve McQueen and his prisoner friend Dustin Hoffman end up on Devil's Island, the prisoners were unimpressed. Exile! Cottages! Crayfish for supper, small gardens, sun and wind—the Iraqi POWs watched, scratched their beards, saw Devil's Island and wished that they could live in such a place.

They watched Steve McQueen test the wind and tides and launch his final escape from the cliff into the ocean on a bag of coconuts. But cruelly the Iranians cut the final dubbed dialogue, the epilogue,

'Papillon made it to freedom... and for the remaining years of his life he lived a free man', so they did not know that he had made it. The broken prisoners wept and became depressed and discussed Papillon's courage, his opportunities, his plans. 'He should have done it this way...'; 'If only he had known that...'

On January 21, 2002 several hundred of the men were released. Thayr was not among them. This was very hard; his four closest friends left him. On television he saw them meeting their families at the border, the television cameras, reunions, exhortations. Those who were left behind were told: just another ten days and they would be sent home too. They looked through the windows for signs of buses, they asked the guards if they knew anything, but the guards said nothing. Depression settled over them; Thayr did not even want to watch television any more. Why had they been left behind? Why had the others been chosen?

He was not released. Another year passed. News mounted of an impending American invasion; they were sending troops to Kuwait again. In March 2003 Iranian television was reporting that the Iraqis were ready to fight. Thayr was not convinced. He saw that Iraq had already surrendered to all sorts of American demands. He dreamed of his father and he thought that this was a good sign; somehow the release that was rumoured even imminent, would really happen.

On March 17, 2003—three days before the Americans invaded—Thayr and the remaining POWs held with him were released from Iran and sent back to Iraq. He had been held captive for nearly twenty-one years.

It was a time when everything stopped and everyone watched television. Blair was firm, Bush gave his ultimatum, Colin Powell held steady, the Iraqi Information Minister denounced them all. The days ticked down: the UN, France giving their *non*, ElBaradei, Blix; Bush and Blair and Aznar in the Cape Verde Islands, press conferences, microphones and flags. I was in the north, in Kurdistan, where the Kurds packed their belongings into tractors and taxis and headed for the mountains or insulated their houses with sheeting against gas attacks. The prisoners' return was lost in the larger hanging moment, but for the Iraqi media it was a story to be covered as other prisoner returns had been, a nice patriotic staged event, and the cameras were accordingly sent down to the border.

The Iraqis had broadcast the names of those to be released on television. Their families came along, together with hundreds of families of missing men whose names had not been listed. Thayr was in the first group of prisoners across the border and people clustered around him, calling names, holding up photographs. To loved ones, Thayr was able to say, 'Don't worry! I know him! He's on the next bus!' but others he could tell nothing. A microphone was put in front of his mouth: what did he think about the situation of the coming American invasion?

Thayr had been back on Iraqi soil for just minutes, he was full of patriotism. He scanned the pressing mass of people for his brother (surely his brother would be the one to come, perhaps with the nephew he had never seen?). Thayr smiled, he had seen his brother—he thought it must be him—and thrust his hand in the air as a salute. 'We are all willing to fight again and to die for our country!'

Thayr pushed past the microphone, found his brother and they embraced, a few hurried words and tears. A great cheer went up from the crowd, but Thayr noticed that the general sent to oversee the repatriation did not greet them warmly. There were no garlands or handshakes, no tanks or salutes. There was no parade or honour guard. The general counted them through, Thayr thought, like animals, and said nothing.

The ex-POWs were driven to an army base at Jalawla to be processed home. Forms were filled in: name, family, rank, unit, date of capture, health status. Thayr looked around him; it was a large room, dusty, filthy. There was no furniture except broken chairs; Agents from military intelligence stood around the walls. Former POWs, now back in uniform, told them, half whispering, that times had changed and they should not expect to see things as they remembered them. They were offered new suits, but Thayr was tall and none of the trousers they had fitted him. Some of the released prisoners stood up and gave patriotic speeches and read poetry in praise of Saddam while Iraqi TV filmed them. Thayr stood in his prison clothes, holding his documents in one hand and the prayer mat and Qur'an the Iranians had given them as a parting gift in the other. He felt no happiness in freedom. It was choked off by the dirty room and the broken chairs: is that what they were worth? A couple of soldiers came up and asked him to give them his prayer mat or the Qur'an.

'These Iranian things? Why?' Thayr hardly realized he was still carrying them. He noticed the cracked leather of their shoes; they did not even have proper army boots. He saw that the army was hungry and he thought: if the army is hungry... He realized that they had been in that room with the broken chairs for several hours and there had been no food offered, not even tea.

His brother drove him home to Samarra; two nephews sat in the back, quiet. Thayr asked everything he could think of. How was everyone? What was his job? What was he doing? How was everything? His brother answered some questions—they had moved, the family was much larger now and their father hadn't wanted to stay in the house from which they had lost Thayr, people were fine, friends were married, children, cousins, nieces.

Thayr looked out of the window. The roads had loose grit on their verges and there were checkpoints everywhere. They passed soldiers standing in shallow trenches with thin metal helmets. There were not many cars; the houses along the road were crumbling.

'And our country, how is the country?'

His brother paused.

'Let's leave that aside now... You have been separated from us for so long, let's leave the subject of our country alone.'

The house was in a new area that Thayr remembered only as outskirts and waste ground. Thayr could not identify anything; the streets looked like familiar Samarra streets but everything went in the wrong direction. His house was not his house and there were a hundred people he did not recognize gathered there: uncles and cousins and children, scores of them looking up at him reverently; everyone smiled and clapped him on the back and said how happy they were. The women were in a separate place inside the house. He went to his mother, fell in front of her, kissed her from her feet to her forehead. She looked very old and tired to him; he wept into her lap.

'Where is my father?' he asked, and then they told him he was dead.

Thayr spent the brick of 1.5 million smooth Saddam-faced dinars he had been given by the government on two sheep to be slaughtered for the guests. He could not imagine being a millionaire and the money was strange and everyone spoke strangely, it was a blur. The Americans were coming; people were cursing Saddam. Thayr told them not to shame themselves and they looked back at him, haggard and sad.

'You do not know what has been happening, but everything has changed and God knows I will kill the Americans myself if they come. But if I could, I would kill that bastard too!'

Thayr was shocked to hear such talk. He had not seen the money run out, the dinar devalued, the corruption, the encroaching fear, the queues for exit visas. One man who had been a POW and was now back in the army said, 'Everything has changed for the worse. Even my neat uniform is a disguise. We carry a lot of pain.'

Others said, 'We know you have suffered, but our situation has also been difficult, maybe even more difficult.' They complained about the oil-for-food rations and the cheap quality of flour, the excess of beggars in the city. People were sick now and the hospitals did not have any medicine. People began counting the executed: this man was executed and then this other man was executed.

'Ali Asyan?' Thayr asked about a neighbour, a friend, a loyal party man.

'Killed.'

Thayr thought, if Ali Asyan had been executed then things must be very bad.

A retired officer told him, 'Whatever they are saying is true. Those who have suffered have the right to complain and those who say good things are generally the ones who have benefited, so listen, because both sides are true.'

Thayr told his brother about the letters in 1983 and how he had kept them next to his heart and would take days to open them. Thayr's brother clapped his hand over his mouth, remembering.

'And our mother, you know, we went to see Saddam because of you!'

And his mother raised her hands into the air, in a gesture that was a comic apology.

It transpired that Tariq Aziz's blind nephew had indeed returned to Iraq twenty years before, and had duly broadcast the names of all the prisoners he had memorized and their plight. Thayr's family had received an invitation from the President himself, that he might give national thanks for their son's sacrifice. Thayr's father refused to go. So Thayr's brother took his mother. The audience was stiff and miserable. Saddam was not pleased that the father and head of the household had not come; this showed disrespect, no matter how they excused it. Thayr's mother had wept copiously and could not bring herself to smile at the platitudes expressed. A protocol officer hovered, a photographer snapped the occasion. When they got home Thayr's mother tore up all the official photographs and cursed Saddam, who was responsible for the war and her son's captivity. Her husband said she was mad and worried that someone had seen her doing this, but she continued her rant. She prayed for the death of Saddam, she cried and railed and yelled, 'I want to drink from Saddam's blood!'

Thayr was aghast.

'Really,' his brother told him, laughing, 'she did!'

The Americans came and Baghdad fell without a fight; the sheikhs in Samarra decided to surrender. Thayr collapsed inwards into himself and stayed in his room and slept and cried. For three months he could not bear to go out. Nothing was explicable; it seemed only to get worse.

By spring 2004 the insurgency had widened. Fallujah had strung up the bodies of four American contractors, in Baghdad militant Shi'a were aiming RPGs at American patrols, in Samarra the American garrison occupying the old Ba'ath Party headquarters was fired on nightly. There were car bombs, 4 a.m. round-ups, detentions, assassinations throughout the country. Thayr was very unhappy about these developments. He told me that since his return, he found himself over-sensitized to the suffering of others. He would see men struggling to find work to feed their families and this pained him. He was lucky to have a brother who had a business and who helped him. One of his friends, a former POW, had a new wife and small son. He had a taxi but the taxi was stolen and he had been reduced to hiring himself out as a day labourer for heavy construction work, and he was worried all the time about feeding his family. The indignity of it made Thayr weep. But the whole country was like this: who had jobs now? One of his friends from prison in Iran was now a policeman in Tikrit. 'Hah! Working for the Americans!' Thayr rolled his eyes ruefully.

One day Thayr came to our interview looking proud and sheepish. He had dyed his hair jet black. He made a face.

'My mother made me do it!' he said.

I knew he could not, after all these years, refuse his mother anything. And then he beamed: 'She has found me a wife!' and he showed me a photograph. A stocky, tall woman in a field, half smiling for her brother behind the camera.

'Ah! She's very beautiful,' I congratulated him.

He sighed a little. Yes, she was tall, and that was good. But she was not so educated. He had always wanted an educated wife. One of his relatives was a minor sheikh and he had six daughters and he had always wanted to marry one of them.

'But they were all married years ago.'

Thayr told me about his betrothal ceremony, which took place in the bride's home and among women only. The bride's father and brothers hid in the garden or other rooms of the house, making sure first there was enough Pepsi and fizzy orange and chocolate cream cake and date pastries and foil-wrapped sweets, but were not allowed in on the proceedings. The only man allowed is the bridegroom who sits, abashed, next to his betrothed, who must sit demurely, eyes cast down, responding only with the shyest of grace to the greetings of her cousins and friends. Thayr gave his fiancée the required gold (bought by his brother), a thick gold-rope necklace with a pendant bearing the name of Allah, four bracelets and two rings. The women threw candy about like festive confetti, sang and danced to Araby pop and croon, let their headscarves slip and showed off their glittery high-heeled sandals.

Thayr sat through this, awkward and pleased. He had not met his bride before and he tried to get her to talk a little. He teased her and said how beautiful she looked in her apricot meringue lace ballgown. He told me he wanted to put his arm around her shoulders but she had wriggled.

'My brothers! They will kill you!' she told him. Still he managed to put his hand over hers when they cut the cake together.

All went well and when he got home he related everything to his mother, who had been too infirm to attend, and to his brother. They sat at the kitchen table drinking tea and talking until one of his nephews came in from the garden and reported that he had found a green US military glow stick in the garden—consternation!

Thayr recounted me this story, laughing but serious.

His mother was worried immediately: what did it mean that there was a green glow stick in their garden? It was from the Americans; they were marking something. They had marked their house!

'Oh. Allah! They will come and arrest everyone. Yes, it is late now, just the time for tanks and arrests.'

Everyone was very concerned and a great debate raged: should they move the glow stick, because then they would not be marked, or would it be noticed that they had moved the glow stick and then they would be punished? If the house was searched, where should they hide their gold jewellery—sometimes the Americans stole gold! What should they do with the Kalashnikov? Every house was allowed one Kalashnikov— but should they hide it, because it would be better to have no guns at all, and maybe they would take the Kalashnikov away if they found it? But if they hid it and the Americans found it then they would be accused of hiding it. Maybe it was better to leave it out in plain view.

Thayr calmed them all down.

'I convinced them I was a military man and I knew about these things.' He told his nephew to bring the glow stick in from the garden. 'And you know,' he said, twinkling a little, 'the electricity was off, so we had some use from it!'

The last time I saw Thayr was at his brother's car showroom in June 2004. We drank fresh melon juice and talked. A couple of men, relatives or acquaintances, came in and sat down beside us. 'How is Samarra?' I asked. 'What is going on up there?'

Thayr allowed himself a knowing smile and nodded to the men who had come in. 'Why don't you ask them? They are the resistance there.' Thayr almost winked at me. The two men, reasonably dressed, polite, pleasant, told me that they had shot down an American helicopter the week before and that everyone had been very pleased and things were going quite well with the insurgency.

I remember (and writing this, remembering, I miss him) how he could laugh and smile and joke. I did not feel bitterness in him. A hundred times I asked him: but why? Why were you loyal? It was Saddam! It was this horrible murderous regime that betrayed your loyalty!

He would shrug and say, 'Yes, now it is clear it was like this, but not then.'

Once I teased him about coming back to Iraq and the first words out of his lips were 'Long live Saddam!' Thayr laughed and rolled his eyes. 'I know! Don't remind me! What was I thinking? It was like we had been hermits in caves returning home and finding another world.'

He hated the waste and the lies, and the memory of those many prisoners, brothers to him, who had died in Iran hung heavy. 'Their blood was wasted. It was a crime. People should make sacrifices for something that is worth it. They didn't know. They hung on to something that was not true. They were fools.'

But mostly he carried his sufferance proudly: 'Pride, this is what I see in people's eyes. They want any word from me, just to give them an order. I see how much they respect me; they are proud of what I did. Everyone is destined to die. Only your deeds and your history are left behind you.

'I did not sacrifice myself to get a reward. It was twenty-one years and I swear I do not regret a second of it. I feel it is my manhood and my honour. I, as a man, was not weak in front of the enemy. I can see this in people's eyes. They say, "This is a man."' □

GRANTA

IN THE CLEARING

Andrew Brown

The double-decker bus had wing mirrors that protruded on stalks and between them, above the driver's head, was a row of bug-eyed headlamps, extinguished now at half past seven in the morning. It had been light for five hours. We were driving northwards on a broad, empty road through the forest. Soon everything brightly coloured or square-edged was far behind us. There were no more fields with ripening crops, or any other patches of yellow or red. All I could see were low green and brown hills beneath a huge sky that was blue and purple and grey. When the road passed by the side of lakes the horizon would suddenly recede and then the most distant hills were a deep greeny-grey, as if they were made half of sky and half of forest. This monotony continued; it could have continued for days, since the forest extends unbroken for 500 miles across northern Sweden and Finland. But I climbed off after six hours, in Sorsele, a town on an island in the middle of the Vindelälven river. There are no other towns for fifty miles in any direction, but here there are 1,500 people, two supermarkets, a few shops, a library and a branch of the state-owned off-licence.

When you enter a supermarket, you leave geography behind. Like airports, they are all the same place with the same lighting, equally distant from the world around them. But in Sorsele, the country around kept breaking through on to the shelves. There was canned tuna from Alaska, canned sweetcorn and fresh garlic. But at the meat counter there were cuts of elk and venison as well as beef, and half-litre tubs of reindeer blood for cooking with.

I must have looked out of place as I browsed for supplies, because a tall elderly man with a cast in one eye pushed his trolley up to mine and started talking urgently but without haste about setting nets under the ice in winter. He just wanted to share what was at the top of his mind. In the background I could see people turn their carts sharply when they caught sight of him. But he seemed reasonably sober and terribly lonely, so I listened and his discourse expanded. He lived ten miles out of town, on the river. He had started mining at sixteen, when he'd learned to set charges by hand in holes he had made with a hammer and spike: when he told me this, he mimed the invisible hammer blow. We stood between the stationery and the canned vegetables, but his hand was somewhere else and in another time.

The mines where he'd worked had shut down decades ago. He

was only seventy-one, he said; he wanted to be taken on as a teacher at a new mine. He didn't want to be paid—he had his pension—but he'd love to teach the mining skills he had known all his life; besides, his wife didn't like him hanging around the house. He seemed to recollect himself then and wished me a courteous goodbye.

I had arranged to stay on the Vinblads' farm in a clearing on the river four miles downstream, reached in a taxi on a metalled track through the forest. It was the most remote place I'd been able to find that still had electricity. I had travelled here to work on a story that had appeared unreachable: I suppose that I, too, was setting nets under an imagination that had frozen.

The next morning, after a shower, I sat for minutes on the spare bed, just listening to silence ringing in my ears. There is a sort of concussion that persists for three or four days when you leave behind the sound of motors, for even when cars seem inaudible there are almost always electric motors whirring all over a modern house.

Behind the farm the road I had come along rose up a fairly steep hill through replanted forest and I walked up there before breakfast. It was so quiet that I heard the crunch of my shoes on the loose surface but also, after each foot lifted, a second noise of displaced gravel shifting back into the depression my heel had made.

At the top of the hill was a small, shallow pond that had killed all the pine trees around it, so that they stood with grey, peeled trunks and blackened limbs as if they had all been poisoned when in fact they had just drowned. A little beyond the dead lake the north side of the road opened up into an enormous logged clearing, with about every hundredth tree spared, so it didn't look as awful as a clear cut; but it was still a desolating sight.

In that vast silence, not oppressive, but inescapable, everything I could see felt alien to human concerns. We might be happy for a while here, but we could never belong, and in the cool shadows of the forest there is almost always a sense that whatever elusive spirit does belong there wishes us no good. In the early years of the twentieth century, Swedish children who had to walk long distances to school would do so with their coats turned inside out to ward off the trolls. That word conceals a whole taxonomy in folklore— the *vätt*, the *näck* and even the *tomte*, now shrivelled to the comic status of a leprechaun—but these creatures as they appear in folk tales display towards humans almost exactly the indifference, blazing sometimes into cruelty, that peasants show their animals, and sometimes on an isolated farmstead I have wondered whether we are the tamers of the forest, or its pets.

Such thoughts recurred as I worked through the next few days, and walked by the quiet reach of the river past the farm. I was staying in an annexe, with a bedroom, a bathroom and a kitchen with a table where I could type and watch the rain gurgling off the gutters of the main house and falling past the window boxes, when I was not counting the mosquitoes patiently waiting on the screen window. Most days there were thirty at least. Towards the edge of the clearing where the farm stood there were two purpose-built *stugor* or cottages for holidaymakers.

Late one evening everything grew still on the broad, smooth flat of the river here. I stood on the sandy bank, looking towards the far shore about a quarter of a mile away. There were rises clearly visible out on the stillest water. I heard noises and excitement downstream on my shore, and found two middle-aged couples from the cottages in the grounds loading a little motor boat with fishing gear and bickering happily while they did so. 'Where do you want me to sit?' asked a rather fat wife. 'On your bottom,' replied someone. I asked whether any of them knew what was rising, and they suggested *sik*, a sort of white fish. They were going upriver two or three miles to spin for pike in the pool below the rapids.

The next morning I saw them again. They had caught ten pike from the boat and would now try laying a net across from the farm. When they returned, they had four fine *sik*, a small pike, and a small perch which one of the husbands—a short, round, bearded, gleeful man— was carrying carelessly, with its head cut off and tiny streak of bright red blood running over the white flesh and green flanks. 'They get so tangled in the net it's the only way to get them out,' he said.

The wasteful fecundity of the river fascinated him: 'The river is full of pike,' he said. He pointed to a set of large iron hooks, high under the eaves of the barn. 'There,' he said, 'they used to store the spatchcocked bodies of the pike all summer, sheltered by fine mesh so the flies couldn't reach them. They would dry in the sun and the wind, and all winter you would eat little bits of dried pike, as a snack, or with a beer. But no one bothers nowadays.'

The next morning, as I wrote at the kitchen table, there was a bang on the door and he presented me, grinning, with a paper plate of three newly fried perch, bulging like yellow pillows and dusted with gold where the butter had burned a little; also a polythene bag full of little ones smoked with their skins on so they had gone the dark green of pine forests. I was almost dumbstruck; explained that I had had breakfast and would put them in the fridge. But before I could do so, I had to eat one in my fingers. It was just perfect. I knew I must go fishing myself, and when the rain stopped, a little after one, I decided to chance a walk to the rapids.

I had been walking for about forty minutes, when the first car to pass me stopped and a young man gave me a lift to the point where the path down to the river leaves the road. The path across the clear cut soon vanished into chilly woods all bright after the rain. I walked down to the rapids on one of those narrow, irregular, descending Scandinavian paths that look as if they have been cut by water and maintained at night by busy trolls: stone, moss, damp earth form successive sections, and everything is veined with pine roots. A noise of rapids could be heard, and after about ten minutes the path came down to the glorious smooth reach just before the whole river vanished into five or six hundred metres of white water.

Downstream, the path soon brought me to a deserted, locked wooden shack, with a porch and an inverted rowing boat on the ground in front of me. This was where I had the first shock of the day. I was congratulating myself on not only performing a thorough toilette with jungle oil first thing this morning, but remembering that the bottle went in one particular pocket of my Gore-Tex jacket— that one—yes, the pocket with the zip open and nothing in it. I think I gasped in horror at the discovery: I certainly had to spit out a mosquito immediately afterwards.

So I changed into my waders down by the river, where there were slightly fewer insects than under the trees, assembled my rod, threaded the line, and thought. When I started I could just see another boat at the foot of the rapids from which people were fishing, but by the time I had tackled up it had vanished in a brief shower, and I saw no one else the whole time I was there. Not that I was looking for them. I was looking for fish, and wondering where in this crazed, frothing wilderness of water they might be. It is almost always the wildest parts of these big northern rivers that hold the trout and the grayling. They have more oxygen in hot weather than the placid stretches, and the bottom is so irregular that the rocks will always provide shelter while plenty of food rushes helplessly past in the adjoining currents.

Grayling are rather delicate fish, purplish-black on top and a bright silver everywhere else, a colour that is only really visible in the air: in water it is so perfectly bright that it becomes invisible by reflecting the weeds and gravel all around them. Any writer might try for a style like a pane of glass, but only a very great one could find a style as luminously invisible as a grayling's skin. The body is streamlined, with a fine wrist before the forked tail. The grayling has one superb extravagance—a long dorsal fin shot through with purple lights that dry to turquoise in the air. It is almost as high as the body beneath it is deep, so that when you see a grayling appear in clear water with its dorsal fin flaring it seems as if the river were waving at you a banner made from the Northern Lights.

A few hundred metres below me there was a long stone bank curving out into the water—this was built to narrow the rapids when the river was still used for floating timber. On my bank there was the usual jumble of boulders sloping into the river, most of them about the size of an armchair and difficult to walk over. I looked across them, up towards a small island close to land, wondering how best to reach the hard current in the middle of the rapids, and thinking that if this were a normal river, there should be fish in the stretch where the two streams from each side of the island reunited beneath it, and as I watched this, I distinctly saw some tiny splashes in the choppy little waves there.

I picked my way out across the rocks until I stood on a flat-topped underwater rock at the foot of this run, able to cast upstream to where the two currents joined. I couldn't actually see any flies in the air, but in that kind of water it was a safe bet they would be sedges—little drab, delicate flies that look like moths in flight, but on land settle with their wings folded to form a long, narrow ridge that conceals their bodies entirely. Their wings, under a magnifying glass, are covered in tiny hairs, but if you want to imitate them you must forget all such refinements and just make a fly that is dark and narrow, and will float through any waves. I put on an especially small and scruffy one of these, and from the first cast grayling made little splashes at it with a discretion that quite concealed their real size.

The first one took me five minutes to persuade to land, and was the largest I had ever caught. I slipped him back into the water as a thanks-offering to the Vindelälven and on the next two casts caught two more, only a little smaller, which just about hooked themselves: I saw nothing, but simply found them there when I lifted the line. I thanked the Vindelälven but I didn't want to presume, so I changed my fly; and changed it again, and again, and again, until I found something else that I could see and that the fish appreciated. Then I caught two more, which I put back, and kept the next one. I had been fishing for three hours, and for part of that time I felt completely human. Looking down the river, into the clear water, with a grayling that I knew I would eat knocking furiously on my rod, I felt this was about as close to happiness as one could come and know it.

When I returned to land the forest air was muggy and full of midges. By the time I had climbed out of the clear cut I could feel my whole face streaming sweat, like a baked tomato just before it bursts. I trudged the two miles home. It was easier once I was up on the hill, for the breeze cooled me down a bit. But I was carrying ten or twelve kilos the whole way, and none of it was flat.

It took an hour to walk home with a full pack. I fried the grayling fillets in bacon fat, with dill. I could not have spoken, even if there had been anyone to hear.

The rain returned next day. I worked. My senses refined. The less there seemed to be to see and hear, the more clearly I could apprehend what there was. At the table in the kitchen I kept typing, looking back to a past that seemed as grey and impenetrable as the clouds clamped over the valley. For days I seemed to be struggling through a bog in my work, measuring progress only in exhaustion. But at least I could attain exhaustion. It seemed to me, from where I sat with nothing to watch but the swallows, that trying to work as I normally do, with a telephone and an Internet connection, was like trying to think in a cloud of mosquitoes. In the evenings, if I did not fish, I would walk by the still reaches of the river. One day I realized that my story had almost reached a point where it moved by itself without needing to be pushed every inch.

That evening I spent an hour by the river being hardly bitten at all and slowly overwhelmed by the silence. The various ducks and divers out in the main stream seemed restless and boisterous, though they seldom called; they were constantly splashing and resettling on the water, seeming to jostle one another. Right on the far bank at the other end of the old ferry route I could see a white blurry sausage and a dark one and hear the occasional hollow noise of a wooden boat being moved around. The noise was much more distinct than the sight. After about half an hour of this, the blurry sausages spoke— there was a child there, too, and their voices, at normal conversational pitch, carried right across the river. I remembered an earlier evening walking on the shore when a car had driven along the gravel road and it seemed so loud and distinct I supposed it was a train.

After I had been staying for a while, the Vinblads, who owned the farm, started to make small friendly noises. I had approached them cautiously, with a nonchalant display of harmlessness, as if we were creatures meeting in the forest. I had been visibly conscientious about cleaning and sweeping. I borrowed their washing line when I needed to dry the clothes that I washed in the kitchen sink. I waited for them to speak.

They were both short and firmly built. Sture had an expression of mild, amused determination and a handshake that felt like rusted iron pipes. Ulla had short ash-blonde hair and a face, kindly when she talked to me, that filled with brutal determination when she thought. Some people look vulnerable when their thoughts are elsewhere. Ulla seemed to leave behind a face of stone, like an effigy on a tomb. But whenever we talked she was considerate, thoughtful and easily amused, and when she learned that I planned to walk into town to go shopping, she offered me a lift, and on the way told me a little of their story.

The farm had belonged to Sture's parents; he and Ulla had bought it from his widowed mother in 1970, after she had a stroke, and lived there ever since. For twenty-five years Sture had worked full-time, mostly as a logger, and farmed in the evenings, until he had a heart attack in 1995—it was the stress, she said—when the work became impossible. They sold the cows, and built the annexe where I stayed and, later, the two *stugor* in the grounds.

Ulla had brought up six children—that was all she told me then.

They had eleven grandchildren. One of their children lived in the valley, two in Sorsele, two on the coast and one in the far south. She only thought of the son who actually lived in their house as living 'here'. The two in Sorsele had 'moved away', though only four miles.

On the west coast of Sweden, a thousand miles, more or less, from where I now was, I'd had a friend who could distinguish between the different dialects of adjacent fishing villages—except that no one nowadays spoke in anything but television mulch. In the high north, this seemed to be less true. Ulla and Sture both spoke a dialect with all the word endings missing, at least to my ear, and the vowels shifted towards the back of the mouth. Remembering winters further south, when snot would freeze hard on my moustache, I imagined it as a language pinched and chopped off by the cold, arranged so that you spent as little time as possible with your tongue exposed. But they could hear differences in it too fine for an outsider to notice. Ulla came originally from the Skellefteå district, about a hundred miles away, on the Baltic coast. When she took Sture to meet her parents in the early Sixties, and her father and grandfather talked to each other, he couldn't understand a word of their dialect.

Sture and Ulla were puzzled that I did not have a car. I don't think they believed that I actually wanted to walk as much as possible, and I couldn't see any way to explain to them that in fact three or four hours' fiction writing counts as a reasonable day's work, when their own definition of work was so much harder. Ulla offered to dig out an old bicycle for me from the farm's abundant store of broken-down machinery, so that I would not have to walk the whole way to the water; and at about five o'clock one afternoon this was produced. I think it was younger than me, but not by much: an ancient, upright, foot-braked lady's bike with swept-back handlebars and flecks of rust all over the cream skin. But there was a baggage carrier, on which my rucksack fitted. I rode it around the yard, upright and wobbling like the schoolmistress in *Butch Cassidy*, and then piled everything on the back to explore the path to the bottom of the rapids, which led, I was told, from another settlement upriver. The road along the shoreline that I would have preferred to follow didn't exist, for the fairly obvious reason that it would be destroyed by the floods every year.

So I pushed up the hill, feeling like a superannuated Vietcong. It was a very long hill, even with a bicycle to help. But nearly at the top, I turned left to Stridsmark (which means battlefield), the hamlet at the foot of the rapids, and whirled down a succession of switchbacks, very upright, with my cap wedged down hard, rejoicing in the rush of air on my bare arms in the sunlight.

After a mile or so, I braked where the road petered out at a house and barn. A man with browny-yellow hair, and browner, yellowing teeth set widely and at irregular angles, was fixing something with a spanner. He wore trousers, sandals, and nothing else. He had a rich, hay-coloured beard, a large, pale stomach bulging over his jeans, and blue eyes of astonishing brightness and depth. He looked at me as if I were strange and possibly mad.

I asked where the path was to the rapids. He looked at me as if all his suspicions had been confirmed. He said nothing.

I asked again, recalibrating my accent to the flutingest BBC Swedish I could manage.

'You can't get there,' he said.

'But I'm sure there's a path,' I said.

'Well,' he said, 'in that case, it's the path from beyond the barn. But it's a good two kilometres, and it's very bad.'

He studied my expression.

'Well,' he said, 'maybe a kilometre and a half.'

But something inside me rebelled. I determined to go home and not to wear myself out fighting through another tangle of mosquito-infested undergrowth. I wheeled the stately bicycle around and prepared to mount.

'Did you come from Sorsele?' asked the farmer. His manner suggested that if I had, it was the funniest thing that had happened all week.

No, I said. I had come from Sikfors. He absorbed the disappointment. I cycled slowly away up the gentle rise and, when it became less gentle, dismounted and pushed.

The rain returned the next day; bright puddles formed in all the declivities of the road. In the pauses when the drizzle died away, I bicycled down the valley, away from town. This stretch of the road, or track, was where the earliest settlement had been built, when the first farmers and trappers pushed up the river in the 1670s and built a 'Lapp chapel' on the island of Sorsele. Before that time the whole valley was pure unsettled wilderness. Now, of course, every tree you see, in all the apparently endless forests, has been replanted or allowed to grow by man. There are only a few scrappy fringes of primeval woodland on the borders of Russia and Finland, deliberately preserved.

Coming down one little slope I saw a fox so red and snub-nosed that I thought it must be a lynx; otherwise, the forest seemed empty. Reindeer and elk left tracks on the sand when they came to the river to drink; the local paper had stories about bears and even wolves. But most days I did not see any animals at all. So I told Ulla that I thought I might have seen a lynx. She was delighted; in all her years up there, she had only seen one once, and that had been sixty or seventy miles away, where the mountains rise out of the forests towards Ammarnäs. But she knew there was supposed to be one hunting along this stretch of the river. There were also red deer there, which the farmers kept alive in winter by putting out hay, since deer can't scrape down through the snow for food as elk and reindeer can.

She gave me a lift to the library so that I could look the mysterious animal up. It was an airy modern space that seemed unusually warm, with a huge chamber off the hall for hanging outer clothes in winter. There was a display of children's books in Turkish, as well as glass cases with handicrafts from the wooden cabins where the poor had lived. I found an encyclopaedia and discovered that the animal I'd seen must have been a fox; a lynx could not have had so long a tail, even as a kitten. I told Ulla this as we drove back. It was a shame, I said, that the beautiful story could not be true. She seemed to accept this. It was perhaps a way to chip myself off from the undifferentiated block of tourists.

She was determined to show me the sights of Sorsele. We went together around the junk shop, where clothes, books and ancient plastic gadgets were sold second-hand. It looked like a collection of all the unwanted Christmas presents in the country. I imagined that each of the regular customers must have owned something in it at least once. As we drove back, Ulla said that she must take me some time to see the church. There was also, she said, a very beautiful woodland graveyard.

In the morning I wrote in my diary, 'Today it is raining and looks as if it will get rainier and colder all day. I hate it that the days go past, and that this must come to an end. I want to spin here like a capsule far above the earth, just watching.' But around one-thirty that day the drizzle evaporated, leaving the skies grey and cold enough to wear a jacket over a flannel shirt even when cycling. I piled everything on the bicycle and set off for the river. I seemed full of strength and determined to walk down to the very tip of the rapids. But I found that the other path led through a fresh, rain-soaked berry bog. It would have been fun in waders. It smelled deliciously fresh, but soaked me from halfway down my calves, and grew at last quite impassable.

So I returned to the first place and stuffed my soaking feet into dry waders, swearing loudly in English at the empty river. There were no rises. I decided to catch the fish down at the bottom of the river, where they feed on the larvae, or nymphs, of flies. I waded carefully out to a run I had spotted at the very start of the rapids, put on a large and hideous bead-head stonefly nymph, and caught nine grayling, all returned, and none much above the minimum size. Still, nine grayling in three hours is not bad.

Just as I was sitting down to peel off my waders and put on my soggy cold shoes again, a middle-aged man and his son picked their way over the stones towards me. He was lean, blue-eyed, with a short, full, fox-coloured beard; the son was taller, clean-shaven but for a blond goatee beard about four inches long and a habit of tipping his chin in the air to stroke it. The son had a fly rod and waders; the father wellington boots and a long spinning rod. I was feeling absolutely exhausted as we chatted (I thought this was the effect of flickery sleep patterns in the light) and making silly mistakes in my Swedish. Then I happened to look up at the father's spinning rod, which was about my eye level where I sat on a rock with my waders round my ankles, and saw on the end of the line a curiously misshapen silver and metal fish about ten centimetres long, so much bigger than the fly I had been considering grotesquely huge that I burst out laughing. He stiffened like a terrier and demanded to know why I was laughing.

It looked so big, I said, in comparison to the flies I had been using.

'I made this myself,' he said. 'I have caught more than five hundred trout on it: thirty of them weighing more than five kilos.'

He looked ready to fight a duel for the honour of this little wobbler. I was impressed by the engineering and the skill that must

have gone into such a thing and I told him so, as his bristling
subsided. I realized his whole life turned around the wobbler, as mine
might turn around my work.

Once I had cycled home I was slumped over the remains of a plate
of meatballs, as exhausted as if they had been fired into my stomach
like grapeshot, when Ulla banged on the door. Would I like to come
out with them and lift a net this evening? It must be done now,
because this was the rotting month.

I didn't understand the urgency until we were all sitting in their
fibreglass dinghy. The outboard motor had been Sture's fiftieth-
birthday present, sixteen years ago. He sat at the oars and Ulla at
the engine. I sat in the middle with a camera and we set off across
the calm river at its broadest point. After about ten minutes we
reached the empty detergent bottle bobbing on the surface that
marked the end of the first net. For these were gill nets, long sheets
of clear nylon about a metre deep, which are simply left out to hang
in the current and entangle the fish that pass. They choke there and
are almost all dead by the time the net is collected, or as near to it
as makes no difference. If they had been left overnight, they would
have spoiled in the ruthless fertility of summer.

Sture rowed the boat backwards up the line of the net while Ulla
lifted the cord on top of it and peered down the mesh for tangled
fish. If she found one, she lifted a stretch of net on board, and pushed
the fish and pulled the net with her broad hands until it came free,
when she flipped it into a plastic bucket. But in the whole length of
the first net there were only three small *sik* and a perch; when I saw
that some were still alive, I pulled a Leatherman tool from my belt
to use as a priest and clubbed them on the head with it. In the second
net there were only three plump perch where a shoal had passed in
the night. These fish seemed much more wrongfully (and
unexpectedly) dead than the ones I had caught myself.

As we stood afterwards around the gutting table, in the usual
cloud of small bloodsucking things, their eldest son, Lars, walked
up in jogging shorts and a T-shirt, as if there were nothing in the air
but air. I have watched Ulla negotiating with a couple of Polish
tourists while a mosquito moved slowly along her forehead under
her woollen hat with ruminative pauses and she just didn't seem to
notice at all, though I twitched trying not to brush it off.

I was introduced by my distinguishing characteristic: 'This is Andrew. He puts back the fish that he can't eat!'

Walking up to the house with a bucket of headless, gutted fish to smoke, Ulla pointed out the potato patch. The plants are nearly three feet high now and some are flowering. They are going to pull the first ones today and have promised me some. This is about two months later than one eats the first new potatoes in the south—on the other hand, these ones were only planted on June 13. That was less than six weeks ago. The light is so strong and continuous that plants never pause in their growth for a moment.

Later we sat in their kitchen drinking rosehip tea and talked. Hugo, the Norwegian forest cat, made up to me in the most shameless and flattering fashion. He placed his front paws on my thigh and stretched his neck right out, twisting it to expose new bits for scratching and at the same time to rub the back of his head against me. 'Is it true,' Sture asked, 'that in England it gets dark at night in summer?' He knew such places existed, but he asked the question as if summer dark were unknown in about half the world.

As a young man he had worked on logging crews in the woods in winter; out there for a month at a time in a steady thirty-below. 'We used to burn wood in the evenings, and then it would be beautifully warm—twenty, twenty-five degrees inside the cabin with ten men there. But the cabins were badly built, and when you woke the next morning to make coffee, there would be ice on the water bucket. Of course, once you were out in the woods and working, you don't feel the cold.' Did the chainsaws mind the cold? I asked. No, they were reliable. But the tractors were always breaking down when there was more than thirty degrees of frost, so they used horses instead.

Ulla's father, who was eighty-five, had been in the Stockholm paper because the first meteorite to land in Sweden for a century had struck the ground right in front of him, leaving a charred circle in the grass. But he was a remarkable old man in other ways, a dowser, too. He could dowse not just for water but for electric cables buried in the ground. Here Sture mimed the leaping of bent copper wire in the hands of his father-in-law as he walked over a cable. Then he said that his wife had a gift of her own. Oh, don't, she said. No, really, she could see the *vätt*. It took me a moment to recognize the word for the forest trolls who lurk around dwellings as if on their way to domestication.

'I don't like to talk about it,' she said eagerly. 'Even as a child, I had feelings about them, but I didn't want to tell anyone, because they would have thought me silly. But when we moved out here, there was clearly something in the barn. There was one cow that would be milked overnight sometimes when no one was there. Once I found a trail of milk drops going back into the woods from the barn, but even before I saw that I could feel there was a path to the woods. I told Sture not to park the tractor there, but he just laughed. The next day, the big back tyre was flat and he had to take the whole wheel into Sorsele to mend it. But when they got there, there was no puncture. The tyre was fine, and so was the valve.

'Then, about three weeks later, he parked the tractor there again, behind the barn. It was the most convenient place. Again, he came out the next day and found the tyre punctured; but when he took it into Sorsele there was nothing wrong with it. After that, he never parked the tractor there again, even if he didn't completely believe me. But a few years later, forgetting, he parked the snowplough there at the end of the winter. When he came out to look at it, four of the long split pins that hold it to the tractor were missing. They were heavy steel things—' She held her hands up, about twenty centimetres apart. 'Sture came in and said, "Someone needed those", meaning that they had been stolen. He was going to order fresh ones. But I told him that he should move the plough, and this time he believed me. Three days later, two of them were back where they should be.'

Sture took up the story. 'I found the other two a couple of months later, behind a big slab of Sheetrock that was resting against the wall in the barn. I know I didn't put them there.'

She looked at me. 'Andrew doesn't believe us,' she said.

No, no, I said. It was just the way that these stories took place in a world of tractors and cotter pins. But still, I said, there was no reason why the *vätt* shouldn't adapt to a world of refrigerators; after all, Hugo had.

She rose to make more tea and, as she walked across the kitchen, her hips seemed stiff and high. It was the first time I had ever seen her look tired, but after that I could not forget that she was also old.

Back with fresh rosehip tea, Ulla told another story: she had been lying in bed one morning at about five when she heard a great bang at the front door and someone come into the kitchen. But she was tired and didn't bother getting out of bed. She thought it must be Lars. Yet when she came down, the fridge door was open, and the front door, and no human had been there.

Once, she had actually seen one: a little grey man, about so high—her hand a couple of feet above the table. The grass had been high, then, but not yet cut. The long wooden frames on which the hay is dried stood empty in the meadows. She had been on the tractor in the big meadow down the road (she used a dialect word for meadow, and Sture said 'in Swedish', so then she used the word I'd understand). Just as she drove past the frame on her tractor, she saw from the corner of her eye a little grey shadow standing on the top pole. She stopped the tractor and looked again. Three times she stopped and restarted the tractor. Each time, when she looked at the pole, the creature was there. She was sure he wanted something. But what? She thought at last that he must be warning her. So she drove straight back to the farm and told Sture that they must get in the hay on the big meadow at once.

She told him why, and he believed her. So he took his tractor down and they made hay of the whole field. The storm came over the hill just as they placed the last forkful on the stack. Then it rained without stopping for a fortnight. In this short summer that would have lost them all the winter hay.

This meeting seemed to her unequivocal proof that the *vätt* were benevolent spirits, happy to exchange favours with humans.

Do you have such things in England, she asked. No, I said: we have driven the wilderness out, and ploughed it over, and gardened it for a thousand years now. Nothing like that could live there any longer. I looked out at the bright evening. It was twenty past eleven and time to go to bed.

The next day, Ulla took me to the graveyard. We were supposed to be shopping, but she said she wanted to show me the sights of Sorsele, and so we drove from the supermarket to the church, but when we reached it, she continued over the bridge, to a spot where she said there was a beautiful forest graveyard. She drove past slowly, me making the right sorst of noises: it just looked like a sparsely forested slope with unusually regular outcrops of granite. As we went past, she said, 'Sture and I will be buried there. We have chosen a spot. It's just up there—we had a little boy who only lived four and a half hours, and he's there.'

She drove on for a few hundred metres until we came to a

junction. A road ran off, completely straight, into the scrubby forest on our left and she slowed down to turn. 'You can go down there and get to the rapids,' she said. 'Lots of the fishermen go that way.'

On the way back past the graveyard, I asked when the child had died. 'In 1965. He was our second child... We could stop,' she said, as if the idea had just occurred to her. 'I want to check the grave is all right.' I caught her eye and rather wished I hadn't.

At the gate, she turned left and walked down a straight asphalted path. I walked for a while through the upper regions, photographing the heavy, ornamented gravestones, and when I thought she had had enough time, walked to the upright marble slab that said VINBLAD, FAMILY GRAVE. There was a bucket on the grave in front, half full with flowers no more than a day old. 'It's all tidied,' she said, as if she had only been tidying. 'They say it stops hurting,' she said. 'It never does.'

We drove back over the bridge into town. Opposite the church was a substantial three-storey house. 'It used to be the parsonage, but now it is just offices. I was friendly with the parson's wife—she said it was a lovely house, but terrible to run. Imagine how much it cost, and how much time, to put up all the curtains!'

That night, I fished almost until eleven. I wanted to catch one more fish on a dry fly, and so I tried once again the place below the island where I had fished the first time that I came to the river. Almost immediately I hooked a nice fish. I was in a hurry to release him, so I put the rod down and started to pull the nylon directly. Just as I noticed he was foul-hooked near the eye he broke free, with the fly still in him. I felt horrible, and rather guilty, and resolved to net everything from then on.

As if to punish me for wounding the fish's eye, my own glasses started to steam up terribly whenever I tried to concentrate, so that the fly would vanish as soon as it landed and, after it had floated down for a while, it was all I could do to distinguish the river from the rocks. I looked longingly downstream at the breakwater, where there were three people fishing, and wondered if I could go down and ask them for splash of jungle juice. But I manoeuvred myself into a new position and managed the long, perfect cast that had eluded me for an hour. The fly had hardly settled on the water before it was taken by a large fish which did not diminish, as so many large fish do, when it approached me.

In the water, it was the biggest grayling I had ever seen, let alone landed; it was definitely too big for my net, and after three or four farcical attempts the net broke away from its frame, but somehow retained the grayling inside its remains so I could hoist it in and kill the fish on the rock at my feet. I felt nearly as shattered as the fish myself, and walked very slowly home through the liquid light of the woods, thinking about trolls and immortality.

The next day, something strange happened. I walked by the river around noon—wonderful silence, elk tracks in the sand; and a neat pile of yellowing reindeer bone: a skull, a shoulder blade, a bit of a jaw, half of a shin.

After lunch I hauled the armchair into my bedroom so I could sit in front of the window and read. But then I didn't read; I just sat, looking towards the north. I was too low to see anything but sky, the top of an empty flagpole, and round it swallows hunting in the bleak and blue-grey light. I didn't think, or move much in the chair. I didn't watch in any active sense either: my eyes were not hungry; they were simply clear. It was as if the silence that had been in my ears for so long had finally reached my eyes.

I felt that I was eavesdropping on myself, and when I became aware that I could hear my thoughts, they were all in Swedish, with long vowels stretching out under the sky. Beneath that sky, I didn't feel small. I felt transient. I knew I would flicker away soon like everything else, a swallow, or a grayling, or one of the large, cautious ants on the edge of the road. Every living thing in the landscape would be dead, hidden or fled in six months' time; and the river would freeze up four feet thick. In spring the water would return in a flood that would tear boulders the size of cars; as this receded, hundreds of millions of fish would be born in the shallows, and billions of insects in every swamp and pool.

The fecundity of the river, renewed every year, seemed the most powerful force on earth. It had been here long before humans; but even the river was weaker than the ice. Twelve thousand years ago the whole valley was bare rock pressed in the grinding darkness underneath a glacier; one day the river would vanish again.

Long before that I would die. I'd be as dead as the grayling I had eaten by the river; and as dead as everyone I'd loved; everyone I could even remember. Everyone who could ever remember me would die.

I didn't want anything else. Up against that huge sky, there was nothing else to want. But this wasn't a revelation for my benefit: there would never be an apocalypse or a reason. It just was.

I thought of the river again and how much more valuable it seemed than human life. So I did want one thing: that the grayling should not die out until after the humans had all gone.

For a time I sat, assenting, until the silence was broken by two mosquitoes. I killed them as quickly as I could.

The next day it rained incessantly while I packed to leave. I woke in the middle of the night, imagining that the whole landscape was a kind of quilt, soft as unleavened bread, which I could pull round my giant self, with warm prickly pine trees like a pelt, and the cooling rivers and smooth, comforting rocks. Then my foot started twitching and banging the bed and I heard these as the thumpings of a dying perch's tail on the floor of the boat. Then just a huge silence and grief. I wept a little without any sound, stretched on this abyss, and when I next woke it was the morning when I must leave.

I walked along the river for half an hour before breakfast, touching the reindeer skull for luck. It was so sunny that there was even a hint of yellow in the tips of some wild sprouting rye on the bank. I have the greens, I thought. Up here, all blues turn green.

At the bus stop I embraced Ulla on the tarmac and promised to try to return in the winter. Even before the bus moved, the rumbling blurry noise and smells had whisked me away from the forest as soon as I climbed on board. Then the journey started, and at once we were back in the middle of nowhere: the trees and lakes and rocks outside were all an undifferentiated smear against the windows that stretched as far as I could see, and in the middle of the broad daylight I thought of a line from Donne's 'St Lucy's Day': 'I am re-begot, of absence, darkness, death—things which are not.' The radio hissed and clicked like scorpions in the roof.

Several times we passed cars parked by the side of the road with groups of berry pickers beside them, holding white plastic buckets for their harvest. There, along the roadside, summer was almost over.

□

GOD AND ME
John McGahern

I grew up in what was a theocracy in all but name. Hell and heaven
and purgatory were places real and certain we would go to after
death, dependent on the Judgement. Churches in my part of Ireland
were so crowded that children and old people who were fasting to
receive Communion would regularly pass out in the bad air and have
to be carried outside. Not to attend Sunday Mass was to court social
ostracism, to be seen as mad or consorting with the devil, or, at best,
to be seriously eccentric. I had a genuinely eccentric school-teaching
cousin who was fond of declaring that she saw God regularly in the
bushes, and this provoked an uncomfortable nodding awe instead
of laughter. In those depressed, God-ridden times, laughter was seen
as dangerous and highly contagious. The stolidity of the long empty
grave face was the height of decorum and profundity. Work stopped
each day in shop and office and street and field when the bell for the
Angelus rang out, as in the Millet painting. The Rosary, celebrating
the Mysteries, closed each day. The story of Christ and how He
redeemed us ran through our year as a parallel world to the solid
world of our daily lives: the feasts of saints, Lent and Advent, the
great festivals of Christmas and Easter, all the week of Whit, when
it was dangerous to go out on water; on All Souls' Night, the dead
rose and walked as shadows among the living.

Gradually, belief in these sacred stories and mysteries fell away
without my noticing, until one day I awoke, like a character in a
Gaelic poem, and realized I was no longer dreaming. The way I view
that whole world now is expressed in Freud's essay 'The Future of
an Illusion'. I did not know that the ordinary farming people I grew
up among secretly viewed the world in much the same terms. They
saw this version of Roman Catholicism as just another ideological
habit they were forced to wear like all the others they had worn since
the time of the Druids, observing its compulsory rituals cynically,
turning to it only in illness or desperation. Yet none of this is simple.

Before the printed word, churches have been described as the Bibles
of the poor, and the Church was my first book. In an impoverished
time, it was my introduction to ceremony, to grace and sacrament,
to symbol and ritual, even to luxury. I remember vividly the plain flat
brown cardboard boxes in which tulips for the altar, red and white
and yellow, came on the bus in winter when there were no flowers
anywhere.

In 1903, Proust wrote to his friend George de Lauris:

I can tell you at Illiers, the small community where two days ago
my father presided at the awarding of the school prizes, the curé is
no longer invited to the distribution of the prizes since the passage
of the Ferry laws. The pupils are trained to consider the people
who associate with him as socially undesirable, and, in their way,
quite as much as the other, they are working to split France in two.
And when I remember this little village so subject to the miserly
earth, itself the foster-mother of miserliness; when I remember the
curé who taught me Latin and the names of the flowers in his
garden; when, above all, I know the mentality of my father's
brother-in-law—town magistrate down there and anticlerical; when
I think of all this, it doesn't seem to me right that the old curé
should no longer be invited to the distribution of the prizes, as
representative of something in the village more difficult to define
than the social function symbolized by the pharmacist, the retired
tobacco-inspector, and the optician, but something which is,
nevertheless, not unworthy of respect, were it only for the
perception of the meaning of the spiritualized beauty of the church
spire—pointing upward into the sunset where it loses itself so
lovingly in the rose-coloured clouds; and which, all the same, at
first sight, to a stranger alighting in the village, looks somehow
better, nobler, more dignified, with more meaning behind it, and
with, what we all need, more love than the other buildings,
however sanctioned they may be under the latest laws.

When a long abuse of power is corrected, it is generally replaced
by an opposite violence. In the new dispensations, all that was good
in what went before is tarred indiscriminately with the bad. This is,
to some extent, what is happening in Ireland. The most dramatic
change in my lifetime has been the collapse of the Church's absolute
power. This has brought freedom and sanity in certain areas of human
behaviour after a long suppression—as well as a new intolerance.

The religious instinct is so ingrained in human nature that it is
never likely to disappear, even when it is derided or suppressed. In
The Greeks and the Irrational, E. R. Dodds proposes this lucid
definition and distinction: 'Religion grows out of man's relationship

to his total environment, morals out of his relations to his fellow man.'

For many years Dodds was a sceptical member of the British Society for Psychical Research. He distinguishes between two approaches to the occult, though he admits they are often mixed in individual minds. The psychic researcher he describes as wishing to abolish the occult in the clear light of day, while the occultist seeks experience rather than explanation. If the true religious instinct as described by Dodds—our relationship to our total environment—will not go away, neither will its popular equivalent seeking signs and manifestations and help in an uncertain and terrifying world.

Not very many years ago, a particularly wet summer in Ireland became known as the Summer of the Moving Statues. Rumours circulated that statues of the Virgin Mary in grottos all around the country were seen to move and had given signs that they were about to speak. Many of the grottos were constructed during the Marian Year of 1954, when no housing estate or factory was built without a grotto of the Virgin and a blessing by a bishop; and there were also grottos from much older times, often set in a rock-face with dripping water, or by a holy well that was once a place of pilgrimage. Crowds gathered in the rain to stare at the statues. There were pictures on TV, reports on the radio and in newspapers. The journalist Dick Walsh decided to travel around Ireland to investigate this phenomenon. He saw many small groups gathered in all weathers staring at the statues as if willing them to move and speak. When he returned, he reported that the statues looked steady enough but he was less certain about the people.

Whether it be these humble manifestations or the great soaring spires of the Gothic churches, they both grew out of a human need. This can be alleviated by material ease and scientific advancement but never abolished.

Still sings the ghost, 'What then?' □

GOD AND ME
Nadeem Aslam

One night some years before I was born, my mother balanced a ladder on two thick branches within the canopy of a tall tree and climbed upwards, emerging out of the leaves and flowers, her arms free and outstretched as she arrived at the topmost rung.

The tree was a jacaranda, *neelum* in Urdu, its high flowers a delicate blue-violet, as though the floor of an English bluebell wood had been made airborne. It stood behind my grandparents' house in Pakistan, and I have seen it, have imagined a young woman rising above the blue haze of its flowers. Just beyond the furthest rung, her mother was leaning out of a window and she pulled her young daughter into the house safely, the ladder falling away.

That evening my mother had attended a performance of devotional Muslim music at a house in the next street. Her brother, my uncle, had become a follower of a strict unsmiling sect of Islam which forbade such gatherings; on discovering where his sister was, he had installed himself at the front door of my grandparents' house waiting for her return, a cane in his hand.

On the very first page of my first novel, I wrote about an adult who takes children's toys from them and hands them back broken. Islam forbids idolatry. Toys can be considered idols and are to be smashed. My uncle did that to me: he snatched from my hands a mask that I had just bought from a vendor in the street and tore it to bits. I can still remember my feelings of shock and incomprehension. My uncle's version of Islam was the same kind practised by the Taliban regime in Afghanistan three decades later. It would be state policy in the Taliban-ruled Afghanistan to ban children's toys, as well as music.

In Turin, Italy, in the spring of 2005, I went to a reading given by the Syrian poet Adonis. He would read a few verses in Arabic and then pause while they were translated into Italian for the audience. I know neither language and yet, not long into the reading, I discovered that my eyes were full of tears and realized that if I did not exert control I would be weeping openly. I was puzzled and when I told my friends about it later, they were amused. It is only now, months later, that I think I know what made me cry.

As a child I was made to read the Qur'an without any understanding of the grammar or idiom of Arabic. I had to learn the words by heart simply because they were sacred. My mind, even then, did not work like that, and I was regularly slapped or beaten with a cane on the hands and body by the clerics for not having memorized the verses. Even more frightening than the thought of being punished myself, was the thought that my brother would be beaten. I remember him crying out under the blows one day at the mosque. My uncle, who was feared by everyone, including my mother, would sometimes wake me at dawn with his loud chanting of the Qur'an. As a result of such associations, the very sound of Arabic came to sicken me.

I cannot be certain but perhaps there is more—another layer to this revulsion towards Arabic. During my teenage years, Pakistan was changing under the military rule of General Zia-ul-Haq, who legitimized his regime by promoting what he called 'Islamic' values. The Qur'an came to be chanted on television and radio at every opportunity and people began to give their children archaic Arabic names. These 'Islamic values' also meant the flogging of criminals and public hangings, as in Saudi Arabia. This was new to Pakistan and I found it horrific, this brutalization of my country's civil society.

I loved—and continue to love—the pages of certain copies of the Qur'an: the lovingly illuminated borders, the geometric designs on the title pages; a small chrysanthemum flower employed at the end of each verse instead of a full stop. One of my oldest notebooks has the following sentence: *Allah will surely prove his love for his creatures by filling Paradise not only with wine and beautiful girls and boys, as promised, but with arabesques as well.* The sinuous calligraphy of Arabic was greatly pleasing to my eyes but I stopped myself from pronouncing the words.

I left Pakistan in my mid-teens. Here in England, I had no real contact with spoken Arabic—any more than with Chinese or Greek—until I began to hear the taped interviews and finger-wagging pronouncements of Osama bin Laden and his fellow terrorists; and they too were full of hatred and the firestorms of Hell.

I have not lived a very cosmopolitan life. My parents to this day do not know any countries other than England and Pakistan. (They have a few memories of India where they were both born before Partition.) I only started to travel when I became a published writer. And so that day in Italy—on one of my very first trips abroad—when the great Adonis recited the poems I had known in English translation for many years, it was a struggle for me to reconcile the hated sounds with the loved words that were echoing in my head. *Her name was walking silently through the forest of letters.*

I have read widely in Arabic literature, beginning, yes, with the *Thousand Nights and A Night.* I have read the Qur'an several times as an adult, and of course there are the novels of the magnificent Naguib Mahfouz; pre-Islamic pagan poetry; the fables of Kalila wa Dimna; extracts from a sorcerer's manual from eleventh-century Spain; the wounded and wounding lines of Mahmoud Darwish. But I have read them all in English, silently in my study. The aural connection was severed long ago. Until that day sitting in front of Adonis. And then there was confusion because how could a sound that spoke to me of brutality, express words of love, of kindness, of longing? There lay the source of my tears. *Qays used to say I have clothed my body with Leila and clothed the human race.*

Of course if I can change the other side can too. One day I saw my uncle become fascinated by a small intricate bird I had folded out of red paper and left lying around. After a few moments he seemed to remember himself and closed his fist around the shape, crumpling and tossing it aside. But for a few moments he had encountered wonder and seen the possibility of beauty within something he loathed, something he went on to destroy.   □

GRANTA

PLANET OF THE YIDS
Gary Shteyngart

Papa and I are walking down the wide, frozen Leninskiy Prospekt. It's my favourite part of Leningrad. I'm ten years old and I've seen the English Golden Peacock clock at the Hermitage a hundred times, thrilled to those mechanized peacock wings and dancing twenty-carat mushrooms that every fourth-grader loves so much. (With shit like this, who *needs* acid?) But that old-town Petersburg is not for me. I'm a citizen of the future.

This is the future. Or rather the present. Same difference. Apartment blocks that have landed from the Andromeda Galaxy: long cumbersome rows of flats, a greyish, intergalactic colour, flanked by ten-storey towers on which the words GLORY TO SOCIALIST LABOUR! and LIFE WINS OUT OVER DEATH! lord over us in fantastic block letters. *Karablyi* we call these new apartments—ships.

Spaceships, I think, as I have read Ray Bradbury and Isaac Asimov, and anyone else the censors have let slip into the country. You don't have to tell me twice: the Andromedans have landed and now our entire neighbourhood is set to take off for the stars.

'Do you have on your spacesuit?' Papa says.

'Is it time for the Planet of the Yids?' I ask.

'What did I say?' Papa takes a swig from his flask. 'Put on the spacesuit, my little turd, and off we go.'

I make the motions of donning my helmet and slipping into my cosmo-galoshes. The temperature is twenty below on the Celsius scale, the street sweepers have fallen asleep somewhere, leaving about a half-metre of January snow for us to traipse in so that we are, without a doubt, treading on one of Jupiter's outer moons, the apartment buildings enormous granite cliffs against which the winds of Io make long screeching sounds.

I've spent the whole day dreaming of the Planet of the Yids. It's so much better than my usual fare, the Soviet classics about Timur and his Band of Red Commandos. I think my father is the H. G. Wells of our time.

Papa starts us off with a battle. He's very excited, jumping up and down, falling a bit into the soft, all-forgiving snow, his *shapka* askance, his spittle forming a frozen arc in the phosphorous glow of street lights and our cheesy Soviet moon.

A battle! The Yids are under attack from twelve Brezhnev-class galactic cruisers the Space Slavs have launched against the Yids' gorgeous black-market planet, where you can chant the Mourner's Kaddish at the top of your lungs and pick up Hennessy cognac and silky-smooth cotton underpants (and for a good price, too, you'd be pleasantly surprised). This time the Yids are surrounded; even Supreme Leader Sharansky has not expected this kind of onslaught and is hiding out in his wife's *mikvah* (a ritual bath for girlies, Papa explains), crying into his *yarmulke*, the coward.

'Maybe Captain Boris can use his circumcised space-*khui* to energize the Shputnik shield,' I say. 'That way he can protect the ionosphere.' You can always count on Captain Boris to save the day, while Supreme Leader Sharansky shows off in front of foreign reporters, being witty and profound, the darling of the free universe.

'Oh, you'd think that,' Papa says, taking an extended swig from his flask, 'but then, before Captain Boris can get his underwear off, *boom!* the goys start bombarding the planet with *salo* space-torpedoes.' *Salo* is salted raw pig fat, lard, a lumpy cousin of English suet. Slathered across a piece of rye bread and followed by a crunchy cucumber, *salo* is my favourite food ever, but these days Papa's Planet of the Yids stories often have a moralizing aspect against this fine Russian staple. (I am only ten years old but already the idea of a God who would deny his people *salo* seems cruel and far-fetched to me.)

'And then what happens?' I shout.

But Papa has turned around and is staring off into the snow-swept distance, where a short figure, bundled in what looks like several coats, is leisurely making his way towards us. 'Aha!' Papa says, a smile cracking his frozen lips. 'Look at that! They're tailing me!' He grabs me by the arm and drags me, cosmo-galoshes and all, towards the figure, which, upon our advance, veers off to the left, then to the right, then stumbles backwards. 'Allo, you!' shouts my father. 'Following me and my son, eh, you KGB scoundrel?' I'm scared, but Papa is laughing. 'Let's have some fun,' he whispers to me, and winks.

The figure stops and puts out his mittened hands as if Papa's about to belt his mug. Two small blue eyes, teary from the wind, are staring at us from inside a scarf wrapped around his head babushka-style. 'Why are you yelling at me, Citizen?' the fellow says to Papa, his slipshod pronunciation reminding me of our building's janitor, Drunken Shurik. 'I'm walking home, that's all. I live in—'

But as he points to a row of ten-storey futuristic flats, he loses his balance and falls unceremoniously into the snow.

'You're drunk!' Papa says. 'They sent a drunk after me!'

'You're lying, Citizen,' says the fallen man. 'It is you who are drunk, and in front of your son, too! I should drag you to the nearest police station...'

'Listen to this drunkard!' says Papa, spitting into the snow. 'Here! You want some?' He waves his flask at the man. I'm hiding behind Papa, taking in the scent of his coat, the mixture of coal, frost and dead rabbit.

The fallen man looks at the flask as if the naked Gina Lollobrigida has walked down Leninskiy Prospekt and asked him to mount her in the snow. 'Gaaah,' he says. 'Mmmmwah?' He crawls towards Papa and the flask, then somehow manages to stand erect. Now I can smell his breath mixed with Papa's breath—it's the familiar smell of a crowded streetcar in the morning.

'Rrrrr...' the man says. 'I'm a...' He points to a little blue pin glowing cheaply on his torn coat. 'I'm a...mmmm...' One more glance at the proffered flask. 'I'm a...mmmm...a member of the All-Union Society for Sobriety... We have an alcohol-free meeting every Wednesday in the men's toilet at Finland Station. We have sardines and fresh bread and...a-a-a-apple juice... Come see for yourself!'

Papa throws the flask to the ground. 'I can't believe they sent a drunk after me!' he cries. 'What am I... A nothing? Who marched in front of the synagogue last Friday chanting WE ARE JEWS! Who? Sharansky?'

'I know nothing of your Zionist activities, Citizen,' the fellow says, his eyes, like my father's, fixed on the fallen flask, which is already covered by a thin layer of snow. 'And where did you get such a nice fur hat? Perhaps you're a speculator as well as a Zionist. Such a shame for your small child...'

'Oh, go to the *khui* already,' Papa says, picking up his flask and uncapping it once more.

'No, *you* go to the *khui*, Citizen!' cries the insulted man, as he starts to hop towards one of the buildings, glancing behind him at the silver flask being emptied into Papa.

At home, Papa stomps around the floor in his galoshes so loudly that Drunken Shurik's wife downstairs starts threatening to call the militia again. 'Am I not a man?' Papa hollers.

My mother, who is the most cultured woman in our building, a graduate of both the Musical Conservatory and the Fine Arts Academy, comes over with a frying pan and makes as if she's going to hit Papa over the head with it. 'No one's following you,' she says. 'You're not a dissident. No one cares about you.'

I'm hiding in my nook by the gutted television set—the insides filled with Papa's clandestine stash of matzo—trying to read about Timur and his Band of Red Commandos as they outwit the invading Nazis yet again.

'Hit me!' Papa cries. 'Go ahead! I don't want to live! You bitch! I'll rip your tits off!'

'Shithead,' says my mother, in a quiet, cultured voice.

In her home-made sweater (patterned on an Italian design copied from a German magazine smuggled in by a Polish friend), her eyes the fading blue of the Catherine Palace, the frying pan handled as deftly as if it were a tennis racket, my mother is the most beautiful woman ever. 'I *wish* they'd put you in a labour camp like Sharansky,' she says. 'First thing I'd do is buy an entire jar of *salo* and eat it with some pickles.'

'WE ARE JEWS!' Papa screams his mantra.

'YOU ARE AN IDIOT!' shouts Drunken Shurik's wife from below.

My mother lowers the frying pan. She surveys my now supine Papa, determines that he's out of breath or out of vitriol, or, more likely, out of alcohol, then returns to the bedroom where we soon hear the rat-a-tat of her American sewing machine. I want to read aloud to her from the Timur book, the artillery of her sewing machine an ideal backdrop to the battle at hand, but then I don't want to leave Papa alone. *Paff! Paff!* I draw a segmented bullet line from an illustration of Timur holding a rifle to the picture of a German soldier on the opposite page. *This one's dead.*

Papa motions for me to come and help him. 'Let them send me to the gulag!' he says, as I roll his bulk over so that he can achieve a four-legged hold on the world. 'I'll tell my American relatives to stop sending her parcels. See how much *salo* she'll buy then.'

Papa crawls over to the couch beneath the Uzbek wall rug embroidered with primitive-looking birds and animals which so perplexed me as a toddler. 'You'd come visit me in the gulag, wouldn't you?' Papa asks, as he tries to drape his legs over the couch. Little whistling noises escape through the two bent cylinders of his nose. His round body gives off the heat of a mustard compress. His face is yellow and black in places.

'Maybe *mamen'ka* will let me move with you to Siberia,' I say.

'I'll lose some weight,' Papa says. 'Some people are made for prison. I'll share a bunk with Sharansky, that Moscow bastard, and we'll while away the night chatting about *Eretz Yisroel*, about how one day we'll play volleyball on the beaches of Tel Aviv with some tanned *sabra* bitches, spend our Fridays talking Kabbalah with the mystics of Safed. He'll understand me, Sharansky. We'll have a bottle of kosher wine on the eve of the Sabbath and then two more on Sabbath morning. I'll turn him into a stinking *alkash*, see if I don't!'

'I know you will,' I tell Papa. 'Your stories are better than H. G. Wells's.'

'You want to go pee on the anti-Semitic pooch?' Papa asks.

'Maybe later,' I say.

'You're my best friend,' Papa says. 'It's important to have friends, don't you forget. I'm your mother's best friend too, and she doesn't even know it.'

'Siberia will be fun,' I say. 'Wild bears chasing after us... Mushrooms and berries for dinner... Planet of the Yids day and night.'

'That's how it'll be,' Papa says. He grabs me by the collar and pretends he's my dog, licking my face until I can no longer breathe; I'm knocked out by the vodka fumes. 'Oi, oi!' he cries. 'Look at what I'm sitting on!' He pulls out a copy of *The All-Union Guide to Boys' Development*, the well-thumbed tome with its cover drawing of perfect naked little boys ascending from age six to twelve, their miniature Yuri Gagarin faces dreamy and heroic, their tiny scrotums progressively fuller. Papa flips to page forty-six, the dreaded Genital Development page. 'Aha!' he says, pointing to the shrivelled sac of goods labelled LENINGRAD MALE, AGE TEN. 'Let's see what you've got to show me! Let's see Corporal Sasha's uncircumcised space-*khui*.'

He's on top of me. I'm twisting down into the couch, cupping myself with both hands. He tries to prise my arms apart. We're both screaming like madmen, ashamed and excited in equal measure. The book falls to the floor. The rot of his armpit in my nose. My mother comes out with the frying pan.

It is time for bed.

And now a few words about the anti-Semitic pooch. Bublik was an overactive yellow-and-brown English terrier who chased after his own tail with a single-minded purpose, creating the blurry appearance of a yellow poppy-seed-sprinkled roll (in Russian, a *bublik*). The dog had been genetically programmed to chase after grouse in the Anglo countryside but somewhere down the line his life had gone terribly wrong and he now found himself in a starchy Leningrad courtyard, hemmed in by icicles, brown sleet, empty vodka bottles and the belching exhaust of the passing trolleybus. That Bublik was an anti-Semite was clear to my Papa. His owner was Colonel Bezpredelkin of the Leningrad KGB, a man barely capable of addressing the lowly residents of our building from beneath his bushy silver moustache, a man who even in the middle of a February blizzard stood as silent and still as a malachite column in the Hermitage Museum. According to Drunken Shurik, who vied with my Papa for the title of our building's Most Unreformable Alcoholic, the otherwise silent and haughty colonel had once shared a New Year's bottle with him and in the throes of merriment told Shurik that he had taught his Bublik to recognize Jews by their garlicky smells and to bark at them with special ferocity.

Why my father chose to listen to Drunken Shurik (the name alone!) and to take on Bublik we will never know, but, in Papa's defence, the dog did embark on a crazed barking spree whenever any garlic-scented Yiddle from the building passed by and, in all fairness, his shrill bark did sound like, 'Ev...ev...ev...ev...ev...' followed by a growl of 'RRRRRRRRRR...RRRRRRRRRR', *evrei* being the Russian word for Jew.

And so my father decided we should pee on him. In the psychologically destroyed Russian village in which my father grew up, trapping an adversary and peeing on him was considered the equivalent of a Sicilian blood vendetta. It was really the end of the road as far as revenge went. One night, with my mother perfectly asleep and dreaming her cultured dreams, and Papa perfectly drunk and ready for trouble, he and I grabbed a wooden milk crate and set out on our midnight score-settling.

Colonel Bezpredelkin was good to his Bublik. Recognizing the dog's outdoor nature, he let Bublik roam freely within the confines of our courtyard during warm weather. And so Bublik was a regular fixture in our crappy courtyard; some of the neighbourhood children, aware of his owner's exceptional pedigree, even saluted him as they passed by.

On an unseasonably warm and dry April day we found Bublik licking his favourite parts under the courtyard's solitary oak tree, his thoughtful expression that of a connoisseur awarding a third Michelin star. Papa stumbled towards him with a piece of pork salami dangling between two fingers. Intrigued, Bublik let go of his small pink appendage. As he drifted closer to us, the fine animal with his slender chest and perfectly docked tail let out a single bark, 'Ev!' and growled softly, 'RRRRRRR.'

'I'll show you who's a Jew,' my father muttered. He waved the pork salami and Bublik traipsed behind him, his head held low as if he was scouring after my Papa's garlicky scent. I followed behind with the milk crate, my heart beating fast in my mouth, the way it did whenever I was privy to my father's fantastical life. 'To the rocket!' my father whispered. Corporal Sasha's Special Space Rocket was a drainage pipe carelessly slung across a neighbouring building. Beneath the rocket a small ditch had been dug which the courtyard's men had quickly turned into an impromptu receptacle for beer bottles and cigarette butts. Papa dropped the salami into the filthy ditch, waited for Bublik to sniff his way over there and said to me, 'Now, Corporal!'

As if in preparation for my impending weight gain, I was developing a unique kind of walk where I propelled myself in sudden jolts, as if I was flicking a long tail behind me. For the manoeuvre at hand, my imaginary tail proved a boon. I did a small run-up to the dog, propelled myself over Bublik and, with the efficiency of a top-notch African-American depositing a basketball, squarely smacked the milk crate around the animal.

As Papa held his boot over the makeshift cage, we watched the dog through the two peepholes we had carved into the milk crate. Bublik, momentarily distracted by the salami on offer, twirled around and started growling the low, humiliated sound that comes with loss of freedom, a kind of unofficial Soviet anthem. Papa unleashed his bulbous turtle-like *khui*, took aim at one of the holes in the crate and, with an expression of perfect contentment long denied, started chanting: 'This is for Israel... This is for Moshe Dayan... *Chai, chai, chai, am Yisroel chai...*'

Bublik could not believe what was happening to him. A life of being coddled, saluted, overfed with choice cuts of mutton and veal kidneys, of being cared for by Leningrad's best veterinarians, and now, after a warm spring night of licking his own pink nozzle and howling at the moon, a drunken *evrei* was pissing over his fine double-barrelled snout. The dog responded as would any high-placed Soviet citizen under the circumstances. 'JEW!' Bublik barked with all his ferocity, his slick trimmed coat gleaming with Papa's pee. 'JEW! JEW! JEW!'

'Quick!' Papa shouted to me. 'Do what you must!'

I lowered my pants and held myself, rather apologetically, in front of Papa. By the lights of *The All-Union Guide to Boys' Development* my *khui* was about three centimetres short of average. Maybe that's why, no matter how much I strained and bothered, nothing issued forth but a weak little childish *spritzle*. 'I told you not to go earlier,' Papa admonished me. 'I told you to save some for Bublik.'

The milk crate trembled beneath my father's foot. The light came on in Colonel Bezpredelkin's window. 'Bublichka!' the normally unflappable man shouted. 'Bublichka! What's the matter, puppy?'

'Run, Corporal!' Papa said. We kicked off the milk crate, unleashing the bewildered urine-soaked terrier, and ran for the street, collapsing on top of each other near the faded light of the empty-shelved grocery store, my Papa's arms nearly crushing me as we giggled and shouted and danced, four-legged, on the cracked asphalt of the ruined street. 'We're free!' Papa shouted. 'We're free!'

'I'll piss on him next time, Papa,' I promised dutifully. 'Oh, how I'll piss on him.'

'I love you, son!' Papa wept happily. 'Everything I do is for you. For you and *Am Yisroel*.'

'WE ARE JEWS.' I whispered his magical mantra and soon we started chanting it together, our voices rising through the murky darkness, as if we could wake every last shit-stained citizen from their nightly stupor and make them listen to us, love us, even *fear us* into the bargain.

Colonel Bezpredelkin never found out who had relieved themselves on his Bublik although he delivered a venomous speech at the meeting of the local district committee on the subject of 'Who is the True Animal among Us?' Meanwhile, a change had come over Papa. He drank less. He avoided arguments with my mother. And he spent a lot of his time thinking greater thoughts. The Americans might have said that peeing on the anti-Semitic dog had 'empowered' him.

The colonel no longer allowed Bublik to play in the courtyard but Papa and I kept devising new ways to urinate on the poor animal, while Papa expanded his activities in a time-honoured Soviet direction: he wrote anonymous letters to the colonel's KGB superiors, complaining about how a man in Bezpredelkin's position could own an English terrier, 'a murderous fox-hunting associate of the class enemy, member of the pawed Gestapo'. But Papa wasn't done yet. He wanted to be recognized. He wanted to be admired. This was his nature. According to my mother, he had fallen into a terrible funk after I was born, sensing he was about to be instantly and irrevocably displaced in my mother's meagre affections. Likewise, when I became a giant florid kike in my early teens, he felt diminished by contrast, like a circus monkey chained to an elephant.

For years after the first Bublik incident I could sense that Beloved Papa was plotting something extraordinary, but no one quite expected what came next. After his release from prison, Papa told me he had entertained a few scenarios all involving urine, a canine and the Big House—the block-sized headquarters of the Leningrad KGB which even to this day mars the exquisite southern bank of the Neva river. First he wanted to kidnap Bublik and pee on him in front of the Big House, then he wanted to kidnap the colonel and pee on him in front of Bublik, then Bublik and the colonel together... Anyway, we can all feel sympathy for the terrified and entirely innocent tomcat my Papa finally ended up disgracing in front of the KGB headquarters as he sang his trademark 'Am Yisroel Chai'. (Colonel Bezpredelkin and Bublik had long been transferred to Moscow.)

Hooliganism, the lesser charge for which my Papa was sentenced, reflected the tenor of the times. Papa had waited so long to execute his plan that not only the colonel, but Brezhnev and his desiccated replacements had gone as well. It was the glasnost era. Gorbachev was in power, prisoner-of-conscience Natan Sharansky was free and living in Israel, and the authorities wanted to ignore the Jewish question as far as possible. So after entertaining the idea of putting my Papa in a mental hospital, they settled on the non-political charge of hooliganism.

When they let Papa out I was already an enormous teenager, 120 kilograms, with a set of thick squishy fists that could do right by my Jew-baiting schoolyard enemies, the big boys with untrimmed nails and two-scoop Adam's apples who used to throw me on the floor and play out the Soviet anthem on my head with xylophone mallets ('Unbreakable union of sovereign republics... Tra la la la...'), but who now crossed to the other side of Leninskiy Prospekt when I walked by. 'Dog-pisser,' my few friends called me in honour of my father's exploits, a moniker I wore proudly.

Papa came out in 1992, the year after the USSR was unceremoniously shut down to make way for something more profitable. I was standing by the prison gates with my mother, chewing forlornly on a bagel. Mother was in the middle stages of the throat cancer that would kill her, her voice already silenced, fingers too shaky to wield the frying pan that used to keep my father in check. A formidable Volga sedan, the kind that used to take Colonel Bezpredelkin to work every day, idled by the kerb. We imagined it was waiting for the prison director himself.

The first thing we noticed was his gait. Erect and *biznes*-like, Papa strode towards us, the ends of a new cashmere scarf inching towards his genitals. The yellowness and blackness had been stripped from his face, leaving him positively rosy and newborn, if a little arch around the eyes. My fat feet propelled me towards him (*'Papochka!'* I cried), until I was clasped in his embrace, surrounded by his fine Jewish laughter and the expensive German aftershave that wafted around him. One of his palms was freshly tattooed with a star of David, another featured a skull with eagle's wings, the sign of a budding criminal's authority. Across the wrist I saw the misspelled English word SUPERBOS.

Three of Papa's former cellmates came out of the Volga sedan, all dark-skinned and curly-haired, one wearing a woolly ethnic hat. These boys could tap into a gas pipeline, throw a landmine on the roof of a moving vehicle, kidnap an enemy's invalid grandfather, win a provincial election. They nodded to my father respectfully, 300 kilograms of Georgian and Chechen muscle searching for a Jewish brain to guide them.

Papa stepped back and looked at his fat, weeping son, then at his silenced, dying wife and then upwards and beyond at the half-dead country surrounding him. The Planet of the Yids hazily circled the polluted sky above us, broke free of orbit, floated off into the cosmos. The space torpedoes had missed their target. The Shputnik shield had been deactivated. We were all alone with each other. □

GOD AND ME
A. L. Kennedy

Faith: the greater it is, the more unsupported it must be and the more it will force you to operate beyond your senses, with the possible exception of that vague intimation of being watched, of a presence beyond imagining standing much too close behind you with something unnerving in mind.

Or perhaps that last part is just me: the Calvinist heritage, the forty years of not-doing-so-well putting a certain spin on my preconceptions concerning the Beyond. The largest preconception being, of course, that there is a Beyond and that Someone is in it, outside it, omnipresently giving the infinite eternal oversight.

My personal experience of the Beyond and the Something is, of course, intangible, unspeakable. I can only attempt to portray it by traditional means—the illustrative story with accompanying gloss. So this is the story where I climb Mount Sinai.

And it's a true story: I really did climb Moses's mountain in the small hours of a clear February night after very little rest and no breakfast. I'd been too cold to sleep and one of my room-mates (life's character-forming experiences always involve communal and rudimentary sleeping arrangements) had some kind of respiratory infection and managed to breathe over-loudly and squeeze out irritating little coughs throughout the few hours I had to lie and fret about hypothermia.

So I was tired, even before I began the climb, and not bursting with love of my fellow man. I was calling my journey research because that seemed less trivial than travel and less embarrassing than pilgrimage. Still, my attempts to keep things prosaic were already being undermined by the painfully naked stars, the slightly reptilian crests along the type of mountains I seemed to remember from my *Children's Illustrated Bible*, or from Tolkien, or from C. S. Lewis: some long-ago, tender place where faith in many things was easier. It began to seem almost churlish not to expect the numinous.

And, in the purely literal sense, I was not alone. The foot of the mountain was thronged with an assortment of nuns, camels, priests, camel-drivers, marshalled groups of Eastern European Orthodox and Korean Christians and straggling mobs of hikers, high-rent crusties, hippies and undecideds. There may also have been a number of spiritual frauds and cowards, much like myself.

The climb (more of a walk, really) took a while: about two hours along a comfortably wide and occasionally steep path that wound between moonlight and shadow, folded along the spine of vertiginous slopes and then tucked itself into clefts. It taught me that nuns are almost invisible at night, that pilgrims are prone to chatter and that camels are remarkably dainty and can follow you soundlessly— although their smell will overwhelm you before there's any danger of their treading on your heels. Beyond that, I was offered no insights. I had no gloves, so whichever hand I used to hold my torch slowly gave up the ghost and then had to be jammed into my pocket while the other began to freeze. I hadn't realized I'd need gloves, let alone one of the nifty little head torches that a few of the wiser hikers were sporting. And perhaps I might not have brought them along anyway— a touch of controlled suffering seemed quite in order; comfortable.

Just shy of the summit, the path meets and is then replaced by the last section of the Steps of Repentance—a suitably punishing route built of irregular boulders. This demands scrambling and stamping for ten or fifteen minutes of purging effort. (And is best done in the dark, thus avoiding sight of the litter and soiled toilet paper tucked to either side of the rocks.) I duly scrambled and stamped and reached the usual small satisfaction of an effort ended, or an object achieved, or a series of mild pains concluded.

The summit was moderately and quietly, crowded. I bought a glass of chocolate from a little stall—odd to smell something so close to familiar in such strange air: each breath dry, clarifying, lively. After my exertions, the chocolate tasted especially fine. The glass was cracked and the liquid was gritty, but this only improved it. I sipped and wandered about, padded round space blankets and huddles of sleeping bags where people had spent the night aloft. People smoked—not always tobacco—there was quiet talk, anticipation, groups and individuals just sitting, or standing, waiting. It was easy to tell which way was east: among the brown and dim jumble of sandy soil and rock, everyone was facing the same direction, as if the sun were already here.

And if I was going to have an epiphany, it should have happened then. I was light-headed, I was undistracted, I was a person of Christian upbringing in a place of biblical significance and a glory was beginning to unfold—a holy and unholy glow of blue that was rolling out ghost upon ghost of mountains, an ocean of misted shapes, and everyone intent around me. I felt that first piercing of sunlight, that lick of whitegold over a sense of the earth's curve and all of us, everyone, felt this together and somebody started to fly a kite in the shape of an eagle—all we could hear, the flutter of this eagle—and colours now, an absurd generosity of colours: layering purples, crimsons, yellows and each new tone seeming to add a new solidity to the range of peaks below us—as if the earth were not quite formed and now it was beginning, becoming itself—and the Korean Christians were singing hymns: simple, gentle hymns—and surely to God this was more than enough to create what I need for a Sign, a Revelation, a Hint, a Clue—and the world shone, warmed, brimmed up to meet me, changing and changing and never anything but lovely.

No Sign, though. No epiphany. Nothing.

So I gave up.

I even moved away a little: at least shifted my feet, scuffled a bit. And I no longer expected anything at all.

Which is, of course, when it happened. A swoop of feeling dropped into me like some kind of phantom piano and I dropped with it to my knees and was, naturally, crying—and for a moment, just a moment, filled with being not alone and with joy and with the awareness of a very large sense of humour.

So where is the lesson in this? We can take the psychological option—and say that having determined I would have a spiritual experience, I managed to, once I'd relaxed enough. Hardly a lesson there: to say that someone who decides to do something will then do it. We can take the medical option—sleep-deprived person almost faints. Even less inspiring. Plus, when I was younger, much younger, I would now and then be taken by a view, an angle of light, some detail of nature that would tap me down on to my kneecaps for a while. All very mild, but not unheard of and no prior expectation necessary. And going without food and sleep?—never makes me faint—it's more my standard operating procedure. No, the lesson has to be spiritual—the old, old tiring axiom that when all hope is lost, that when we despair and then pass beyond despairing, Aid from Someone Beyond will duly arrive.

And I don't deny that can be true. We've all known times when we've beaten our heads against walls of one kind or another until we're sick of it and stop—at which point the other option emerges, or the better alternative becomes clear, a sense of mercy perhaps becomes tangible for a moment—and possibly the cosmic Sense of Humour that lets us educate ourselves, because no one could do it more brutally.

But, of course, it isn't always true. The people we love can still die, or go away. Our hopes cannot all be fulfilled. Sometimes we leave the beating and the wall and we are rewarded with silence, emptiness, another wall, a different beating. And there's no point playing the game of right, now I really give up, now I really am letting go and commending myself to Your care. That care includes cancer, house fires, betrayal and pre-emptive war.

Here I am: forty, childless and alone, perpetually alone—but the same person who fell to her knees for joy at the sight of a landscape. I was made with a capacity for joy. Now I keep low on sleep and food because it means I feel less and I no longer care if I've given up or not, because I know it makes no difference. And beyond me are the people with real problems: a world of apocalypses and quiet lives that try to bind themselves round wounds that seem not only savage, but perverse.

My story tells me that Someone demands I should give up all expectation and surrender to the bone. Sometimes this will be rewarded with the colour of a love I'll never know—a view into the nature I won't fulfil. Always this will remind me of the monumental Trickster behind creation, the one who overloads coincidence, who works on a scale where mercy is a terror and life is a pantomime of blood and wonder. It's a story of the last laugh—when we find out that no matter what we do or don't abandon, no matter how accepting or rebellious we are, in the end we all lose everything. □

Islamic Imperialism

A History
Efraim Karsh

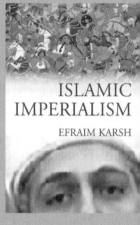

From the first Arab-Islamic Empire of the mid-seventh century to the Ottomans, the last great Muslim empire, the story of the Middle East has been the story of the rise and fall of universal empires and, no less important, of imperialist dreams. So argues Efraim Karsh in this highly provocative book, which is a fundamental challenge to the way we understand the history of the Middle East and the role of Islam in the region.
288pp. £19.99

Saints and Sinners

A History of the Popes
Revised Edition
Eamon Duffy

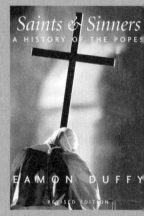

This acclaimed book encompasses the extraordinary history of the papacy from its beginnings nearly two thousand years ago to the present day. In this new edition, the author has brought the story fully up-to-date to cover the last years of John Paul II and the election of Benedict XVI.

"[A] minor masterpiece which is everything good, popular history ought to be . . . The most comprehensive single-volume history of the popes in print."—John Adamson, *Sunday Telegraph*
496pp. 47 colour illus. Paper £10.99

YALE UNIVERSITY PRESS
tel: 020 7079 4900 • www.yalebooks.co.uk

GRANTA

THE LORD
IN HIS WISDOM

Jackie Kay

Jackie Kay and her adoptive mother on the Mull ferry, 1960s

Jonathan is suddenly there in the hotel corridor leading to the swimming pool area. He's sitting on a white plastic chair in a sad cafe. There's a small counter with a coffee machine and some depressed-looking buns. He's dressed all in white, a long white African dress, very ornately embroidered, like lace, and white trousers. He's wearing black shoes. He's wired up. My heart is racing. 'Jonathan?' I say.

'Yes,' he says, standing up and turning slowly to meet me.

I hadn't meant to meet him here. I'd been sitting in the swimming pool area at a nice table by the bar, waiting for two hours, looking up at every elderly black man coming through the opening in the wall. It's a strange thing looking at one black man after another wondering if he is your father. It seemed this morning that everyone was. Several handsome black men appeared, all of an age with Jonathan, wearing more and more elaborate outfits in all sorts of vivid colours: bright green, bright blue, burnished gold, tangerine orange. It was like sitting watching a fashion show of old black men walk the gangway to the pool bar. Each one made some kind of entrance, it seemed, because each one could have been my father.

I wasn't sure that the staff at the hotel reception would definitely pass on my message to send him to the pool bar, so I kept going back to check. Jonathan had said he would arrive some time in the afternoon. Everybody told me that afternoon in Nigeria could be anything between twelve and five. I went to the reception and asked if anybody had called for me. 'No, nobody,' they said. Then I rushed to my room to double check by phoning the hotel operator. 'Yes,' she said, 'Somebody called for you.'

'When?'

'About three minutes ago,' she said.

I tore along the corridor and pressed the lift button. Downstairs I saw the man in white sitting in the odd little cafe. It's the first time I've ever seen anybody sit there since I got to the hotel yesterday.

'Can we go straight away to your hotel room?' he asks me.

'Can we go to my room?'

'Yes, I would like to go to your room now.'

We walk along the corridor to the lift and all the lights suddenly go out. Another power cut. I take his hand and lead him towards the lift in the dark. I grope about in the darkness holding my father's hand. Then the lights suddenly come back on again and we get into the lift. He doesn't talk. I know he won't talk until he gets into the room. He doesn't look at me. He looks down at his black shoes and clasps his hands. He's carrying a plastic bag. A white plastic bag. When I met my mother, she was also holding a plastic bag. Both my birth parents, on first sight, looked like some homeless people look, who carry important papers in carrier bags.

They met in 1961 in the Dance Hall in Aberdeen. Jonathan was a student there and my mother was a nurse. They kept in touch during my mother's pregnancy, then Jonathan returned to Nigeria and my mother went to a mother-and-baby home in Edinburgh to have me. I was adopted five months later by a couple in Glasgow—the people who are to me my real parents. They are lifelong and committed socialists. When I traced my birth mother some years ago I discovered that after her relationship with Jonathan, she had become a Mormon. The Latter day Church of Jesus Christ Saints or whatever. The Mormons, she told me, believe that adopted people cry out to be adopted while they are still in the womb. When I told my mum that my mother was a Mormon, she said, 'Jesus Christ that's the pits. Why not have a wee half bottle and forget all about it.'

And now we're in the room. After forty years I'm about to have a conversation with my birth father for the first time.

Jonathan is moving about from foot to foot, shifting his weight from side to side, like a man who is about to say something life-changing. He begins: 'Before we can proceed with this meeting, I would like to pray for you and to welcome you to Nigeria.' I feel alarmed, frightened that he is going to try and get me to receive Christ. Religion scares the hell out of me. Extreme religion seems to me like a kind of madness, a strange state of mind with crazy, paranoid, superstitious justifications for everything that happens. But it is obvious to me that Jonathan won't be able to talk at all if I try and skip the sermon. So I say, 'Okay then,' and he says, 'Sit please.' And I sit. He plucks the Bible from the plastic bag. Then he immediately starts whirling and twirling around the blue hotel room, dancing and clapping his hands, above his head, then below his waist, pointing his face up at the ceiling and then down to the floor, singing, 'Oh God Almighty, Oh God Almighty, Oh God Almighty, we welcome Jackie Kay to Nigeria. Thank you God Almighty for bringing her here safely.

She has crossed the waters. She has landed on African soil for the very first time. Oh God Almighty!' He does some fancy footwork. He is incredibly speedy for a man of seventy-three. He's whirling like a dervish. Suddenly, he takes off his shoes and puts them on my bed and kneels on the floor and reads the first of many extracts from the Bible. He seems to half read and half recite them; he appears to know the Bible by heart. As he recites he looks at me directly, quite a charming look, slightly actorish, the sermon for him is a kind of performance; his whole body gets thrown into it. 'God has given you this talent. You are a writer. You have written books. You have been blessed. God already knows about you. Don't think for a second that God hasn't been waiting for you. Now all you must do is receive Christ and your talent will become even bigger and you will become more focused. Amen. From this moment on you are protected. God protects the talented. Amen. You can walk through fire, you won't get burnt. You can swim in dangerous waters, you won't drown. Don't even bother with your hotel safe. God is looking out for you.'

I shift uneasily in my seat. Christ almighty, my father is barking mad. He spins and dances and sings some more, singing in the most god-awful flat voice, really off-key. The singing sounds like a mixture of African chanting and hymns. It's a shock. Despite the fact that he can't sing, his performance is captivating. I watch his bare feet dance round the room and recognize my own toes. He looks over directly into my eyes again to see if I'm persuaded. 'I see in your eyes that you are not yet able to put your full trust in God. And yet you know that that would make me happy. At every reading you do, you could take the message of our Lord. Think of the people you could convert.' (I think of the twelve people at a reading in Milton Keynes central library on a rainy Thursday night.) 'Think of all the people you could bring to the Lord if you get ready to receive Christ.' I look as non-committal as possible. I start to think that I should try and get this to stop. It feels like a kind of assault. He senses me thinking this and says, 'Just one more extract from the Bible. I prayed to God you would be attentive and you are being attentive. I prayed to God you would be patient and you are being patient.'

He wants me to be cleansed, cleansed of his past sin. 'If animal blood can cleanse sins under the Old Law, how much more can the blood of Jesus Christ cleanse us and prepare us for glory?' As

Jonathan says this his eyes seem to light up from behind like a scary Halloween mask. 'For if the blood of bulls and of goats, and the ashes of an heifer sprinkling the unclean, sanctify the purifying of the flesh, how much more shall the blood of Christ, who through the eternal Spirit offered himself without spot to God, purge your conscience from dead works to serve the living God?'

I realize with a fresh horror that Jonathan is seeing me as the sin, me as impure, me the bastard, illegitimate. I am sat before him, evidence of his sinful past, but I am the sinner, the live embodiment of his sin. He's moved on now, he's a clean man, a man of glory and of God, but I'm sat on the hotel-room chair little better than a whore in his eyes, dirty and unsaved, the living proof of sin. Christianity has taken away his African culture and given him this. I'm thinking about colonialism and missionaries and not properly listening. I go in and out of consciousness like somebody very ill. I hear his voice in the background. God knows how long it has all been now. I keep trying to rouse myself to ask him kindly to stop. 'And from Jesus Christ, who is the faithful witness and the first begotten of the dead, and the prince of the kings of the earth. Unto him that loved us, and washed us from our sins in his own blood. And hath made us kings and priests unto God the Father; to him be glory and dominion for ever and ever. Amen.' I've zoned out now, drugged by his voice. I can't see properly. Pages of the Bible are flying around the room like hummingbirds. I am desperate for a drink. My glass of wine is sat there at the table in front of me but it seems disrespectful to drink alcohol in the middle of my own personal service.

'Thank you for your patience,' Jonathan says again after another half hour has faced up to eternity. The tears are pouring down my face. I can't stop. It's a flood. It's self-pity. Jonathan is delighted to see them. He thinks maybe I am ready to receive Christ. He thinks I'm moved by his sermon. I am moved; my cheeks are soaking wet. I wipe them with my bare hands as Jonathan's voice goes deep and he lifts his hands into the air and claps and spins like a windmill. I think maybe it's nearly over. *Dear God; I'll believe in you if only this will stop.* I look at my watch. He's been praying for a solid hour non-stop. The man can talk. We have that in common too. 'I prayed you would be docile. Thank you for paying attention.' I shuffle in my seat ready to get up. Then he starts up again more whirling and twirling and shouting to God almighty. More clapping and foot tapping and spinning and reciting. A whole big wad of the Bible rolls out of his mouth like bad money. 'For the grace of God that bringeth salvation hath appeared to all men, teaching us that, denying ungodliness and worldly lusts, we should live soberly, righteously, and godly in this present world. Open your heart to him. Repent of your sins. Allow me to purify and cleanse you. I want to pour out my glory. Believe what I am telling you.'

I try and think of all my sins. True, there are a lot of them. But the fact that I was born out of wedlock? That is not my sin.

Jonathan still wants me to receive Christ. 'You won't give me that assurance? Why won't you give me that assurance?' I don't reply at first because I'm not sure I'm supposed to answer. Then there is a tiny moment's silence where I say, 'I would like you to respect my beliefs as I respect yours. I'm not comfortable with being born again.' I don't want to hurt his feelings and if I told him that I was an out-and-out brutal atheist he'd have to sit down. Even if I said I was an agnostic, he'd feel dizzy. He tells me of meeting a man on the way to the Nicon Hotel in Abuja who was a non-believer and how much of a blow to him this man was, how he'd had to get away fast before the man pulled his spirits down. Jonathan needs believers; he needs believers like some people need cocaine. He needs the fresh hit, the new blood of a beginner believer. I start to see him as a kind of holy vampire, dressed in white, ready to take me in, to help me receive Christ. There's not even a wee wafer or anything in the room. 'God has intended us to meet after I became a born-again Christian. We should deliberate on the issue of new birth. Your talents are even greater than mine. You are going to be very big and God is going to help you. All you have to do is receive Christ and everything will blossom from there. Your whole career. You won't believe the big changes that are going to be happening to you.'

The man won't let go; he won't give up. He's desperate. He's trying to bribe me with my own career! The writer in me perks up for a couple of sick, ambitious seconds. Nope—not even for my writing could I receive Christ. My head is pounding, a tight headache as if somebody had been screwing nails into my forehead. Perhaps I'm being crucified! I think he's about to stop when he cranks himself up again. 'So the people shouted when the priests blew with the trumpets; and it came to pass, when the people heard the sound of the trumpet, and the people shouted with a great shout, that the wall fell down flat, so that the people went into the city. Do you see it? Are you ready to take your city and our land for Jesus? Repent now of every single sin in your life. Receive healing. Follow the six steps to Salvation: Acknowledge, Repent, Confess, Forsake, Believe, Receive.' He has the whole list of extracts written down on a tiny scrap of lined paper which begins with 'Welcome Jackie Kay to Nigeria in blue biro' (chapter such and such, verse such and such). He starts up again. He's like a bad poet who doesn't know when to quit, reading one poem after another to a comatose audience. I think, *Oh fuck it, let me drink that wine.* I reach out and knock the whole glass back in one gulp. It's been two hours, two hours of nonstop praying. I'm exhausted. All the blood has drained out of my face. I can feel how pale I must look. My father has drunk my blood.

I say, 'You definitely know your Bible,' and he beams with pride. There is clearly no compliment I could pay him that would be higher than that except perhaps, 'You're a good looking man for your age.'

And then all of a sudden it stops like the end of the rainy season. Jonathan sits down, shattered. 'I thank you again for your patience. And now the time is yours. I will eat with you. I will have a drink with you. I will stay for as long as you like. I am in no particular hurry.' I have a terrible headache; the idea of spending an indefinite period of time with my father is not now as attractive as it was on the aeroplane.

At the bar, I knock back another glass of wine and ask him if he is glad to meet me. 'Yes,' he says, 'because you are evidence of my past. Once I used to go clubbing and such, and drink wine and meet women and now I am a preacher. You are my before; this is my after. You are my sin, now I lead this life.' Sin again, how dreary it is to go on and on about sin. 'You obviously have my genes. None of my children are dullards. Not one of them. But if people were to know about you, they would lose their faith in God,' Jonathan says. Goodness, I think, I never knew I was that powerful. 'The only way I could be open about you would be if I was able to showcase you, and you agreed to be born again. Then I would take you to the church and say "This woman is my daughter. She is my before. This is my after." But you have given me no assurance that you would receive Christ and even if you did I would still have to think about how all this would affect God. I have discussed it with God and God agrees with me that for the time being it is best to keep quiet about this. I have told nobody that I was coming here to see you today. I have not told my young wife. My wife is also high up in our church. She is head of the women, I of the men. If I was going to tell anybody I would tell her.'

So I'm a secret, a forty-year-old secret, and must remain one unless I accept the Lord. I'm surprised that it seems so difficult for him to tell his wife given that she was not married to him at the time. 'What age is she?' I ask.

'She is your age,' he says. 'God—in his wisdom—has provided somebody for my sex drive. We are trying for a baby.' I like that: *God—in his wisdom—has provided somebody for my sex drive.*

'You are seventy three!' I say.

'So? A man can do it at any age,' he shrugs. 'God would like us to have another baby.'

How lovely it must be to believe in God, to be provided with young women for your sex drive, to tell straight lies with impunity, to hide your past in God's name, not to feel a second's guilt. To be religious in this way must be great fun. When I tell my mum about it on the phone, down the incredibly clear line from Abuja to Glasgow, how he doesn't want to tell any of his children, and how I must remain a secret, how he feels I am his past sin, she says, 'By Christ, did we rescue you!'

□

GOD AND ME
Geoff Dyer

Best just to come out and say it at the outset: all my religious experiences—if we can call them that—have been drug-related. Drug-*related*, note, not drug-*induced*. Were it not for LSD, Ecstasy and, most consistently and reliably, good old marijuana, I'm not sure I would have had anything approaching a religious experience. I'd still have had peak experiences but the peaks would have been lower. That is my core belief: any experience, however intense, can be enhanced by drugs. Up to a point. Up to a point in terms of both the degree and kind of enhancement you're trying to achieve (the dose) and the point in your life at which you're doing so. After that point—these points—attempting to enhance the experience can end up diminishing it. Having suspended all psychedelic activity a couple of years ago, I have, effectively, reached that point in my life. Normal service, it is hoped, will be resumed in my mid-fifties but right now—aged forty-seven and counting—I'm reluctant to proceed any further along the entheogenic path. (I'm too scared to take the drugs I want to take, stuff like DMT and ayahuasca. Snakes seem to feature prominently in the visions unleashed by the latter, and the fact that I'm terrified of snakes virtually guarantees their appearance.) Perhaps that's why I've not had anything resembling a religious experience for some time.

Which is a shame, because these are the experiences that make life worth living. Take, for example, the apocalyptic afternoon of November 5, 1987, when my friend Chris and I did a trip on Clapham Common, where all the trees from the hurricane were being burned in huge bonfires. The question is this: would those fires have been burning had we not done the 'shrooms? I've lost track of the number of times when something extraordinary happened while tripping. It's as if the act of taking a trip—quite apart from the effects it induces—causes things actually to happen.

Several years later, while living in Paris, I went to the cemeteries of the Somme. I wasn't sure exactly where I was heading but at some point, stoned, I ended up in front of Sir Edwin Lutyens's memorial to the missing of the Somme at Thiepval. I wrote afterwards that some part of me would always be calmed by this place. Well, I certainly got that wrong. More than a decade on, I'm not calmed at all by the memory of Lutyens's memorial. If anything I'm somewhat agitated by it, because I wonder if my capacity for feeling that way has been permanently arrested. (Has it perhaps been arrested by the very things that played such a significant part in bringing those feelings to life?) Will anything rival that or the experiences I had, over the course of several years, at Burning Man, the annual freak-out in the Nevada desert? Is it possible that I gobbled down the best part of a lifetime's worth of peak experiences at Black Rock City? Is there a finite number of these experiences?

The signs at the entrance to Burning Man read WELCOME TO NOWHERE, tacitly dividing the word in two—now and here—and thereby emphasizing the way that peak experiences are always time- and site-specific. For me, more specifically still, they have usually occurred in places where I've had a sense of time standing its ground. Often these places were established with pretty much that effect in mind in that they were intended as places of worship or ritual. Sometimes they were established at a particular place because that site was already invested with some special power or aura. Either way, over time such sites achieve a force—what Lawrence, at Taos Pueblo, termed a kind of 'nodality'—that seems simultaneously to have guaranteed their survival and underpinned their foundation. But here it gets complicated and interesting for two reasons. Firstly, this is never felt more strongly than when such places have fallen into ruin (have, in other words, *almost not survived*) and their primal circuitry is laid bare. Secondly, ruins acquire a force of their own even if no sacred impulse lay behind their foundation. This was palpably the case at Leptis Magna in Libya, where I was conscious both of its nodality and of how I had to strain to feel it—of how much more intense the experience would have been had I been stoned or tripping. To be precise, I kept thinking how much better it would have been if I'd been stoned, but then I started to think that if I had been stoned I would have become paranoid about being in Libya on my own, or bummed out at the prospect of having to return to my wretched hotel. Neither state was quite right. Each engendered a longing for the other, but since only one of these states was available the longing for the one that was not became a source of torment. Discontent is inimical to the religious experience. If you're wondering if it could be made better—more full of wonder—then it's not happening.

Burning Man is ostensibly at odds with this point about time standing its ground in that the event is predicated on its transitoriness. But the desert is timeless. Burning Man introduces an element of the temporal in the time-free desert. Time is not standing its ground but it is, at least, making its mark—a mark which is then painstakingly erased. No trace remains. It's like a condensation into a week of a process that usually takes hundreds or thousands of years (and the process, usually, is not completed; at the very least some vestige survives, endures).

The common thing in all these varieties of 'religious' or peak experiences can be traced back to that deluded idea I had about *always* being calmed by the memory of having been at Thiepval. Never content with saying 'I love you' we invariably add 'for ever'. Why? Because what makes the moment or feeling special is, exactly, the sense that it is already touched or inflected by eternity. 'Sweet Helen, make me immortal with a kiss,' implores Marlowe's Faustus, speaking for us all.

On the day I began writing this I read in the papers about the aftermath of two murders. The mother of Anthony Walker, the black teenager who was attacked with an axe by a pair of racist yobs in Liverpool, said that she forgave her son's killers. Not only that but she found something to 'admire' in one of them—Paul Taylor—because he expressed a degree of remorse. 'His mum must have instilled some goodness in him,' she said. The important thing about this remarkable expression of forgiveness is not the effect it might have on Paul Taylor—who could be eaten by rats for all I care—but on Anthony's mother, Gee. She has not allowed her heart to be shrivelled or hardened by what happened. This struck me powerfully because I was also reading, in the *Camden New Journal*, about a sicko called Daniel Archer, who killed a prostitute, hacked up her body 'and carried the remains on a bus before dumping them'. In a diary, Archer wrote that he had 'a brick for a heart'. Most of us do not even come close to murder—but the heart can easily begin the process of hardening that can lead, eventually, to its becoming a brick. I have gone through a long Nietzschean-Bolshevist phase of despising Christianity but then I look at Gee Walker and think that if a silly superstition helps keep your heart alive then that superstition is obviously a force for good. But then I think, wouldn't it be great if these Christians—these best possible advertisements for their faith—could go the extra mile, could abandon their belief—their delusions—and retain all their niceness, decency and open-heartedness?

Maybe a conversion to Christianity would have prevented Daniel Archer or Paul Taylor becoming a killer, but in a sense that shows how conversion is often most effective at the lowest levels of personal development. 'The further one advances in life,' writes E. M. Cioran, 'the less there is to convert to.' The paradigmatic conversion occurs in jail, when an ex-gang member embraces the Nation of Islam. Personally, I long to convert to *something*. It would be so nice, so comfortable and cosy. But of course one must never convert to anything. (A side question: can one *convert* to atheism?) Like almost everyone who goes to Burning Man, I was evangelical about it for many years. In talking about it you cannot help sounding like a member of a cult. But there's nothing, actually, to convert *to*.

Burning Man has been described as a post-religious event. Last year I went for the fifth time and doubt I'll go again—which means what? That as well as being in a psychedelic interregnum I'm in a post-post-religious phase of my life? And what, in turn, does *that* mean? That this, logically speaking, is the *beginning* of my religious life proper? Or does it mean that the last afterglow of religious feeling has faded? If so, how do I feel about that? Well, not ecstatic, not *stoked*, but I am content, these days, to play for lower stakes.

Over the centuries there has been a pretty stable consensus about which qualities are worth cultivating: goodness, kindness, honesty, reliability, consideration, compassion, generosity. At various times certain additional qualities get thrown into the mix; previously excluded qualities get called up (by Nietzsche, by various political ideologies) or promoted or relegated. But the core list has remained fairly impervious to historical change. (Don't we love Nietzsche partly because his life adds up to a kind of tragic parable, for the way that, having excoriated the notion of pity, he ends up throwing his arms around the neck of a horse that is being beaten—and then goes completely mad?) All the evidence is in—and has been in for centuries. And yet we still find it difficult to demonstrate our faith in the qualities we admire. We admire generosity of all kinds—and yet we succumb to meanness and pettiness. Given that we find it difficult to live up to our own standards, it's best, surely, to keep our expectations low. In *Black Lamb and Grey Falcon* Rebecca West lowers the bar until it is almost on the ground. Even to summarize her position as a preference for the delightful over the horrid is to put it in too

Manichaean a way. Her preference is simply for the agreeable over the disagreeable. The problem, though, is that:

> only part of us is sane: only part of us loves pleasure and the longer day of happiness, wants to live to our nineties and die in peace, in a house that we built, that shall shelter those who come after us. The other half of us is nearly mad. It prefers the disagreeable to the agreeable, loves pain and its darker night despair, and wants to die in a catastrophe that will set back life to its beginnings and leave nothing of our house save its blackened foundations.

West also hints at the kind of brutish logic that reaches its apotheosis in—and animates the actions of—the Archers or Taylors of the world: 'All men believe that some day they will do something supremely disagreeable, and that afterwards life will move on so exalted a plane that all considerations of the agreeable and disagreeable will prove petty and superfluous.' (After which, in fact, words like 'exalted' and 'depraved' will be interchangeable.)

For the rest of us, even so apparently simple a thing as choosing the agreeable over the disagreeable is a constant struggle, an ongoing test of our powers of discernment. And *that* is something I can live with. So if, on some kind of official form, I *had* to state my religion then, in spite of all my urges to the contrary, I would pledge allegiance to the agreeable. Whether I can keep faith with it is another question entirely. □

GOD AND ME
Pankaj Mishra

I first encountered God at my Christian-run school in Jhansi, a railway town in north India. It was the late 1970s and until then I had known only gods. My mother, a high-caste Hindu, had pictures and statues of many divine men, women and animals—mythical as well as living—in her miniature wooden temple at home. It wasn't clear which of these little gods in their tinselly splendour was in charge. Certainly, my mother did not feel the need to exalt one over the other. However, the Protestant Christians who ran my school insisted on a religious hierarchy, claiming that there was no god but God—their own; and they expended much effort in trying to rescue the mostly Hindu pupils from their idol-worshipping families.

We began the school day by reciting the Lord's Prayer. A class entitled 'Moral Lessons' continued the drip-drip of Christian wisdom that turned into a resonant flood on Sunday mornings, when we sang hymns at a church near the school, in between listening to sermons that made clear the folly of those who refused to believe in God, and the unlikelihood of them getting past the Pearly Gates.

Only the neediest Hindu students volunteered for the 'Bible Study' classes offered along with tea and biscuits after school, and the more rebellious among us quietly mangled the words of the Lord's Prayer every morning. Our parents had no option but to expose us to the aggressive evangelizing. The few ambitions they cherished for their children in this backwater of modern India could be advanced only by the missionary-run English-medium schools—by people who appeared to be hold-overs from colonial times.

Anglo-Indians and Indian Christians comprised much of the senior staff at school, and they tried hard to behave as if they were part of the white, English-speaking world. Everything about them—their Western-style skirts and suits, their Cliff Richard and Bing Crosby LPs, and their homes—full of framed photos of relatives in Surrey and Sydney—expressed their longing for a connection to the West, and their need to distance themselves from contemporary India.

Indeed, the existence of independent India, the unique victories of the cosmopolitan heroes of the anti-colonial movement (Gandhi, Nehru, Tagore), the remarkable fact of India's continuing existence as a democracy of sorts, were rarely acknowledged at our school— except when we were forced to on August 15, the anniversary of Independence Day. Our headmaster would sullenly unfurl the tricolour and give a short speech about how we must seek Christ's blessings for India, and send the students home for the day.

I couldn't feel the pathos of the Anglo-Indian community, unloved by both the British and the Indians. (It escaped my notice that they were quietly leaving for North America, Britain, Australia and New

Zealand.) I was too resentful, like many non-Christian students, of the preferential treatment given to our Anglo-Indian classmates, who tended to be mediocre students, performing well only with English writing and comprehension. I remember a blond laggard called Desmond, who was widely believed to be spying on the non-Christians on behalf of the headmaster. The 'grace marks' which the Christian students received in exams never seemed to improve his position in the class.

This pampered, unpatriotic Christian minority may have coloured my view of their God. But my own upbringing was also an obstacle to true belief. Hinduism, it cannot be over-emphasized, is a way of life, an evolving tradition rather than a hyper-organized religion with a clergy and doctrine; it can shape your mental and emotional outlook more deeply than a strict monotheism. The first books I read, long before I went to the Christian school, were the Mahabharata and Ramayana. These epics raise, without always resolving, many complex ethical issues; and it was their refusal to simplistically separate good from evil, right from wrong, that helped me, along with hundreds of millions of Indians, to revere Krishna, the incarnation of Lord Vishnu. He often acts deviously in the Mahabharata, and appears in other legends as a hedonist. Indeed, Krishna often reveals his divine being through his ability to make love to hundreds of women at the same time; it was this kind of detail that made the earliest missionaries in India regard Hindus as degenerate.

My early encounters with Christian theology could not undermine my incomprehension of concepts such as 'sin'. Compared to the unabashedly priapic Shiva, St Augustine seemed a bit too tormented by the involuntary movements of his sexual organs. And, when first confronted by the Christian idea of the divine, I could only be perplexed by a God whose son had failed to avoid being impaled upon a cross, but had nevertheless managed to suffer on behalf of all humanity.

I was unfortunate to know a Christianity so tainted by colonialism and racial distrust. My later, voluntary reading of the Bible has made me more aware of its elegant prose and high moral sentiments. The music of Bach, Purcell and Tallis quickly persuaded me, even before I travelled to Italy, that the Christian faith has inspired some extraordinary art; and it is clear to me now that Gandhi and Martin

Luther King could not have done what they did without their particular reading of the Gospels.

But words like *evil* and *sin* still bewilder me. I cannot read *The Heart of the Matter* or the final pages of *Brideshead Revisited* without fighting the suspicion I first had during 'Moral Lessons' classes in Jhansi that there is something vaguely preposterous about it all.

None of the Hindu students I knew at school converted to Christianity and my own early exposure to faith seems to have incited agnosticism; I admire such an intellectual and spiritual regimen as Buddhism, but I have kept well away from institutional religion. The righteousness I knew at school probably also explains the unease that I feel towards many secular intellectuals: people who claim to be children of the European Reformation and Enlightenment, but appear as fanatical as religious fundamentalists in their conviction of possessing a superior truth.

I often run into missionaries when I travel to remote places. Last year, at a Sunday temple service conducted by Mormons in Ulan Bator in Mongolia, I met a young American missionary. This crew-cut native of the state of Utah told me that he had spent the previous two years in the Mongolian grasslands, doing the work of God. His hard work was, apparently, paying off: Mongolia and its neighbours were beginning to feel God's uniquely warm glow.

He pointed to the Mongolians gathering for the service. How young and eager and devout they looked! So they did, but I had also seen equally young and avid Mongolians at the visa section of the American Embassy, wearing the same fake brand-name jeans, anoraks and sneakers. As the fresh Mongolian converts went through the rituals as shiftlessly as I once had, I could imagine their parents praying at home to their many little gods that this big white God, whoever He was, would open up the Pearly Gates to the modern world for their children. □

GRANTA

A CONVERSATION WITH ORHAN PAMUK

Maureen Freely

Orhan Pamuk leaving court, December 16, 2005

1.

Last December—three days before he went on trial for 'publicly denigrating Turkishness'—I interviewed Orhan Pamuk. It was not and could never have been the usual sort of exchange, because we speak often: over the past three years, I have translated three of his books. We have known each other a lot longer than that. I grew up in Istanbul, on the campus of what was then Robert College and is now called Bogaziçi University; my father still teaches there. Pamuk attended Robert Academy, which in those days was on the same campus; I went to the sister school on the neighbouring hill. So the Istanbul that Pamuk describes in his books is the lost city of our youth.

We met at two in the afternoon in the apartment he has used as his office for the past ten years. It is located in Cihangir, on Susam Sokak, which means Sesame Street. Like all the other places where Pamuk spends his days, it is a temple to the book. In the middle of the front room there was a large desk piled high with them. Bookshelves lined the walls from ceiling to floor. There was one armchair between the desk and the window, another in the far corner, next to the large plate-glass window; both were positioned so that the occupant could raise his eyes from the book to take in the sweeping view.

To the right was the Golden Horn, the silhouette of the old city and the humpbacked contours of the Princes' Islands in the Sea of Marmara. Were it not for the derelict apartments to the right, we would also have been able to see the first Bosphorus bridge. Directly ahead of us there was a mosque with two minarets and a dome crowned by a crescent. Between the minarets we could see the sprawling city on the Asian shore. Halfway across the Bosphorus, flecked as always with boats and ships of all sizes, were the dry docks that marked the path of the tunnel soon to link the two shores.

As I looked through the mosque's two minarets, Pamuk told me how, when the mosque was lit up for evening prayers during the month of Ramadan, he could see right through its beautiful large arched windows to the sea. The haze rising from the Bosphorus gave it the dreamlike beauty of my memories. But this was my first day back in Istanbul, and on such days I always looked for what was new in the view. When I told him so, Pamuk pointed over at the Asian shore, where a gigantic Turkish flag flapped at the top of the tallest flagpole I had ever seen.

There was a cloud hanging over Pamuk that day. From the outside, the case against him made no sense at all. Inside Turkey, it was fraught with significance. Even the date—December 16, 2005—had an ominous resonance to some: Pamuk's trial had been scheduled to begin exactly a year after the EU agreed to set a date for accession talks for Turkey, and on the day that Britain, Turkey's strongest friend in Europe, handed over the EU presidency to Austria, Turkey's most vocal opponent.

Why would Turkey want to play into its enemies' hands? Most European observers thought it must have something to do with Islam. Though Turkey's ruling party was officially pro-Europe, it was also overtly Islamist. Did this strange action against Pamuk signal a turn to the East?

This was not the question people were asking in Turkey. For them this was a struggle between what some call 'tutelary democracy' (in which the army holds the reins, stepping in whenever it sees 'the nation' straying from the righteous path) and something more in line with the social democracies of Europe.

It looked as if the democratizers were winning. The death penalty had been abolished. Some cultural rights had been accorded to Kurds. Turkey's old penal code (based on Mussolini's and designed to curb free expression of views deemed dangerous to the state) was to be replaced with a new code reflecting European norms. The EU was funding initiatives to teach judges and policemen what to do if they could not resort to torture, and the army seemed willing to lessen its role in politics. With the new freedoms had come an opening up of the public space, as previously silenced minorities began for the first time to participate in national debates. The burning question was not whether Turkey should face East or West, but whether it was now mature enough to allow for more diversity of opinion, stable enough to tolerate cultural difference—and confident enough to face up to its historical ghosts.

We in Europe like to shiver at the memory of the Siege of Vienna. Had the Habsburgs not been able to beat back the Ottoman army, would all of Europe have fallen into Muslim hands? In Turkey, they shiver at the memory of the Treaty of Sèvres, when the victors of the First World War parcelled out what was left of the Ottoman Empire among themselves. Had Atatürk not risen from the ashes to drive them out of Anatolia, might Turkey have become a European colony?

All countries beginning negotiations with the EU have seen a rise in anti-European and/or nationalist sentiment. In Turkey last year, the matter was complicated by the referenda in France and Holland and the rise of anti-Turkish and anti-Muslim sentiment in the same countries. It was further compounded by more general fears and anxieties about modernization, especially in the more traditional parts of Anatolia—which Pamuk himself explored in his novels *The New Life* and *Snow*, and which he has called the 'Dostoevskian feelings of love and hate towards the West'.

But Turkey has a well-established Western-educated intelligentsia that, far from being cut off from the West, is fully conversant with European debates on Turkey. They were aware of the other obstacles that stood in Turkey's way: the Kurdish issue, the Cyprus issue, human rights abuses and Turkey's continuing refusal to accept that what happened to Anatolia's Armenians in the last days of the Ottoman Empire amounted to genocide. By last year it seemed clear to some of them that Turkey was never going to get into Europe unless the taboo against discussing the fate of the Ottoman Armenians was resolved or debated with dignity.

A group of Turkish scholars, some in US and European universities, and others in Turkey's more westward-looking universities, had already decided that the time had come to hold a conference in Turkey that might bring to an end the ban on open public discussion of the issue. The conference was to have been held at Bogaziçi University. Though it is now owned and run by the Turkish state, it was for its first hundred years an American-owned institution providing tuition in English for the city's elites. It has long been a stronghold of secularism. Since the founding of the Republic in 1923, its graduates have played a key role in building bridges between Turkey and the West. Those behind the Armenian conference may have seen themselves in the same light. Even at Bogaziçi, the questions that gave rise to the conference were still hugely divisive. But at least people were talking about it. Fiery though their arguments were, they were doing what people in a secular democracy are meant to do.

Enter Orhan Pamuk, Turkey's most celebrated novelist. Born in 1952, he has dominated the literary scene in Turkey for the past twenty-five years. But it was only with the publication of his third novel, *The White Castle*, in 1990 that he became available in English. It attracted a small but dedicated following that grew with the publication of *The Black Book* in 1995 and *The New Life* in 1997. In 2003 he won the International IMPAC Dublin Literary Award for his sixth novel, *My Name is Red*. Though he had by then won several prestigious European prizes, it was this book that won him a place in the literary pantheon. His two most recent books, *Snow* and *Istanbul: Memories of a City*, have confirmed that place and brought him admiring readers throughout the world.

But the better he has done in the outside world, the more controversial he has become at home. This is partly due to a powerful ambivalence about Turks who do well in the West, but also due to Pamuk's controversial and widely covered views on human rights, the Kurds and Turkey's power elites. His high profile in Europe and the United States meant that he could sometimes say things that might land a lesser-known writer in deep trouble. But whenever he was interviewed in the West, journalists were inclined to dramatize the political context, especially after 9/11. Sooner or later, these pieces would end up in rather dubious translations in the Turkish media. The increasingly nationalist right-wing press would go on to quote from them out of context and accuse him of making Turkey look bad abroad. It was in their interest, too, to present Pamuk as an anomaly and a lone voice. This was hardly true: as Pamuk himself had pointed out on numerous occasions, there was a long tradition of dissent in Turkey—a tradition for which many writers, journalists and scholars have had to pay with lengthy prison sentences, and sometimes even death.

But in recent years, there had been a gradual easing of sanctions and many in the intelligentsia had seized the moment. It was in the same spirit that Pamuk made his infamous remark to a Swiss journalist who interviewed him in Istanbul in February last year. The conversation turned to Turkey's EU bid and its attitude to freedom of expression. Knowing that there was soon to be a conference on the Ottoman Armenians, he remarked that 'thirty-thousand Kurds and one million Armenians were killed in these lands' and went on to suggest that the time had come to break the silence.

Either this was the last straw for Turkey's nationalists—a loose-knit coalition dominated by old-guard secularists but also drawing support from fringe Islamist groups, the far left and the fascist right—or it was the opportunity they had been waiting for. Their supporters in the nationalist press went mad the next day, with some columnists going so far as to brand Pamuk a traitor and to invite 'civil society' to take steps to silence him. This translated into death threats that may or may not have been linked to fascist-nationalist paramilitaries. During this time Pamuk stayed abroad for a few months, returning from New York when the hate campaign seemed to be dying down. Then, last summer, he was called in for questioning by two public prosecutors. One decided that there was no case to be made, and the other charged him under Article 301 of the new penal code for 'publicly denigrating Turkish identity'.

The news caused a furore in Europe, and it quickly became clear that it had done huge and perhaps irreparable damage to Turkey's dreams of joining the EU. This was just as the nationalist lawyers and prosecutors behind the prosecution had hoped. Though the tabloid press and its nameless, faceless sponsors scared many of his potential allies into silence, the nationalists had a less pronounced effect on public opinion. The majority of Turks still wanted the country in the EU. Moderate voices still insisted that EU membership was the only rational way forward. But as the debate raged on, so too did the hate campaign against Pamuk. Running in parallel were other vicious campaigns against the organizers of the Armenian conference, which finally took place last September after several efforts on the part of the judiciary to shut it down. Perhaps because its organizers opened up public discussion of the Armenian question, they too were subjected to hate mail, death threats and a disinformation campaign. Hrant Dink, a Turkish-Armenian journalist who had played a role in the conference, was also tried under Article 301; shortly after he was given a suspended sentence, five other journalists who'd written columns criticizing the courts for trying to close down the conference were charged under the same article for insulting the judiciary. By then several publishers and scholars had also been charged for insulting the state, or the army, or Turkishness itself. According to some sources, the overall tally of Article 301 cases was more than sixty.

2.

This was the state of play, then, when I walked into Pamuk's office on December 13, 2005. My first question was how it had affected his work. In this atmosphere, how could he write?

Pamuk: Unfortunately, I have hardly been able to write for the last three months. I am still trying. I am extra-pressing myself. I have even set a deadline to finish my novel. But I know my imagination. I need certain things to write with some pleasure and intensity. If we leave aside paper and fountain pen, tea and coffee, what I need most is a certain irresponsibility. It is essential for writing fiction, at least for me: I need a playful irresponsibility, to twist everything in life, to turn situations around, to look for childish irony in the gravest drama, to organize the subtle ambiguities from which fiction arises. But now, I'm expected to be clarifying, clarifying, clarifying my statements. This lost spirit of irresponsibility—this childish freedom—is what I'm hoping to gain back. Because the more this affair grows, the greater the social responsibility that I have to face, and it is suffocating. I really want to do the right thing, to be seen to do the right thing. No author wants to lose the respect, the interest or the love of the nation. Especially when the nation in question is so troubled with its self-image.

This is a central problem for me, something I care deeply about. That's why I always try to clarify, clarify, clarify. And why I fight back when they spread disinformation and lies about me, hoping to damage my reputation here. I always make it clear that what I am criticizing are these laws that prohibit freedom of expression—and the culture that tolerates them, that allows this suppression to continue. The tabloids have the power to manipulate things in such a way that the man in the street may hate you.

But the whole affair is not as bad as it was. It has mellowed so much. Perhaps many of us now realize that the real issue here is tolerance, freedom of expression.

Freely: How do you hold your own in such a climate?

Last spring, when I was in New York, in order not to be sucked in by this, I imposed an ultra-discipline. I would wake up early so I'd be more disciplined and focused on what I'm doing. Here I have an office, and a home, and every day I wake up early and try to write for three, four hours, where no one can reach me, and first do something, write something, for the novel I'm trying to finish. In my view most authors do not write to reflect reality but to invent a second world with a complicated set of rules—the more complicated the better. Though this second world is derived from the first, it is somehow more meaningful, more satisfying, than the real world. If I can accomplish that—if I can visit this imaginary second world and write a few paragraphs, I feel so much self-respect, and so much happier. Just like a child who has played with his toys and exhausted his imagination. If I have been in this imaginary world for a while, if I have enjoyed this happiness, then I can take anything. But if I can't do that, then the void is filled by all the little daily worries of this event, which never finish.

The real punishment will not be the trial or whatever will come of it, but this court case, the dramatization of all this. What I have been through over the last three months has made me forget this second world, and my responsibility to it, so to speak. I am grateful for the international attention, and the backing of the liberal-leftist intellectuals here. It definitely makes me protected. But on the other hand, I feel that I have to answer this attention. One feels obliged. And that affects your imagination. And slowly this responsibility may convert you into a political commentator, or an activist, or a person with strong ideas. I'm not like that and I don't want to be a person who cares about ideas more than life.

So you've been forced into the shoes of a diplomat?

That is the last thing I wanted. But I don't want to misrepresent the nation. I don't want this trial to give an excuse to the conservatives in Europe for not taking Turkey in to the EU, for example. More than anything else this hurts and worries me.

Reading about you in the European press, it's easy to have the impression that you are the only pro-European in Turkey.

In the polls sixty-five per cent of the nation is still for the EU. I take every opportunity to emphasize that I am not the only one here. In interviews and articles I always refer to friends, always making clear I am not alone, that there is solidarity in the opposition among intellectuals, radicals, writers…all these people who have been harassed over the last thirty years. They are not represented in the Turkish media, and unfortunately not in the international media either. I always make sure to mention this—to refer to this tradition of resisting the state.

I know that you never set out to become involved in politics. How did it happen?

As a teenager, I was interested in leftist ideas. Leftism was very prestigious then, and also meant modernity, secularism and democracy. I read all the books. But then I was, as they would say, an 'apartment boy'. Now we all live in apartments, but in my childhood the apartment was a novelty, a Western, modern thing. The other word was 'pudding boy', which means a boy who will not be brave and strong and love his sword and fight through the streets or wherever. I preferred reading Faulkner or Virginia Woolf to politics. Even when I was seventeen or eighteen, I could see that politics, the more radical it was, the more communitarian it seemed. You had to belong to a community. So if you were a leftist, if you were serious, then you had to join these various Marxist, leftist factions. Which was not the kind of thing that I wanted to do. I always said, I will write novels, and postpone that. Or hide myself.

I had good Marxist friends who would come to my house and see lots of books. This won me some respect, but after a while a sort of a resentment, too. Probably they thought that a book-reading person like me who was not interested in politics was wasting his talents, even dishonouring his culture, if he was not serving the cause or the nation. In most people's eyes, art was a minor thing. Naive, proud sentiments like this are, I believe, quite typical in poor countries. But for me, Turkey with its Ottoman legacy was not just a poor country. I felt it was much more complicated and troubled precisely because of its simplistic cultural outlook.

In Turkey at the time, it was commonly thought that if you were not serving a cause, or a community, you would perhaps end up making a lot of money, for example in advertising. There are no

Philip Larkin-types being librarians here. You cannot sustain your life... You have to go into advertising or some other profession. But I didn't go into advertising. So eventually I gained respect for being committed to writing novels—even during those years when I was not being published even in Turkey.

I shouldn't have had anything to do with politics. But then there was the war that the Turkish state waged against the Kurdish separatist guerrillas. The state wanted to hush freedom of speech, they thought it would serve them better if we had a quiet country.

After *The New Life*, which came out in Turkey in 1994, people began to ask me to do things. I did not know why the book was so popular; *The New Life* is my most experimental and poetic book, I would say. Perhaps it tapped into national sentiments, the anxieties of losing tradition and impatience with Westernization and modernity. Anyway, it was selling a record number of copies, so some good people I trust and admire began to ask, would I come here, would I sign this petition, would I come to this meeting to defend this magazine or that person who was in trouble... I think the dramatic moment that everyone remembers took place after a Kurdish newspaper was bombed during the war with the separatist guerrillas. Many of us went out to Beyoglu, the centre of the Westernized city, à la Jean-Paul Sartre, and distributed newspapers there. I was on television with all the others, doing something unexpected for the first time. That was the beginning of my political persona.

Once I'd done that, the establishment, the nationalist media, denounced me as a sort of enemy. This was the beginning of the character-killing campaign. Of course this gets personal, and you get angry. And you gain lots of personal enemies, eternally jealous men full of resentment. It continued from that day to today.

3.

Throughout Pamuk's ordeal, I had been working on a retranslation of *The Black Book*. This was the novel in which he broke with the nineteenth-century realism that most Turkish novelists still espoused; it was also, according to many of his literary admirers, the book in which he found his voice. Set in Istanbul in 1980, nine months before the most brutal coup in Turkey's recent history, it follows a young husband as he combs the city for his missing wife, whom he suspects of having gone into hiding with a relation who also happens to be Turkey's most celebrated and controversial columnist. (Daily columnists exert an unusually powerful influence on public opinion in Turkey; in Pamuk's words, they are 'professors of everything'.) Following the husband-narrator are various shadowy figures who harbour personal and political grievances against the columnist and seem to want him dead.

Despite the darkness of the plot and its ominous echoes, I'd found great comfort in *The Black Book*. Much of it takes place in the streets of old Istanbul; I'd walked these streets myself as a child with my father, when he was writing his first guide to the city. I had so much enjoyed revisiting these streets with Galip, the book's hero. Every day, when I had translated my quota and gone back online to face the sea of emails that campaigns for unjustly prosecuted writers inevitably entail, I'd wonder how long it had been since Pamuk had been able to walk these streets in peace, or even imagine them.

This was why I found it particularly appealing when Pamuk suggested that instead of staying inside all afternoon, surrounded by phones and computers, we follow Galip's steps through the old city and see how much had changed in the twenty-five years since he'd walked these streets.

We headed towards what I still think of as the 'old city' and what the Turks call the Historic Peninsula. This was where the Byzantine Empire built their great monuments and where the Ottomans, after they took the city in 1453, built theirs. From the hills of Beyoglu, its famous silhouette recalled both empires: on the tip on the peninsula, where the Bosphorus merged with the Golden Horn, we could see the buildings and gardens of Topkapi Palace spilling down to the Byzantine city walls. Rising above the hills to their right were the domes and minarets of Haghia Eirene, Haghia Sophia, the Blue Mosque, the New Mosque and (most magnificent of all) Süleymaniye.

But as our taxi crossed the Galata Bridge, the grand contours of history gave way to surging crowds and narrow, tangled streets that— though modernized and concretized and pedestrianized—still sparkle with the lost objects and forgotten details of other ages. In a neighbourhood called Babiali—Istanbul's Fleet Street until about ten years ago—Pamuk pointed out the building where his uncle once worked as editor of *Hayat*, Turkey's most popular magazine in the

1950s and 1960s. Many details from that lost age—the minutiae of newspaper production and the secret codes of Istanbul's *feuilletonistes*—went into *The Black Book*.

In Beyazid Square, he pointed out the locations of various famous bombings. Most dated back to the late 1970s, when Istanbul University was a war zone and there were almost daily pitched battles between rightist and leftist students. Walking through the flea market that now dominated the square—this being the centre of the booming 'suitcase trade' with the former Eastern Bloc—we headed for Sahaflar, the old second-hand book market just next to the entrance to the Covered Bazaar. This, too, had become more touristic.

'I used to spend so much time here,' Pamuk said. 'I'd come here with my mother's car, and park it around Süleymaniye Mosque, and I bought so much. I remember buying the entire *Encyclopaedia of Islam* and carrying it to the car...'

We stepped into a small bookshop, where the bookseller greeted him warmly. He showed us a set of a Turkish magazine from the 1930s called *Seven Days*, the complete works of Walter Scott and a huge nineteenth-century treatise on the construction of tramways. In the quiet, dusty room, the noise of the city seemed far away. Thanking the bookseller for his trouble, we moved on to a stall where they were selling what I took to be bad reproductions of miniatures.

'These things are fakes,' Pamuk said. 'But they're strangely beautiful and original fakes. I was curious to find out how they were made. I had a long and friendly conversation with some of their makers. I thought of writing a scholarly article about their art, because they have unselfconsciously invented a genre. These artists—and they have to be called artists—have realized that when they did accurate copies, the tourists weren't buying them. Miniatures lack perspective and though a picture without perspective is pleasing for the Westernized, it is also in ways disturbing. So they decided to add something to make it more appealing to Westerners. They found a sort of Dadaist solution. They took the old European engravings of Istanbul—which were based on watercolour landscapes by artists like Keith Melling—and combined them with miniatures. So what we have is an inspired collage of engraving and miniature, done with photocopying and colouring. A sort of postmodern cut-and-paste.'

'Look at this one,' he said, pointing at a scene from old Istanbul.

'Ferries like this only came to Istanbul in the 1950s... Details from the recent past are combined with Western images of the Ottoman past and Ottoman miniatures. These bookshops had been fading away, but now they are selling souvenirs for tourists and doing a good business. The sad thing, perhaps, is that they are doing so as replicas of themselves.'

As we continued through the market, he pointed out a bookshop that was once run by a famous sheikh. This was where an old and peaceable Sufi society would once hold its discreet gatherings. 'I mentioned this in *The Black Book*,' Pamuk said. 'His name is still on the door, I think. He was a great bookseller, but when I was a teenager, I'd go in and ask, do you have such and such a book? And they would not have the book I was looking for.'

We went into one last bookshop, where most of the books were foreign translations. He almost bought one. But his rule was only to buy a book if he went home and couldn't stop thinking about it.

As we headed out of the market, a man standing next to an archway asked Pamuk if he was from Iran. 'We're Turks, brother,' Pamuk replied. Pointing at the archway, he added, 'Look at that crack. No one's repairing these things.'

We walked past the building where he studied journalism in his twenties. 'But I never attended. At that time in Turkey you could have a university diploma even if you didn't attend the school but just took the examination. I was busy at home writing my first novel, which took me four years to write and another four to publish.' Pointing at the gate through which students swarmed in and out (quite a few of them doing a double-take when they recognized him). he added, 'The real improvement is that this gate is now open. In my time they had only one gate open so that the police and security could control everything. There was so much political violence among the students.'

We had now arrived at a street where they sold kitchenware. Pamuk pointed out a shop nearby that sold police uniforms. 'There is so much more variety now,' he said. 'There was so little when I was a child, but your eye picked up certain things and enjoyed them. But now, with this flourishing of production, objects of your childhood disappear and you are a bit sad, a bit nostalgic, and you don't feel you belong here. I think each generation is defined by the objects around it. This feeling that we all had the same things! We were living in a detached national culture, unified ideologically, but protected by the state. There was no international infiltration. I'm not referring to books and art and ideology here but to objects. If none are allowed, then your eye gets adjusted. Now, for me, nostalgia is nostalgia for those objects. To be surrounded by those objects is a comfort. And the world is more like a home. The objects to which you are attached are still all around you. The galaxy of objects is your home more than the spaces in which they sit. If you lose them, the feeling of being at home is also lost.

'But there is a second consolation. Objects may leave, objects may change, but they may just come together in particular ways, traditional ways and styles which still carry the memories in a strange way.' He waved his arms, to indicate that it was happening in this very street.

We walked into the courtyard of Süleymaniye Mosque, where the call to prayer was blasting from all minarets. After buying six pink spinning tops from five small boys, we left the courtyard to walk past the Süleymaniye Library, down a well-preserved street much used, Pamuk said, in historical films, and from there into a more ramshackle neighbourhood.

We stopped to look at old houses that had rods running vertically to keep them from collapsing in an earthquake. And restored houses rebuilt around concrete shells. We passed two infamous student hostels—in the 1970s, one had been taken over by rightists and the other by leftists. Gunfire had followed. After passing another beautiful Sinan mosque (Sehzade Cami) and losing our way, and finding a path leading us back to it at the far end of a car park, we arrived at Vefa Bozacisi, where Atatürk had once come to drink its famous fermented-millet drink, and where his glass had stood thereafter on a tiny red velvet throne inside a glass case on the wall.

Before we went in, we stopped to buy a bag of chickpeas. It was, he said, unthinkable to drink *boza* without first speckling it with chickpeas. 'You don't have to drink it if you don't like it, as my mother used to say. Do you like it?'

I liked it. It was smooth and thick and nutty, with a slight kick to it—familiar enough to make me wonder if I'd tasted (and forgotten) it as a child. There was a small amount of alcohol in *boza*,

Pamuk told me, which might explain why it had been so popular in Ottoman times. 'The Ottomans pretended that twenty bottles was equivalent to half a glass of wine. This meant they could say it did not really count as alcohol.' But for him it seemed to be the wrong time of day for drinking *boza*. 'I like to have it at night, after dinner. That's what I'm used to. Do you want another one?'

Before I could answer, a man who had just settled down at the next table with three female relatives, all modestly dressed in headscarves, came over to Pamuk. 'You've been in all the papers lately,' he said. After indicating that they were both on the same side, he added, 'I said that softly, just in case one of *them* happens to be around.' On our way out, the cashier asked Pamuk if he really was Orhan Pamuk and then asked for his autograph. Pamuk gave him the copy of *The Black Book* that he'd brought out with him.

By now it was dark outside, and a cold wind was getting colder. Pamuk suggested going to his house for some tea. We took a taxi and moved slowly through the traffic towards the district of Nisantasi, where Pamuk grew up and lives now. Pamuk Apartments was built by Pamuk's family in the early 1950s after deciding that their old stone mansion was too Ottoman, and therefore not in keeping with Atatürk's Westward-looking dream. As Pamuk described in *Istanbul*, the family was very wealthy then, though Pamuk's father and uncle (who were both engineers and both given to investing in large schemes that never quite got off the ground) would whittle away the fortune in years to come. For a time, every floor was inhabited by different branches of the family. The interior doors were never locked, and as a child Pamuk wandered freely from household to household.

He now lives in the attic apartment, which is another temple to the written word: white furniture, bare parquet floors, bookcases rising eleven and twelve shelves high, and in the centre of the sitting room, another sturdy old desk. I asked if I was right in thinking that this was where Celâl (the famous columnist in *The Black Book*) had his secret flat?

Pamuk: Yes. I had this space in mind. It was different then, but the humming and murmuring of the radiator, the old lift, the cracking of the parquet floor and the slight trembling of the windowpanes when buses pass by—these things give me a sense that this fictional past is still with me.

I think something changed with that book—that everything interesting you've done since stems from what you started there. Is that how you understand it?

In 1982 I published my second novel. At that time there was horror going on in Turkish prisons. And no freedom of speech at all, except that if you wrote a historical novel or a novel which didn't say much about politics, it was permissible. Around that time, in 1985, I met Harold Pinter. He came on a human rights mission to Istanbul with Arthur Miller and other foreign observers. I was their guide. The military proposed a constitution, the whole nation was going to vote for it. Ninety per cent was in favour... But that was not a free referendum by Western standards. One of my cousins was working for an advertising agency at the time, and he called me and told me that some Swiss newspaper people were here and that they were looking for a person who could criticize the proposed constitution on TV. We are still being run by that constitution, by the way, but in those days no one dared to publicly criticize it, and here were these Swiss TV people, looking for a Turk living in Turkey to criticize it, and my cousin didn't know any left-wing intellectuals, so he asked me if I did. He said they didn't necessarily need to see his face. (I used this in the ending of *The Black Book*, when, instead of giving the desired political message, the narrator tells a long story. This may be a good solution for my problems, too!)

Anyway, I said okay, I will find someone. With a friend, for two days, we went to see other friends—professors who had been kicked out of university but were not in jail. We couldn't use the phone, so we went to visit them, to ask them. I hated my position, which made it easy to moralize. These were all good guys whom I respected, but then they were making the right decision not to talk, because if they talked they would get into trouble.

That stayed with me—a man, an upper-middle-class, educated liberal who was going from house to house, making phone calls, a troubled and confused hero who was looking for someone in Istanbul. It was a good frame for a story. But we were frustrated, we couldn't find anyone to speak. My friend said, okay, Orhan, you talk. But at that time I was timid, I was not politically outspoken, I did not know how to criticize the constitution then. They were looking for someone working in human rights. So I did not talk in the end. But Galip, my hero, does.

I was going to include a football match with a major European team. Everywhere my hero Galip went, the whole nation would be there, listening. In those days, Germany–Turkey games would end 7–0. I thought that would be good to demonstrate the national defeat, the anger, the frustration... While Galip searched for someone to make a political comment, not only could he not find them, but on the radio, the whole of Istanbul would be listening to the score. One to zero, three to zero, five to zero...

So *The Black Book* began as a sort of quest novel, set in a big city. But the city is not a Western Cartesian construct. It is a place full of arabesques, twists and turns. I began to write the novel in 1985, and it was published in Turkey in 1990, and in between I managed to invent this texture. Not the story. The storyline is very simple. The wife disappears, and the confused hero, a man who shares my culture and sentiments, walks through the streets of Istanbul. I got the idea of changing Istanbul to an ocean of signs, some of which my hero can read, some of which he cannot understand. And if he doesn't understand them, all the better, because it adds a layer of mystery, which is already there, because of all the layers of history in Istanbul. Later I read that this was called a 'palimpsest', but I did not know that word then.

It is in my character to make a text over-rich, over-abundant. I have a tendency to add more and more. I like to observe details in a space, in a room, in a shop, where the details do not necessarily illustrate the drama in an organic way but eat away at the central story, slyly pulling the story to another corner. Not like Zola's naturalist details. The over-abundance of details is not encyclopaedic, but strange.

The objects become like characters?

I don't know. But it's also related to writing habits. If you are a fast writer—I am jealous of these fast writers—you write lean prose. Which I sometimes do, but which sometimes I cannot do. I have a regressive mind; on the other hand, I'm concerned that the story doesn't go off the track. Every time I have a chapter that I think will be seven or eight pages, it becomes eighteen pages. What happens in those eighteen pages is what would happen in the seven pages. But there are so many signs and symbols that pop up. I like to do that, and to work in various melodies that are related to other things in the book.

But one year after I wrote *The Black Book*, a Turkish director whom I admired and who is dead now, Ömer Kavur, came to me and said, let's make a movie. I told him many stories. But he didn't like them. So finally I told him a story from *The Black Book*—the one about the photographer. I based it on Attar's *The Conference of the Birds*. He said, let's make that into a film. We worked together on the script. But each time I came back to him with my pages, he'd say, 'Orhan you have a tendency to'—he was French-educated—'*surcharge*.' That stayed with me. Because he was saying, don't *surcharge*. Don't overload!

This was a movie and you had to be quick, lean. I learned so many things about writing from Kavur. He had a sense of drama, that something should happen. I would say: so my characters go up the street, and then something happens eventually? He'd say no, they go out, something happens right *then*. Maybe he was exaggerating. But that word *surcharge* stayed with me. I am a *surcharge* person. I know its literary problems and sometimes I try to avoid overloading, but character, I think, is destiny and so I continue to overload.

Borges, incidentally, was interested in *The Conference of the Birds*. He was interested in classical Islamic texts more than is generally known. It is a very simple story, a group of birds is looking for their king, who is lost. They travel, and each bird has an experience, a story. Finally they reach Mount Kaf, which is a sort of Eastern Mount Olympus, and they realize that the king, the god, the person they are looking for, is in themselves. They are the very person they are looking for.

I'd read the book before I read Borges. But Borges's touch made classical Islamic literature look different and new for me. I needed Borges's help for this new approach to classical Islamic literature. Once I had this new outlook, everything, especially old culture, looked new. Galip in my book is in search of something, and he finds it in himself. It's a very Sufi thing: don't look for worldly things, it's all inside.

Maureen Freely

What was it about Borges that opened things up for you?

It was a sort of literary revelation. He taught me to look at those essential religious texts with a radically detached and so inevitably secular eye. Borges taught me that there was something we can call the 'metaphysics of literature'. By following the path of Poe, Coleridge and Valéry, tracing the line from one text to the next, he taught me a liberating way of looking at the old texts which carried so much sentimental weight of tradition and religion. I like the fact that Borges was not influenced by the sentimental content of literary texts, but by the metaphysical joys. He talked about the patterns of literary texts, and that taught me to look at Sufi texts in that light.

Not only Borges but my readings of Poe, Kafka and Calvino also gave me the opportunity to make a distinction between religion and parable, between story and philosophy. I read all these Sufi texts in the early and mid-1980s in Turkey and the United States. My whole Sufi experience was nothing but reading Rumi with Borges and Calvino in mind. But once I had a taste for it...

For Turks, novel writing was a whole political and perhaps ideological package. Reading Balzac, reading Western classics, had a leftist, modernist, occidentalist connotation here, while reading old Sufi or Islamic classics was something very conservative.

You mean it got lost between the cracks of the two ideologies?

Today you can go into a bookshop and find all sorts of religious and modern books. But in my youth a bookshop would either be Western, modern and left-leaning, or Islamic and conservative. The country was more divided culturally then.

For the likes of me, religion was almost a hidden thing. Except for this or that religious uncle or neighbour. And the old guys did not wish to interfere with modernity. They were never propagating their religion. The so-called public space was less religious in my youth, while inside the houses life was more pious, I think.

And what about Sufism?

In my circle Rumi went hand in hand with the spiritualists. They had magazines which mixed Islam with some metaphysics or parapsychology. I later learned that these spiritualists were also involved with sects, and that spiritualism was perhaps a cover for a modernized version of moderate non-parochial sects. In fact, in the 1950s spiritualist sects were occasionally raided as if they were running a brothel. Unless you were protected by some powerful institution, you couldn't be involved in sects safely. All the religious sects that survived had connections with people in power.

Atatürk shut them all down, didn't he?

Atatürk's version of secularism drew a strong line between religious and state affairs. To cut down the strength of religion, especially in the social sphere. He wanted religion to be apolitical, and not radical. But of course to cut the social strength of Islam—that was a very political thing. And not a secular thing. But this is not a subject that exercises my imagination. I like to talk about things and stories.

What about religion and the past? You've written two historical novels.

Look, to put it simply: once you have a major empire, like the Ottoman Empire, you know you can't run it on religion alone. You can run a provincial xenophobic nation like that, but you cannot run an empire. There are so many details that cannot be addressed through religion in an empire. An empire—with its diverse cultures, religions, nations, tribes—has to be worldly. The Ottoman elite was worldly and the ruling elite was close to the military. Later there was the wish to be Westernized, to run the empire along Western lines. After five generations of this, the Ottomans themselves had changed.

During the Republic, Turkey was openly, even aggressively not religious. To prove you belonged to the elite, you had to be Westernized and not religious—at least not openly. These are subjects I described in *Istanbul*. My grandmother used to recite Tevfik Fikret's poetry, which was partly atheistic, saying religion did this, religion did that. Fikret's poetry was very critical of religion. My family would call themselves Muslim, but they were definitely not very religious people.

Maureen Freely

The paradox is that Turkey presents itself to the world as ninety-nine per cent Muslim, but then it's a secular state, so it's a double definition. People outside Turkey don't understand how the two definitions fit together.

Yes. The bureaucrats—they're still sixty per cent of the ruling elite—are always upset when some American or European says it is an Islamic country. Because we Turks are very proud that we are the only 'secular' Islamic state. It's part of our identity. It's part of nationalism, too, unfortunately. Because we can divide establishment conservatives into two now. There are the Turkish anti-Western nationalists. And the Islamists, they are also nationalists. The Islamists are taking us into Europe, while the ultra-nationalists, some of whom are very secular, are using the prestige of secularism and Atatürk as a way of blocking Turkey's road to the EU.

In Istanbul you also made the point that when you were growing up, even in secular households there was still a morality of asceticism, of humility—in other words, Sufi values.

Of course those things change more slowly. I think most morality comes to us through the virtues we learn at home and in school, so yes, Sufism lived on in Westernized houses. You had to be humble. You had to show respect to your elders. You had to do things not for money, but for the thing itself. Now of course all this is fading away, or we are getting old and complaining, perhaps. But I always wanted to make it clear that this old wonderful morality had its very repressive side too. You shouldn't be critical, you shouldn't enjoy glory. This is against the idea of the Renaissance, which is all about worshipping a person's glory. The Renaissance was about Italian princes who, cruel and repressive though they were, also opened a new way of seeing things. Some of this I explored in *My Name is Red,* and I shall also be touching on this culture of ostentation in my new novel, *The Museum of Innocence.* But until recently, as I wrote in *Istanbul,* the culture of ostentation—displaying your wealth, hanging pictures of the wall—was considered to be very unethical. The right thing was to hide your money, and your riches, and objects and images that may represent them, and never say that you're successful. If you did that you were shameless or nouveau riche.

This is your mother speaking...

The whole culture speaks to us through our mothers anyway!

Do you walk around the city as much as you used to do?

I do. After I started doing TV to promote my books, I was slightly self-conscious and of course these days it continues. Some people recognize me on the street. Taxi drivers immediately open up the controversy—but in a much gentler and more friendly way than the right-wing media—though they may disagree with me, we can still give each other respect. For example, a taxi driver this morning: after he recognized me, he made sympathetic noises. Then I complained a bit. He said, 'They made you look like a traitor. They exaggerated everything.' In five minutes we were friends. Although this guy was also an angry nationalist, complaining that the government was selling Cyprus out, we parted friends.

I don't say the things I used to say to such people, I don't like to argue. I prefer to listen. So I just nod and say, yes... yes... yes...

4.

At the trial three days later, Pamuk had no chance to speak and no choice but to listen. For the better part of an hour he stood in the middle of the small, airless, crowded courtroom while six nationalist lawyers explained how he had impugned their Turkishness. There were nasty scuffles between them and the dozen EU parliamentarians who had come to observe the proceedings. Though the judge did not accede to their request that the court be cleared of Europeans, he seemed unable to control their behaviour. He was also unable to decide whether or not to let the case proceed, and in the end he ordered a postponement while he sought the opinion of the Ministry of Justice. Meanwhile, in the corridors outside, 200 people who had not made it into the courtroom were hemmed in by a ring of riot police, while a gang of fascist agitators (said by some to be aided and abetted by plain-clothes policemen) worked their way through the crowd, rounding on Article 301 defendants and other targets, kicking and shoving them and denouncing them as traitors and Jews. Among us were many leading Turkish writers and human rights activists. The most prominent was Yashar Kemal, Turkey's other internationally celebrated novelist, who has himself been prosecuted for speaking about the Kurds.

Another group had planted themselves outside the court with a banner denouncing Pamuk and six other Article 301 defendants as 'missionary children' (the implication being that they had been led astray by their scheming European and American teachers in 'missionary' schools like Robert Academy). Though the banner got a lot of play on Turkish television, the motley crew of fifty-somethings standing behind it was so unimpressive that one Turkish writer next to me joked, 'Where have all our fascists gone?' They seemed to have the protection of the riot police, who did little to protect the rest of us, least of all Pamuk. He was rapped on the head by one agitator on his way into the courtroom and, though he was able to leave the building unscathed, his car was pelted with eggs and stones by a professional-looking rabble. In the nationalist tabloid press the next day, the agitators were applauded ('Again the iron fist!'; 'Again, pelted with eggs!'). Pamuk's face was circled in red and described, though the photograph showed him with normal complexion, as 'ghostly white'.

The case against Pamuk was dropped on January 22, 2006, almost certainly because of fierce pressure from Europe, although the hate campaign goes on. Many other Article 301 defendants are yet to be tried. The law still stands and the nationalist agitators continue to enjoy mysterious privileges. □

GRANTA

ACTS OF GOD
David Graham

David Graham

In August 2003 I took my twenty-three-year-old son to St Tropez in the South of France for the Bank Holiday weekend. After lunch we went for a swim and had a couple of races, which he won. As I went to change, I saw him floating in the sea near the pier. I remember thinking he was fooling around, trying to see how long he could hold his breath. The following events play forever in my mind, over and over in slow motion: realizing he was in trouble, reaching him, the empty look in his eye, his lolling head, screaming for help, kiss of life, consciousness, helicopter, hospital, waiting rooms.

The doctors told me that night it was unlikely that Nick would walk again but I didn't believe them then. All that had happened was that he had dived from a pier and hit his head on a sandbank. I didn't understand, perhaps I didn't want to. Not only had he broken his neck, he had also drowned, and he developed pneumonia within a couple of days. I remember counting the tubes as he lay unconscious for nine days in intensive care. The tubes reduced from fifteen to none as he slowly recovered, but he remained paralysed from the neck down, unable to speak until the tracheotomy tube was removed from his throat and his lung function improved.

He stayed in intensive care in Toulon for seven weeks until he was strong enough to be flown back in an ambulance plane to the national spinal unit at Stoke Mandeville Hospital near Aylesbury in Buckinghamshire. It was there that the reality hit home. I had never given a thought to the people I saw in wheelchairs, who they were and how they might have got there. I used to avert my eyes in the street when I saw somebody in one, as if they could be contagious. I had no comprehension of a life without limbs, incontinent, with little independence.

In Stoke Mandeville I was humbled by the resilience and the public faces of all the patients I saw. And Nick was still Nick—thinner, but with the same sense of humour. He just could not move. In the end you have to get on with it: learn to empty the leg bag, help with pressure relief, give injections, hoist in and out of cars, cut up food, give a drink, light a cigarette. The list is endless, but eventually it all becomes second nature and you no longer notice.

Meanwhile, I changed. I had always been selfish. I still am but I started to think about others and appreciate small things in life. I started taking photographs. I found that being behind a lens was a great way to hide my tears and avoid conversations and thoughts about my son. I'd always had an enquiring mind and photography enabled me to see the world in a different way. It was a way of asking questions.

I never photographed Nick during his rehabilitation. I wanted to but he didn't. So after he came out, I went back to Stoke Mandeville and started taking pictures. Stoke Mandeville is the largest spinal unit in the UK, accommodating 120 patients. The degree of paralysis depends upon the level and severity of damage to the spinal cord. A paraplegic has partial or full paralysis to their lower body whereas a tetraplegic, or quadreplegic, is without use of their hands and arms as well. The higher up in your body you are injured, the more serious the potential paralysis can be. At Stoke, about half the patients are going through rehab following their accidents and the remainder are readmittances with various problems, frequently urinary. Typically a new admission will stay for about eight months, learning to cope with their disability and relearning many of their everyday functions. The progress is slow from bed to wheelchair, learning to feed themselves again and overcome many adversities while having to face the indignity of incontinence and being washed like a baby.

Slowly my photographs evolved. I wanted to show how in an instant, through a simple accident, one's life can be transformed. And accidents happen in such innocent and unexpected ways: falling up stairs, slipping in the bathroom, tripping on the pavement, airline turbulence, the list is endless; it is very easy to become paralysed. I wanted the viewers to feel the pain I felt as a father. I wanted them to see the kind of operations my son had and to understand more about a disabled life. Some of my questions had been too personal to ask, and the camera helped to answer them.

Nick now lives in a flat with a carer. There has been no improvement in his mobility since the moment of his accident two years ago and the likelihood of any recovery remains remote. Our relationship has changed as he has adapted to his new life. The time we spend together is more precious for both of us and, although sometimes lacking in spontaneity, it is also delightfully unpredictable. We see each other when we want to rather than out of duty. We enjoy each other's company and, although he is my son, he is also now my best friend. ☐

The second dive was perfect.
I felt my head strike something hard, heard
a crack and the air was knocked out
of me. I was unable to move. Out of the corner
of my eye I could see light and people
in the water. I wondered why they
were not coming to help me.
I thought, 'I'm not ready to die yet,'
and then I passed out.

Nicholas, tetraplegic

The pier, St Tropez, Summer 2003

Phil undergoing hydrotherapy

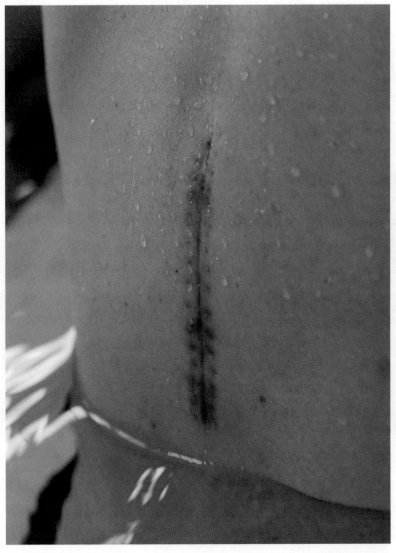

Phil, paraplegic
A balcony gave way during his honeymoon in Barbados

Tadeo, paraplegic
He was putting down a heavy weight

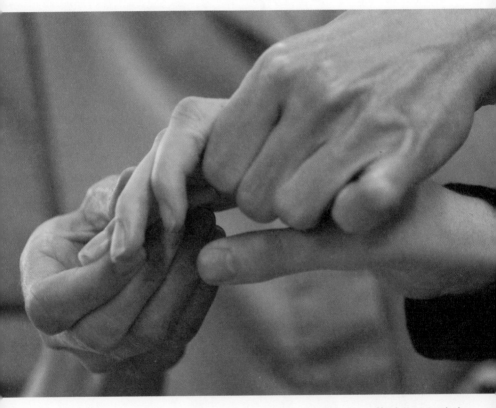

Charlotte, tetraplegic
She was jumping on a bouncy castle

I remember letting go of the car park wall;
it was so much slower than I expected and
seemed to last for hours. Blackness.
A tree broke my fall and saved my life.
The man who found me wasn't sure
at first how I had got there.
I thought, 'If I go to sleep then I really
won't wake up this time.'

Dave, paraplegic

Multi-storey car park, Banbury, Oxfordshire

Troye, tetraplegic
He was injured while playing rugby. He has represented Britain in two Paralympic Games

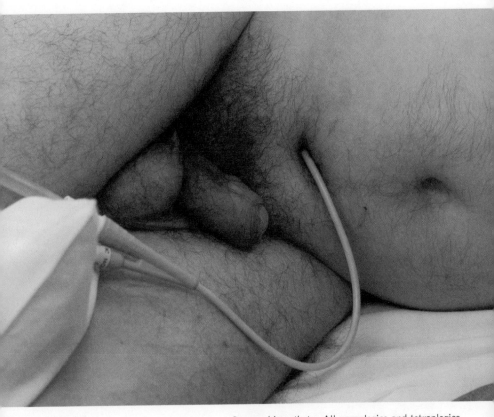

Suprapubic catheter. All paraplegics and tetraplegics
are incontinent, without bladder or bowel control

Robert, tetraplegic
He slipped into a paddling pool

Sandy steering her wheelchair with her nose, tetraplegic
She was admitted for a minor surgical operation

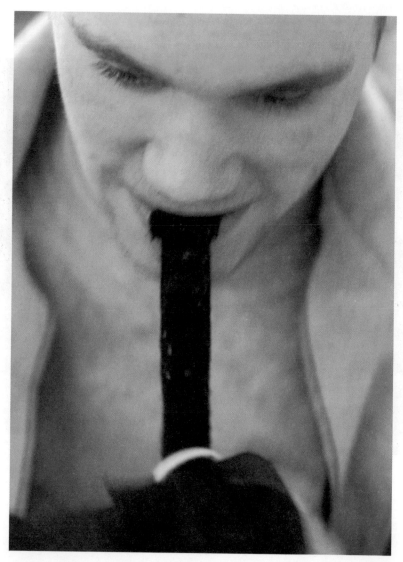

Francis, putting on a wrist strap, tetraplegic
He fell while placing a hat on a Christmas tree

Ali, tetraplegic
He had a motorbike accident in India

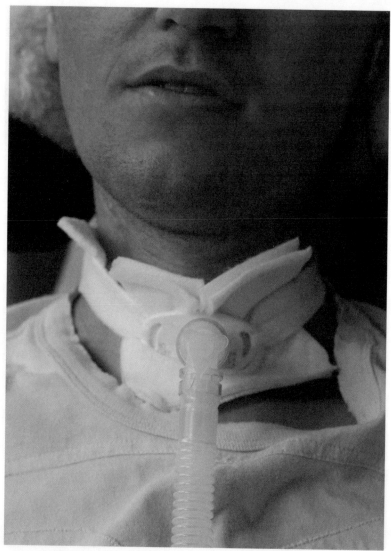

Matt, tetraplegic
A rugby scrum collapsed on him during training

Jean, paraplegic
She slipped while out shopping

I was riding a very talented young horse.
Approaching the twelfth fence on the course
I felt his stride change slightly but it was too late.
He went straight into the fence catapulting
us both into the ground on the
landing side. I thought immediately that I had broken
my back. In fact I had smashed several vertebrae
in my neck. There was no pain.

Paul, tetraplegic

Cross-country eventing course

Dee, paraplegic
She jumped from a second floor

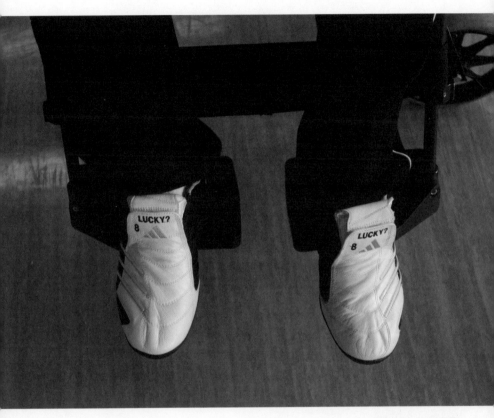

Martin, tetraplegic
He dived from a boat into the River Thames at Windsor

Linda's noticeboard
She is a teacher and was sent cards and photos by her pupils

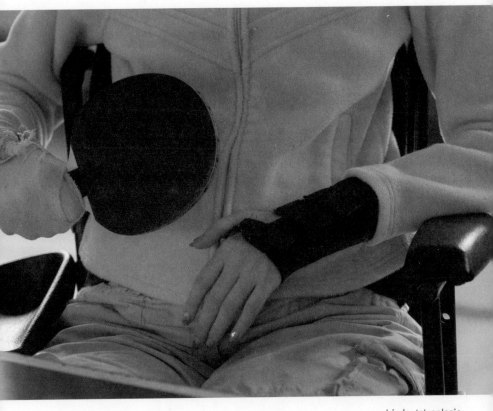

Linda, tetraplegic
A stranger fell on top of her in a London nightclub

Everyone told me it was a dangerous
hobby, but I never thought anything
would ever happen to me. Just to others.
I remember thinking it was a
beautiful day. Then I found myself
spiralling to the ground out of
control. I heard someone screaming
and realized it was me.

Paul, tetraplegic

Hang-gliding site, Coombe Gibbet, Hampshire

James, in a standing frame, paraplegic
He was paralysed at birth

James playing football during a school break

Ian and Linda, who are married, both tetraplegic
They were injured in a car crash

Danny going to work, paraplegic
He was paralysed in a car crash, aged two

ELIZABETH SPELLER

'Beautiful, intense and immediate'
JOANNA LUMLEY

'An enthralling mixture of social history
and intimacy, tragedy and humour'
VICTORIA GLENDINNING

The Sunlight
on the Garden

*A Family in Love, War
and Madness*

GRANTA BOOKS

SUBSCRIBERS GET MORE. FOR LESS!

GRANTA SUBSCRIBERS GET OUTSTANDING NEW FICTON, MEMOIR, REPORTAGE, INVESTIGATION AND PHOTOGRAPHY, FOUR TIMES A YEAR—AT AN OUTSTANDING DISCOUNT ON THE BOOKSHOP PRICE OF £9.99 AN ISSUE.

SO IF YOU SUBSCRIBE TO THE VIEW THAT GOOD WRITING MATTERS—THAT IT CAN MAKE A DIFFERENCE—SUBSCRIBE! OR GIVE GRANTA TO A FRIEND, RELATIVE OR COLLEAGUE WHO SHARES YOUR LOVE OF READING. OR, AT THESE LOW PRICES, DO BOTH:

- ➤ ONE YEAR: £27.95. **30% OFF.**
- ➤ TWO YEARS: £51.95. **35% OFF.**
- ➤ THREE YEARS: £71.95. **40% OFF.**

'THE MOST INFLUENTIAL LITERARY MAGAZINE IN THE UK.'
OBSERVER, 2005

GRANTA

TALES OUT OF SCHOOL
Kees Beekmans

TRANSLATED FROM THE
DUTCH BY SAM GARRETT

I first stood before a class in 1992, when I was thirty-one. For ten years I taught 'bridge' classes in Amsterdam to groups of students who had arrived from abroad and had to learn Dutch. This was long before the current, tougher approach to foreigners, *gastarbeiders*, immigrants, or whatever one chooses to call them; before the present era of immigration quotas and compulsory cultural assimilation. These are stories from that time.

Very bad book for Islam

'This men, he must die!'

Coming from Sallah, this amazes me.

Here at our school, certain topics—religion, discrimination, Dutch mores and the proverbial Dutch stinginess, the Dutch climate—are inevitably discussed from time to time. The students usually bring in the topics themselves, and this time it's Salman Rushdie's turn. Whenever the papers report that the *fatwa* is still in place and that the writer is still forced to live in hiding, the students are sure to come in the next day and test their opinion against mine—against that of 'the Dutch'.

In the few minutes before the bell rings, the two Moroccan friends Sallah and Mohammed, Dunya and Petar from Serbia, and Markus from Finland are the ones who always crowd around my desk. They're all around fifteen or sixteen, and they have all been in the Netherlands for about six months. Mohammed usually comes into the class swearing loudly—not in his own mother tongue, but in Serbo-Croat, to the great delight of Dunya and Petar. The way Mohammed pronounces the words *is* awfully funny, even I can hear that.

But somehow Sallah always makes sure he is the one standing closest to me. When I sit on my desk he comes and stands right in front of me, his crotch pressed against my thigh. He usually takes hold of my hand as well, and holds on to it the whole time we talk. I like Sallah very much, but this is taking things a bit too far for me.

His head is slightly elongated, banana-shaped, his hair is dark and curly, his dark-brown eyes literally veiled by long, black lashes, his teeth a pearly white. On my birthday he brought me a bunch of roses, champagne-pink roses. Sallah is a kind boy with a sense of humour, he would never hurt a soul, he's quick to laugh—and sometimes it's hard to keep him at a distance that's more comfortable for me. He's also terribly sensitive to anything that might resemble rejection; once, when I carefully pushed him away a bit ('Sallah, give me a little room, please...'), I could see he was shocked. He looked at me with big eyes, seemingly on the verge of tears.

Mohammed, equally sensitive to rejection, sensitive indeed to anything that doesn't go the way he wants, tends to react more vehemently. Where Sallah retreats teary-eyed, Mohammed explodes in a rage, throws his books and papers on the floor and stomps out of the room. Or, if he happens to be standing beside a window, he smashes it. But those outbursts blow over quickly. Normally speaking, he's an extremely affable boy.

Yet more and more situations arise in which I am forced to hurt Sallah's feelings. During the afternoon discos, for example, the ones we organize regularly in the school cafeteria, Sallah always wants to dance with me, and although I'm pleased to humour him, I tire of it sooner than he does. When it's time for an exam, Sallah—a slow worker and not the most talented of pupils—is never done on time. Yet when the hour has passed I come to collect his paper as well. When I ask for it he looks at me fearfully and shouts, 'Wait, Sir! Wait!'

'No, Sallah,' I say, 'time is really up, I have to get to my next class.'

'No, wait, Sir!'

Sallah guards his paper the way a little child does its dessert— both arms wrapped defensively around it—but I'm able to get hold of one corner of the page and start pulling. It doesn't help much, though; in fact, not at all. Sallah only tightens his grasp and is now holding on to the paper with both hands. He stares at me fearfully the whole time, beads of sweat on his forehead.

'Sallah,' I say sternly as we both pull on the paper, 'you've had an hour to finish it... If you haven't filled in the right words by now, then you simply don't know them. So give me your paper.'

Still that distressed look—and he's still not letting go. Meanwhile the paper is becoming rather crumpled. His stubbornness surprises me, but now it begins to irritate me as well.

'Okay, Sallah,' I say with a throwaway gesture, 'keep your paper, then, I'm not going to look at it anyway, I'm leaving.'

I act as though I'm about to walk away, and at that same moment Sallah gives up. He lets go of his paper and pushes it across the desk dismissively; now it's his turn for the throwaway gesture. His scowl and the fact that he's no longer looking at me tell me he's angry. I leave him to it and rush off to my next class.

Yet Sallah never stays mad for long—another way in which he and Mohammed are alike. The next day he greets me cheerfully as ever ('Hey, Sir!'), laughing jovially and immediately grasping one of my hands. There is a fun fair on the Dam, Sallah went there yesterday, and now he promises to win a watch for me.

'Please make it a gold one, with the date on it, Sallah,' I say, and Sallah thinks that's funny. His skinny frame creases up with laughter ('Kkchchch'), he slaps his knees with pleasure. 'Okay, sir, gold watch with day on it. Kkkchch.'

Once the other students have taken their seats, we begin that talk about Rushdie. After Sallah has aired his opinion that 'this men, he must die!' I ask the others whether they agree.

'Course, Sir! He's bad man!' Mohammed blurts out matter-of-factly. Mohammed is not the one to ask about Rushdie, I realize now. Ajax, the football team, is more his forte.

Vijay nods in agreement. Vijay is a Pakistani boy, even more gentle in spirit than Sallah, and less forward as well, always a friendly smile for me whenever and wherever I see him.

'Is that how you really feel?' I ask.

Again, Vijay nods. When I keep looking at him, he bursts into laughter, as though he—the old Vijay—is apologizing for the merciless doppelgänger who has now come to the fore, the one I've never met before.

'But why, Sallah?'

'These men he write very bad book for Islam. He must be dead.'

'And what if I had written that book,' I postulate, just to bring it a little closer to home, 'would I have to die, too? Mr Beekmans must die!'

They burst out laughing at that last sentence, it's as though they're laughing away their shame. Only now do they seem to realize what they have been saying. But there is a way out.

'You are not Muslim,' Vijay says.

I look at him questioningly.

'If Muslim write bad book,' explains Vijay, speaking cautiously, 'then he must die, but you are not Muslim, you don't know.'

'Muslim is not allowed to say bad things for Islam,' Sallah shouts.

'But I am?' I ask.

Sallah laughs.

'No one is allowed to say bad things for Islam, but not-Muslim, he not have to die.'

Strangely enough, the mood in the class is anything but grim. Sallah, Vijay, Mohammed, they are all laughing a bit and seem to deliver their draconian verdict almost as a kind of witticism. Their attitude seems to say: come on, that's simply what the law says, there's nothing to get worked up about.

Our Finnish student, Markus—a professor's son who wears his long, blond hair in a ponytail, a remarkably talented drawer with a dry, rather macabre sense of humour—suddenly starts chanting, 'Kill! Kill!' but with a big, fat grin on his face. When I fix my gaze on him, he says, 'These guys are crazy, you can't reason with them.'

The amazing thing is that Sallah and Vijay, these kind-hearted boys, obey a law that literally goes against their grain—and they do so without question, like children. Markus has homed in on that quite well.

Girls interesting also for sex

Kamil, a rather bashful Turkish boy of eighteen with a handsome, intelligent face, comes to me carrying a copy of *Turkish Delight*, by Jan Wolkers. I'm in the school library with my junior class. Of the six books that are required reading this year, they're allowed to choose one themselves. 'Sir…?' Kamil says, holding up the book with a questioning look.

A few days ago, during Dutch class, we had read 'The Membrane of Honour', an article published not long before in the Saturday magazine of the daily *NRC Handelsblad*. The article was about Moroccan girls who, having lost their virginity, had an operation to restore their hymen and so avoid problems on their wedding night. After reading the article, I had asked the students to answer a few questions, including this one: Should a woman remain a virgin until marriage?

'Yes,' wrote Kamil, who has been in Holland for three years. 'Because womens will marry. And a man will never accept that his wife lied in bed with somebody else before marriage.'

Now, here in the library, I clearly recall Kamil's views on virginity.

So I tell him cautiously, '*Turkish Delight*...I don't know whether that's a good one for you, there's an awful lot of sex in it...'

'Oh...no...' Kamil says quietly, then turns around decidedly and puts the book—it must have been the word *Turkish* in the title that aroused his interest—back on the shelf. He would never consider reading such a book, it seems. Somehow, I could have known—Kamil is a serious, perhaps even rather boring, boy whose interests are purely technical, the engineering type, a solid polytechnic student in the making. But the fact that he's not even curious about sex, a boy of eighteen, still surprises me.

The next question, of course, was whether a man should remain a virgin until marriage. That, however, was something Kamil did not consider necessary. 'Because mens cannot be pregnant and has no hymen.' A clearly technical approach.

Murat is a very different kind of boy, a Turk as well, dressed like Kamil in blue jeans and a baseball jacket, but much keener, stauncher than his basically mild-mannered countryman. There is something nasal about his voice that emphasizes that fact. The two boys may share the same rigid morality, but...Kamil seems to submit to it, to bow before it as a law. Murat, on the other hand, wields his principles like a sword, a weapon to keep at bay anything that threatens him and to protect everything dear. During a lesson about boyfriends and girlfriends, Sieu, a rather matter-of-fact Vietnamese boy, asked Murat whether he had 'a nice sister for me at home'. Murat reacted as though stung. He spun around in his chair furiously and told Sieu not to talk about his sister. When class was over, I asked Murat why he hadn't taken it all a little more lightly; after all, Sieu was only joking. 'Where I come from, Sir, honour is the most important thing,' he announced earnestly.

Ali, from Morocco, is a handsome boy, serious too, and although that applies to Kamil as well the two boys have little else in common. In his own, subtle way, Ali is 'cool', but he doesn't lay on that coolness too thickly. With a sceptical glimmer in his eye, this is the kind of boy who sits at the back of the room and takes it all in, who listens well and speaks up only at the decisive moment. His classmates are all a bit in awe of him, and the fact that he is not a leader is probably due only to his own lack of interest: he can't be bothered, he's more of a loner. In his opinions on sex, Ali is definitely progressive. 'As far as I am concerned its okay [to remain a virgin], but it doesn't have to be, because I think girls are also interesting for sex and need it before marriage, and just like men. After all, a girl has to get rid of her needs also.'

Sitting beside Ali is Shahrazad, a pretty, nineteen-year-old Moroccan girl. She is always dressed in modern fashion, you'd barely know she was Moroccan. Her opinions exhibit almost the same degree of enlightenment as her neighbour Ali. Shahrazad feels that it is 'just more exciting, nicer to wait until marriage and give your virginity to someone you really care about, instead of hopping in the bed with the first one you meet and after that say "Oh, I wish I hadn't done that".'

A more modern female standpoint from the Islamic camp is nowhere to be found in this junior Dutch class. Shahrazad's opinion, in fact, seems prompted more by personal considerations than religious ones, even though she calls herself a Muslim.

Mouna, however, sees things differently. She is the only girl in the class who wears a headscarf. For Mouna, a woman should remain a virgin 'even if you don't do that for your husband, then do it for your family and for your religion, because if you don't do that you will bring shame on the family and disobey the laws of the religion, because the Qur'an forbids an intercourse with a non-Muslim or with someone you're not married to, because we are not animals.'

Mouna is a quiet girl, but also a girl who dares to be herself, a girl with character. But she's not the pushy kind, or even the kind to demand attention. She's often ill, and she says it's because she's so tired and has such bad headaches—when I asked whether she ate enough, she told me that most food didn't appeal to her. 'I'd rather not eat anything.'

'But then you can't expect to stay healthy, Mouna,' I tell her. 'You have to eat.' Only now that I speak to her in such a fatherly fashion do I realize how much, in the course of the school year, I have come to like this unassuming girl.

Poles apart from Mouna is Adil, a lively, big-mouthed boy, a stealer of hearts, identical in appearance to any born-and-bred Amsterdam teenager: hair slicked back in the same way, styled with the same gel, dressed in the same tough-guy fashion and with the same brand of nerve. Adil is doing this year over again, he wants to get his diploma, but...life has so much more to offer. There are so many cute girls walking around at this school alone, he can never find the time to court them all. But he does his best. If Adil finds out that one of them has an hour off, he takes an hour off as well. He's skipped classes so often that he's now under a 'contract' with the school.

Because he's never at a loss for words, and because he's so good-looking, he's quite successful with a number of those girls as well. When asked whether a woman should remain a virgin until marriage, our rough-and-tumble Romeo answers: 'if I want to marry then I want a virgin girl in my bed. Not one who is been screwing a few times first and then me last. I don't want secondhand.'

I've often wondered just how much of an Amsterdammer this Adil—who has lived here since he was seven—really is. His answer shows him to be an outspoken child of the streets—hence the 'screwing'—but at the same time a Moroccan. On long summer evenings one often finds Adil down at Leidseplein, where, in his own words, he is 'having some fun, picking up girls or having a beer'. I don't know how far he goes with that picking-up, but he makes one thing perfectly clear: 'If a girl is a virgin, then you bet I won't unvirgin her, if she's Moroccan of course.' Adil, it seems, is unwilling to burn his fingers on this particular taboo. Like so many of his generation, Adil is a child between two cultures, forced to apply double standards.

Latifa, who wears her hair, her gleaming black hair, cut short, lived until the age of eight in the royal city of Marrakesh, with her mother and three little sisters. She has now been living in Holland for an equal amount of time. Her most striking trait seems to me to be her curiosity, or else it's her cattiness, a trait Latifa seems to me much more capable of than her classmates. Her movements also betray a certain restlessness, impatience rather, and so have something spiteful about them. Her light-green eyes, which I've never seen in a Moroccan before, can also flash rather nastily. Latifa's curiosity extends to boys in particular. I know that last year she had a boyfriend, and that when they broke up it made her very sad. Something of that sadness seems to have turned bitter in this dark-haired virago, and to have trickled down into her opinions. She does not, for example, approve of operations to restore the hymen. 'If Moroccan girls find out that you can fix your hymen, and even have the government pay for it, then no one will remain a virgin until marriage.' If she were a physician, she would perform such operations only in rare exceptions, and in any event 'not for someone who has just had intercourse'. If a girl's been raped, that's different, but even then: 'I would only do it if I was absolutely sure. So if someone wanted me to repair a hymen, she would have to answer a lot of questions first.'

'But imagine if a girl like that,' I say to Latifa during the review session in our next class together, 'if that girl loves her boyfriend very much, and thinks she's going to marry him, and then goes to bed with him... And then suddenly her boyfriend drops her! Wouldn't you help a girl like that?'

She shakes her head firmly—the gesture has something unrelenting about it.

'You wouldn't?'

'No, it's her own fault. Then she shouldn't have been stupid enough to listen to him.'

'But Latifa—this girl did what she did out of love. If you don't repair her hymen, she may never be able to marry a Moroccan man. Does she have to pay all her life for something she did out of love? Even if you shoot someone and kill them, you still don't have to spend your whole life in prison...'

Seductive arguments, I believe, but Latifa won't budge, stubborn as she is. 'That's her own fault. She shouldn't have been so stupid.'

'For a mistake she made at a young age, she has to pay for that all her life?'

'Yes.' Not a smidgen of pity.

Undeniably, the students who have nothing to do with the directives of the Qur'an—Sieu from Vietnam, the two Colombian girls ('Sir, is it really true that Dutch men think breasts are more important than rear ends?') and beautiful Sanja from Bosnia—take life more as it comes than do their Muslim classmates. Oh yes, Sanja writes, if she were a doctor she would perform operations to restore those hymens: *'If it pays really well then I will make new hymen for all naughty Moroccan girls.'* When she airs this opinion during our discussion, the others laugh out loud: they pick up on the sarcasm, and seem willing to accept that from Sanja. No one feels the need to convince her otherwise; probably, I suspect, because these Muslims are already quite used to going their own way, amid a divergence of opinions.

Prayer rugs in the schoolyard

Vesna from Bosnia, who is eighteen by now and in her last year of secondary school, tells me that the Moroccan boys in her class no longer look at her, and no longer talk to her either. 'When I come into the class and say good morning, they don't say anything back.'

'Well, maybe you said something they didn't like,' I suggest. But the boys, Vesna says, ignore all the girls. 'They turned into fundamentalists during the summer holiday.'

Because I burst out laughing, Vesna thinks I don't believe her. 'I bet you don't even know that they pray here at school. They stay inside when everyone goes out for a break, and when we come back the whole room smells of old socks.'

It's true that, since the summer holiday, a few of them have started sporting wild beards. Still, I'm surprised at what Vesna tells me, because it's so unlike these boys, all of whom I've had in the class. I know that Vesna is referring to Ashraf, his brother and two other boys, all of whom have been together for almost four years, starting back in the 'bridge' class. And now she's telling me that these boys won't talk to her any more, not even look at her? And that they act the same way towards all the other girls, the girls they've known all those years as well?

I don't teach that particular class any more, so I sound out a few other teachers. I ask their English teacher, for example, whether she has 'noticed that the Moroccan boys in six have started ignoring the girls'. I tell her Vesna says so.

'They don't look at me any more either.' Her voice sounds a little flat, as though she really can't be bothered with my question.

'You're kidding,' I say.

'No, they sit at the back of the class, don't say a word, don't respond to anyone. When I speak to them, they lower their eyes when they listen.'

She says she recently made the mistake of touching Ashraf. 'He wouldn't look at me, so he didn't see that I was trying to hand him some papers. I tapped him on the shoulder and he jumped like he'd been stung by a bee.'

It's not just the English teacher either, so it seems: the boys make a show of averting their gaze when spoken to by their female Dutch and biology teachers as well. They still look at their male teachers, I'm told, but barely take part in their lessons either. And on Friday afternoon it's as though school no longer exists, then they have to go to the mosque.

I listen with growing wonder; I've always known these boys to be inquisitive, hard-working, ambitious pupils. Could it really be true, as Vesna claims, that they have turned into fundamentalists during the summer holidays? Perhaps such things are simply bound to happen at a school like this? More than half the pupils here, after all, are Muslims. I decide to wend my way to the Moroccan boys in the fifth, boys I had in my class last year and with whom I still have good relations. They can probably tell me exactly what's going on with Ashraf and his friends—maybe they've even undergone a similar metamorphosis. Without beating about the bush, but still keeping it a bit light-hearted, I ask them whether they also pray at school these days.

'Yeah…' Ali says, a bit distrustfully. I've always liked Ali, and the feeling is mutual, I believe, hence his honesty. But he also senses that I won't immediately approve of this praying. Perhaps he's even afraid that, if he says too much, the school management may intervene.

'But you didn't last year, did you?'

Ali shrugs.

Younes butts in, 'I've always prayed five times a day.'

'Really?' I ask.

He nods.

'But not here at school?'

'Oh yeah, last year too.'

I look at him in surprise. It's not what I'd expected from this rowdy jokester—Younes has never been an easy student.

'And what about you, Abdeslam?' I ask Younes's brother.

Abdeslam grins. He's not nearly as hard on himself.

'But where do you go to do your praying?' I want to know.

Now they all laugh a bit secretively. 'What difference does it make?' Ali says.

'In one of the classrooms?'

Ali nods. 'Sometimes the gym teacher gives us the key and we go into the locker room.'

Vesna had told me about that as well, how she had gone into the girls' locker room to dress for gym and found a group of boys praying.

'And what if you're not allowed to use that any more?' I ask.

'Then we'll find another place,' Younes says, his tone that of someone who has no intention of letting anyone take this away from him.

I walk back to the building. Standing beside the door is Said, a fifteen-year-old Moroccan mischief-maker who has grown almost half a metre in the last few months. He has two new front teeth now; his own were knocked out, in his own words, by 'this Moroccan who tried to steal my moped'. He laughed when he told me about it at the time, those front teeth didn't seem to matter much to him, more important was that he had run after 'that Moroccan' with a baseball bat a few days later and given him a good beating—and got his moped back. Until then I hadn't realized that Moroccans in Amsterdam could give each other such a hard time—a little naïve of me, I suppose. Whatever the case, I now ask Said whether he 'prays at school too these days'.

Said bursts out in scornful laughter.

So what does he think about the other boys, the ones who do pray? Again, that scornful laugh.

'You should have seen them last year, when they were still hanging around here, making out with the girls.'

Something in Said's vehemence leads me to wonder whether he's had to stand up to them. 'Have they ever asked you to come along and pray?'

'They ask everyone.'

As I go inside, I wonder whether this isn't a task for the school management. It has, in any event, become the talk of the staff room. After a few days the management seems to have picked up on it as well, there has even been a 'talk' with the boys. They've been told that there can be no more cutting of classes of Friday afternoons, that school attendance is mandatory and that here, at a 'public day school', no exception can be made for visits to the mosque. Concerning prayer during breaks, a thorny subject that requires some diplomacy, all that could be said was that one preferred not to see it happen within the walls of the school itself.

That's what I'm told; what I see the next day is six Moroccan boys making a point of rolling out their prayer rugs in the schoolyard. Calmly and in great earnest, they take off their shoes and remain sunk in prayer for a good twenty minutes, standing, then kneeling again, all noses pointed towards Mecca. The whole ritual is undoubtedly not meant as a provocation, it's prayer, but there is definitely something defiant about it.

For a little while it seems as though the whole affair is about to take a grimmer turn, but no: as suddenly as the fire of devotion was kindled, it goes out. Over the next few days I see the boys outside again a few times, on their prayer rugs, but after a week goes by I don't see them any more. And from one of the female teachers I hear—major news indeed—that the boys have started looking her in the eye again. Even Vesna says they have started acting 'almost normal again'.

I suspect it all became a bit too much for them. Teachers talking at them, classmates complaining, a meeting with the school management, it must have got to them. Ashraf, who played a leading role in the whole thing, opened up to the physics teacher—a man for whom he'd always had a lot of respect. He had never, he told the teacher, realized that the way he chose to practice his faith would meet with so much resistance. 'But not looking at women,' the physics teacher told him, 'is something you just can't get away with, not here in Holland.'

They haven't given up the mosque, though, they still go there on Friday afternoon. Now, however, they come back as quickly as possible, so they won't be absent for the whole period, only late. The physics teacher, whose class is the one partly missed and interrupted, has decided to be lenient. 'After all, you have to cut these boys a little slack.'

Ramadan pig

We're halfway through the lunar month of Ramadan when class B3 comes pouring into the room. This class consists only of thirteen-year-olds, all of them of Moroccan or Turkish descent; all of them fledgling Muslims, in other words. They all refrain from food and drink during this month of fasting, from sun-up to sun-down, and for some of them it is the first time they have gone through this ordeal. But they are no less fanatical for that; in fact the opposite. As soon as they are seated and a certain degree of calm has descended, I ask, just to boost their morale, 'Well, people, how's Ramadan going? Are you able to stick it out?'

Of course they are! In fact, they see the question almost as an insult. But still: 'Not Ahmed!' Karim shouts.

'Ahmed ate yesterday!' Abdel sneers.

'Ramadan pig!' Samira hisses.

Ahmed usually sits at the back, beside Mohammed, but today he is up front and all alone. That doesn't necessarily mean anything, friendships and enmities are always switching back and forth in this class. But today, little Ahmed, who can look so innocent and react in such disbelief whenever I catch him being lazy ('Oh, but I didn't know, teacher...'), makes a rather lonely, indeed rather ostracized, impression.

'Yeah, because I was sick!' he shouts back. Then he crosses his arms and exhales loudly, as though all this fuss is becoming too much for him. Those who are ill, I know by now, are excused from the rigors of Ramadan. But I bet that Ahmed, as is the case with almost everything, was simply being lazy here, too. Karim shouts again, 'You just didn't want to go to school!' But Ahmed is no longer paying attention.

Karim is no more than twice the size of the rucksack in which he carries his schoolbooks—at least a head shorter than his classmates. They say he has a growth disorder; his father, in any event, isn't much taller than he is. Karim has what you'd call a roguish look to him, and can be extremely contrary. The best thing to do at moments like that is leave him alone; all attempts at coercion only make him dig in his heels.

Even back in elementary school—most of these students grew up the Netherlands—it sounds as if he was a difficult pupil. In an essay, he writes: 'When I was 6 we went to the third group then we had a teacher, she was 50. Every morning when she come in she picked up her bell and belled two times that means sit down and cross arms.' A little further along in the essay I encounter the Karim I know: 'In fifth group I had to wear glasses then I was 7 I had to wear glasses for 2 years. Almost every morning I tell the teacher I forget my glasses when the glasses are in my bag.' Yes, Karim can be a tough nut to crack, but admittedly the class would be much duller without him.

From where I'm standing, here up in front, it's hard to tell whether Ramadan is really having much of an impact on these students, except that they seem more aware of themselves. They were Muslims before this, of course, but now they *feel* like Muslims as well, and they seem to like that feeling. I can tell, because today is the first time they try to spread the faith—like miniature missionaries. Samira asks me, 'Why don't you observe Ramadan, teacher?'

Karim is the smallest boy; Samira the smallest girl in the class. Neither of them ever backs down an inch. Samira looks like a scrawny little bird, a skinny, sharp-witted girl with big brown eyes who likes to play soccer with the boys. She's the nervy type, and can give an impeccable imitation of a nasal Amsterdam snarl.

'But I'm not a Muslim, Samira,' I say.

'That doesn't matter, it's good for you!'

'Good for my what?'

'For your body.'

'Is that why you observe Ramadan?'

'Not just that!'

'For the poor people, too!' Karim chimes in.

I look at Karim. 'For the poor people?'

'Because then you know how they feel!'

'But why would you want to know how poor people feel?'

'So then you give to them!' Samira shouts again.

'Give to them? What do you give them?'

'Money, of course!'

'You mean you give money to poor people?'

'Yeah!' Samira's voice drops a quick octave, to show her indignation: the nerve of me to even doubt that!

'So you, Karim,' I say, raising my voice a little for dramatic effect, while singling out Karim, 'so now you know how poor people feel?'

Karim, suddenly finding himself in a corner with no idea where this might be headed, is startled. 'Yeah...' he bluffs, still a little unsure of himself. He looks at me, wide-eyed, brash and suspicious all at the same time. The rest of the class is paying close attention now too.

Then, to let the tension fade away into a nothingness the students weren't expecting, I turn back to Samira. As calmly as possible, I say, 'But...there aren't any poor people in Holland!'

'But there are in Morocco!'

'How do you know that?'

'I saw them, when I was on vacation!'

Karim, having recovered from his surprise, launches the counter-offensive. 'There are poor people here, too, y'know. They eat out of trash cans.' The whole class agrees with him laughingly, and Karim laughs too, flattered, his hero-of-the-class laugh.

'Tramps!' shouts Abdel, who always wants the last word.

'Very good,' I say. 'So now all of you know what it feels like to be tramp?'

No one wants to deny that, but no one really wants to confirm it either—after all, who want to be like a tramp?—so the room is quiet. 'What you're telling me then, Karim,' I continue, 'if I understand correctly, is that you give your pocket money to tramps?'

'No way!' The whole class starts laughing again, and headstrong Karim is the hero once more.

Now it's Sarima who shouts, 'Haven't you ever read the Qur'an?'

'What do you mean?'

'Well, if you did, you'd understand.'

'Understand what?'

'About Ramadan, and about everything. It's all in there.'

'Samira's father is an imam,' Abdel shouts.

'Aha!' I cry, raising my voice again. 'So what will the Qur'an tell me?'

'Everything,' Samira says again. 'About how God made the world and people and everything.'

'But God didn't make people,' I say in amazement.

The students begin jeering. And laughing, loudly and a bit exaggeratedly. Obviously, I'm pretty stupid.

'So who did make people, then, huh?' Abdel shouts, glancing around quickly at a few of his classmates, as though to draw their attention to this shrewd retort.

'Nobody made people,' I say calmly. 'Haven't you ever heard of evolution?'

Somewhat to my amazement, it turns out that they have actually never heard of it. 'Well,' I go on, 'once there was a fish that crawled on to dry land, and later it turned into a person.'

Now all hell breaks loose. Abdel, Sarima, Karim, Mohammed, Ahmed, Najib, in fact all twenty of them are beside themselves with mirth. They laugh at the top of their lungs again and slap their knees. My summary of evolution was perhaps a little too succinct to be really edifying. 'So how did that fish get in the water in the first place, huh?' Samira shouts cuttingly.

'If that was true, fish would crawl out of ditches now, too!' Abdel shouts, and everyone laughs loudly again, including Abdel himself.

I calm them down a bit. 'Then tell me what you people think.'

Samira—the others leave it up to her—launches eagerly into the biblical account of creation, and the others help out here and there. Having arrived at the Fall, she says, 'But then he ate an apple from the tree, but he wasn't supposed to, and then they had to leave paradise.'

Abdel even knows that an evil angel tricked Adam, through Eve, into eating the apple, and that the angel was angry because 'he didn't want to serve people'.

'Very good,' I say. 'But wasn't that angel also jealous because God had created man in his image, and because people look like God and angels don't?'

But it seems I've said something stupid again, and blasphemous to boot. 'No one knows what God looks like!' Samira shouts scathingly.

Every attempt to make them take the biblical account a little less literally ('Did you know that that tree was the Tree of Knowledge? It was no accident that God put that tree off limits...') fails ('Whaaat? Man, it was just an apple tree!'). But I'm impressed by how much these young students know about all this. They must have been brought up on it.

There's not much sense in trying to make this lesson descend from the Qur'an to the textbook, so, for the first time this year, the discussion races off of its own accord into matters of faith. And— as has been the case for centuries with all such religious disagreements—both of us, the class and I, stick to our biases. One thing is clear: these first-year students consider themselves vastly superior to me on this point.

When class is over, Najib comes up to my desk. He's the lone wolf in the class, the only one who wasn't born here, and the quietest of them all. 'That's all fairy tales you told us, teacher, all that stuff about us being fish... You should try reading the Qur'an some time.'

Us against us

The boys' names are Asaad, Sayed, Yusuf. They came to Holland by way of Morocco and Turkey, after escaping from war zones. Asaad, Sayed and Yusuf fall under the category 'refugees'.

They're full of goodwill, these sixteen-year-olds, and pleased that the Netherlands has granted them refuge. Asaad, a Kurd from northern Iraq, writes: 'I wont staying in Netherlands I think Netherlands very good land.' 'Wont' here should be read as 'want'. Were it up to me, I would grant Asaad a permanent residence permit on the basis of that sentence alone. I'm prejudiced, though, I admit, because I know Asaad. He is tall and friendly and he stutters, but he likes to talk. I know Asaad, but I'd like to know more about him. For that reason, I ask the students to write a short essay in class about their native countries, and about why they came to Holland. I've only just got around to doing this with Asaad's class, because their Dutch wasn't up to it before this. But now, after about five months, they can probably handle this assignment. What's more, they also feel comfortable enough with me by now to actually feel like writing something.

That definitely goes for Asaad, who knuckles down to work right away. Twelve sentences in an hour is all he can produce, but they're meaningful sentences, perhaps precisely because Asaad still formulates so clumsily. They hit hard, these sentences, because their clumsiness stands in such stark contrast to what they say. 'I live in Iraq in the north,' Asaad writes, 'there two leaders Talabani and Barzani both want my city. He comes many people get dead, other too if comes many people dead.'

Leaders who have started fighting among themselves now that Saddam has stopped bothering them—the reason why Asaad, as the eldest boy ('I am old in the house my father and mother choose me'), was sent to Turkey with his uncle and fled through the mountains. From Turkey, Asaad and his uncle drove to Holland in one week. In summary, Asaad writes of his country: 'in Iraq many war every day people dead there I think cant people live.' Indeed, Asaad, no place for a person to live.

Sayed and Yusuf come from war zones as well. Sayed is from Algeria (Algiers) and Yusuf from Somalia (Mogadishu). In Somalia, rival clans have been fighting each other for years. Yusuf, who loves to tell jokes, who always acts cheerful and is, I believe, cheerful as well, nevertheless writes: 'when I was lidle I seed many problem for my country. I can not think about what I seed there. I remember what I seed, some evenings I dream of.'

Some evenings I dream of. Yusuf is here on his own. He's what they call an 'IMA', an independent minor asylum-seeker; there are a few others at this school as well. 'Also I not know where is mine families. When I leaves Somal till now I not have contact with mine families.'

Algerian Sayed came here because 'In Algeeri they muny problem', because there are a lot of problems in Algeria. Sayed can barely write, because he can barely read; he mixes the letters all together. He's a fast talker, though. After our Dutch composition class, if you can call it that, I talk to Sayed, Yusuf and Asaad about the violence where they come from. Sayed comes up with a striking observation, one I hadn't expected from him, and one that continues to haunt me: 'All people is crazy there, teacher. In Somalia, Iraq, Algeria is crazy war. Everybody us against us.'   □

GOD AND ME
Diana Athill

I suppose a good many people who, like me, cannot accept the teachings of any organized religion, or even conceive of anything one could call 'God', have nevertheless occasionally experienced some flicker of what seems to be the numen. To me it happens very rarely, but I still have a clear memory of its first occurrence, some eighty years ago.

It was in an orchard through which I went every day, running back and forth between our house and my grandparents'. At one point an old and untidy tree beside the path had leaned over so that even a child had to duck or swerve to avoid its branches. It was not a tree that had ever interested me, because the apples it bore were cookers, too acid to be eaten raw, but one day, when I happened to duck instead of swerve, I found myself within it, surrounded by its gnarled branches all heavy with very large, smooth, intensely green apples, and they stopped me in my tracks. They were so beautiful, so powerfully still, so...I didn't know what. Alive? I stood gazing at a group of three of them, a huge one and its two slightly smaller companions, shining serenely among their equally green leaves, and their stillness seemed almost to be humming. I began to feel that I was on the edge of something, that in a moment something was going to happen...and when it didn't there was a vague sensation that it was my fault: that if I had been able to go as still as those apples, whatever was humming in them would have sounded in my head. The moment passed quickly, I ran on, not—as far as I can remember—bothered by it. But what happened in my head was that those apples continued to *be* in it, even into my eighty-ninth year.

They, and from time to infrequent time other similar experiences, led me to fancy that had I been born at the right time and place I might conceivably have accepted a really primitive form of religion: belief not in a One and Only God, but in many little localized gods, gods of trees, rivers and so on, dryads, naiads, satyrs—I might even have enjoyed believing in them. They would not have offended reason by claiming the absolute and exclusive power with which we burden our One and Only Gods. Or, to be more serious, Buddhism might be the answer—it does not bother with a god and seeks, as I understand it, the achievement of stillness. But I have never been able to take the elaborate imagery through which one form of it expresses itself and I am too self-indulgent for its central disciplines. But at bottom what those experiences have suggested to me is not any specific answer, but a feeling that however little one may believe in any of the gods, big ones or little ones, awe should be respected, because it is so undeniable that a reason for being awestruck does exist: the thing that hummed in those apples—life.

The more one thinks about it, the more astounding it is that here and there in the universe, out of the whirl of particles came forms of life, some of which developed into beings complex enough to be aware of themselves, even to try to understand themselves and their relationship with their environment. It is astounding beyond our ability to be astounded, hence our attempt to tame it into systems which, because we ourselves have invented them, are within our grasp. Once—and this, like the apples, was a key moment—I was on the river at Oxford, with a man I'd met that evening and would meet only once again, because he was about to leave Oxford for good. It was an exquisitely moonlit summer night, we had taken out a punt and were talking, as one tends to talk in one's early twenties, about what we did and didn't believe. I said something about the puzzle of what had begun it all, because 'after all, there must have been a beginning', and he said, 'Perhaps not. Perhaps it's just that the human mind is incapable of imagining anything that doesn't begin.' I don't think anything said to me has ever pleased me more than that dizzying little remark. It was as though he had pushed open a door and given me a tiny peep through it into the Unexplainable, and it was thrilling. And ever since then I have been content to listen to and love the humming of life in everything without minding at all that I don't understand it.

So often people say, 'Without God what would be the point of life? How could one go on without believing that it has a meaning?' It does not seem to occur to them that any 'point' granted them by their god has been provided by the human imagination, and cannot therefore be trustworthy, however comforting. Of course, it does not have to give them what seems to be good reason to blow up skyscrapers full of people or to send in the bombers to countries they happen to disapprove of—a 'point' imagined by someone gentle and generous will be different from one imagined by a fanatic or a fool—but it is observable that in spite of the omnipotence which is usually claimed for a god, he always seems to be concerned only with human beings on this particular planet, and often with only some of those human beings, not all of them. And yet we know—we ourselves, astounding phenomena that we are, have laboriously discovered—that Earth is no more than a grain of sand in the immensity of what surrounds it, and that like any other of the worlds whirling through space it will continue to harbour life only if it continues in exactly the right relationship with its sun. Although we have developed into this tiny planet's dominant form of life (indeed have overdone it, probably to the planet's detriment, but that is another story)... Well, fleas have developed the ability to live and prosper on the bodies of animals, including us, but it doesn't occur to us that they are therefore capable of understanding, or trying to understand, the workings of the human mind; and we in relation to the universe are infinitely more trivial than fleas are in relation to us. It seems to me odd that while on the one hand this is common knowledge, on the other hand a great many people choose to believe and find comfort in the minuscule myths provided by their religions. Whistling in the dark: that is what it is.

And so, of course, is finding comfort in the awe-inspiring unexplainability of life. To me, it just happens to be the tune which sounds least silly.　　　　　　　　　　　　　　　　　　□

GOD AND ME
Blake Morrison

Between the ages of nine and fourteen, I sat in church each Sunday, waiting for God. My hopes weren't high, even to begin with, so I felt no bitterness when He didn't reveal Himself, merely bemusement at what all those prayers had been in aid of. If honest piety couldn't flush Him out, even as a passing shadow or sudden gust of wind, what could?

The nearest I came to a sense of the numinous was once, playing football, when without intending to I dipped my body one way, and took the ball the other, and left an opponent behind me. It was only a feint, not a swoon, let alone a trance, but the sense of forces beyond my cognition or control left a strong impression. Occasionally, since, I've had that with writing: the thrill of doing something, however small, I didn't know was in me—and maybe wasn't.

After giving up church, and cutting down on the football, I began writing poetry. Part of the impulse was a feeling of awe for the world bodied over against us—earth, city and sky—and the unknowability of the universe beyond. But even at twenty I'd not have called myself spiritual and by the time I was forty the material realities of existence had driven out what little spirituality was left. Was it having a job that did that, or becoming a parent, or reading more widely, or getting older? Whichever, I've lost all sense of wonder—and of God.

This feels like a failing, especially in a poet. But most of my poet friends aren't spiritual, either, and would be embarrassed to see the word applied to their work. Through love, sex, drink, drugs, music, mountains, sunsets, grief, meditation, insomnia and physical exhaustion, I can still experience a heightened perception of reality or transcendent surges of rapture. But science can explain these altered states of consciousness. I don't delude myself that an unseen divinity or supernatural powers play any part.

If God's gone at last, that's a relief. To suppose an active intelligence lies behind Creation is to point up, as Kingsley Amis once put it, the ignorance, insensitivity and downright nastiness of the Creator. Amis thought of himself as a non-militant unbeliever. But these days his secularism seems brave, heretical, even blasphemous. Which newspaper now would dare to take his poem 'New Approach Needed', which addresses Christ on the cross ('you won't get me/Up on one of those things') and advises him, should he ever come back, to 'get some service in, Jack... Tell your dad that from me'?

My own form of unbelief is milder. Orwell used the phrase Anglican Atheist to describe the kind of people found 'wandering about the ruins of the C of E', and that's how I see myself: as someone fond of singing hymns in whitewashed rural churches but honour-bound to stay away on Sunday; someone who would never restrict another person's right to religious worship but thinks belief in deities or an afterlife childish nonsense; someone who no longer hopes that God will turn up and would want him imprisoned or executed if He did.   □

GRANTA

KISS DADDY!

John Borneman

For several weeks Ziyyad is adamant about a visit to his home, but I delay. Another visit to another family, I think. On display the whole night! Again! I know that a good ethnographer never turns down an invitation. But every night of my final two weeks in Aleppo I have committed myself to activities, including several lectures outside the city. I'd already met Ziyyad several times at other students' homes, where the women in the family had cooked for us, or someone had purchased take-out food from a local restaurant. In these Muslim households, we eat and discuss with only the other men and boys. Ziyyad plays on my guilty conscience about delaying a visit to his family and begins to ask personal questions: 'Who are you seeing today?' 'Why are you unable to come?' I cannot say no for ever. He has actively sought my friendship. I agree to the Saturday evening before my departure.

Ziyyad is in his final year of completing a bachelor's degree in English literature. As a pious Muslim, five times daily he is bound to perform a fixed ritual of prayer, called the *Salat*. So if we spend more than a few hours together, he routinely asks me, 'Can I go pray now?' Or, 'Is there some place to pray here?' I invariably find the question, and his politeness, charming. But why ask me? In the souk, men pray regularly in front of me: they roll out a rug, fall to their knees, mutter their prayers, stand up, roll up the rug and go on with business.

'Go. I'll wait,' I say. If we are with other students, they take turns going to pray, leaving someone with me at all times. With so many mosques in Aleppo, and with prayer rooms in most university buildings, there is bound to be a place to pray around some corner, so it is relatively easy to perform the required ritual. But why am I in a position to tell Ziyyad whether or not to pray? It is none of my business, I think, it is his obligation, his duty, his choice. But he thinks otherwise and solicits my agreement before disappearing—for about fifteen minutes each time.

Once, after I voice some criticism of the university, Ziyyad says, 'It is a curse to ever have been born in this country.' I am taken aback by the intensity and generality of his complaint. This kind of sentiment is the opposite of the pan-Arab solidarity Syria's Ba'athist regime tries to produce. Ziyyad thinks of himself as a social outsider, and he harbours a sense of deep cultural alienation, much deeper than he is capable of expressing, perhaps deeper than he himself is aware of. He wants desperately to avoid being identified as Syrian. Being American would be best.

'Who would Americans think I am?' he asks. I tell him Syrians are very diverse and it is hard to characterize them, they fit no physical stereotype, and, anyway, Americans have no clear image of what Syrians look like. He is immensely pleased when I tell him that in neither pronunciation nor looks—he has light, innocuous brown hair, clear brown eyes, medium-muscular build, hairy chest and legs (a friend who saw his photo called him 'a cute bear')—would Americans think he is Syrian. 'They might think you are from anywhere,' I say. 'Spain, England, even southern Germany.'

'Really?' he asks sceptically, and repeats this question frequently.

When I first meet Ziyyad, he guesses that I am from 'near Canada'. 'Close,' I say, 'northern Wisconsin. It is the vowels.' He declares his major interest to be 'dialectology' and asks if I would be interested in giving a lecture on this topic.

'Tell me what it is first,' I reply. 'I have no idea.' When I use words Ziyyad has never heard spoken, he repeats them several times, carefully, precisely, and then gives me one or even several dictionary definitions he has read.

He asks questions like, '"Had to go"—do you pronounce that "hada go", "hadda go", or "haD To go?"'

I say, 'Enunciate the D and T, keep them separate. Don't slur or people will think you are lower class.'

But Ziyyad does not care about class, he is interested only in being recognized as American. Even without ever having visited the United States he is able to detect and reproduce exactly several American dialects—culled from American movies and National Public Radio, which he listens to daily. I tell him not to mimic American actors, most of whom have bad diction, but to pay attention to NPR or the BBC.

'I don't want to learn British English,' he says. 'I want to learn American.' He sometimes reads for me in English and asks me to correct his pronunciation. But I tell him he is fluent. He speaks better English than most members of my family.

'How is that possible?' he asks.

'Your vocabulary is larger,' I explain, 'your understanding of grammar and control of syntax are better. Most Americans do not speak good English.'

'How can that be?' he asks. 'It is their language.'

Often boys ask me what I like about them. When Ziyyad and his friends who study English literature ask, I say, 'Your curiosity.'

'What do you mean?' they ask.

'For example, for language. You are curious about learning languages,' I say.

'What do you dislike about us?' they ask. 'What are our faults?'

'Your faults are not for me to tell you but for you to discover,' I reply. 'But I would encourage you not to focus on language because of its technical qualities alone. You already speak well enough. Appreciate the poetic qualities of language; appreciate tone, what can be done in writing and talking. You should now aim for cultural competency.' Cultural competency! They had never heard this term before, so I throw out some names of contemporary authors: J. M. Coetzee, John Updike, Doris Lessing, Joan Didion, Toni Morrison, Tony Kushner. All unknown. I encourage them to enjoy reading, not to memorize or read for class alone but to read as a form of pleasure, like eating. They do not react to my exhortation. Their relation to the activity of reading appears limited to memorizing and reciting the Qur'an, which certainly involves poetic appreciation. But that reading has little to do with the pleasure of critical scrutiny and interpretation about which I speak. Later, I give Ziyyad some old *New Yorker* magazines I had brought with me. 'Read these,' I say, 'and you'll have cultural competency.'

On the night I am to eat with his family—father, mother, brother, sister—there is a constant drizzle and chilly wind. We meet downtown and walk about two miles to his parents' apartment. He shows me a paper, taped to the refrigerator, with a list of English euphemisms for going to the toilet. 'You want a copy?' he asks. I decline the offer. I recognize perhaps half of them. Take a leak? Water the horses?—yes. Going for a Jimmy Riddle? Siphon the python?—not a clue.

'I downloaded them from the Internet,' he says, proudly and mischievously. I go through and point out the ones he can safely use in public without offending anyone.

His mother, who works as a high school French teacher, has cooked for several days. She serves all the traditional Arabic dishes—Kurdish hot cheese pastry, baba ghanoush, falafel, hummus, mouttabel, mouhammara, peppers and onions, along with a main dish of chopped lamb baked with tomato slices on top—and a sautéed chicken salad, a more modern concoction which his father had prepared. As usual, the table is laden with dishes, each overflowing to the point that makes taking the serving spoon out impossible without creating a mess. There is hardly room for our plates, and my own is precariously balanced, half off, half on my corner. I eat way too much, everything is truly superb, and I thank them profusely throughout.

Ziyyad and his father sit on chairs across from me, while I sit alone on a small sofa. The father, who teaches agriculture at a secondary school and does odd plumbing jobs, often with Ziyyad's assistance, is tall, slender but muscular, partly bald, a very handsome man about ten years younger than me. He sits quietly, smiling but never fully relaxed, saying very little and perhaps not understanding much of what we say. As Ziyyad and his brother are English majors, most of our conversation is in English. They all speak other foreign languages, the mother only French, the father Romanian and French, the two sons only English. Ziyyad occasionally translates into Arabic.

His younger brother looks much like him, except he has no beard, and his hair is long, shiny black, and his eyebrows frame racoon-like eyes. He is, in other words, a stunning beauty. He wears a sweatshirt, sweat pants, and a stocking cap pulled tightly over his head. Not cultivating a rap look; just for comfort. For most of the evening, he squats next to the father, stroking his arm and holding his hand, but every time he gets up to carry dishes to and from the kitchen he has a spring in his step, almost as if dancing. The mother and daughter stay in a separate room off the kitchen, and they either shut the door or switch off the light the several times I walk past to wash my hands or use the toilet.

The fact that the women serve us and yet remain out of sight, though a common family arrangement in Syria as well as in many parts of the world, nonetheless makes me uncomfortable. I also feel awkward because I want to speak Arabic, just to include the father, but the boys want to practise their English. I relent, perhaps out of relief more than deference to their wishes. Once Ziyyad's brother comes over and sits next to me, and asks, 'Do you really hate your father?' Ziyyad must have told him something of our conversations about psychoanalysis.

'No, just some disagreements.'

'Why do you conflict with your father?' he persists.

'I love my father. He is dead now,' I say, 'but having conflict does not mean I did not love him.'

Their father sits passively through this exchange, smiling now and then. This conversation is about him, of course, and there is something queer in talking about him, the silent father, my host, in his presence.

After we finish the meal and just before dessert, the daughter, who is still in high school, comes out of the bedroom and joins us. She sits on the other sofa, along the far wall, and listens, saying nothing. Perhaps they have brought her out to interest me in marriage.

Indeed, Ziyyad's brother asks why I am not married, and why I have no children.

I say, 'Different opportunities. If I had a wife and child, I most probably would not be here with you.'

'Why don't you want to remarry?' he asks.

'Once is enough,' I say.

Ziyyad confides in me, almost as an aside but with a nervous giggle, that the whole family would like to leave Syria, that they had planned to emigrate. His father is underemployed and has no better prospects in Syria. He received his doctorate in Romania, and he financed it on his own by alternating years working in Syria with years studying in Romania. But the best jobs go only to those with good contacts, either educated in Syria or sent by the government to study abroad, and he lost those opportunities by going to Romania without government support.

He tells me of an embarrassing episode of family history. Four years ago, they paid $3,500 to a company in London to emigrate to Canada, but they have heard nothing back.

'That is a lot of money,' I say. Perhaps two years of both his parents' salaries! 'Did you contact them about the status of your application?'

'Yes, once. They said, "Don't contact us, we'll contact you."'

'What makes you think they are honest?' I ask.

'We know another family that was successful. They are in Canada now.'

'I would write a letter, and send a new letter every month until they answer.'

'I guess we've lost it,' he scoffs. 'There must be a curse on this family.'

Around 10.30 I stand and suggest I might leave, but Ziyyad's brother pleads, 'Oh, but we're enjoying you so much. Don't go.'

I sit back down. The mother, who has remained hidden the entire time, finally comes out after hearing I am ready to leave. She sits on the other sofa by her daughter, and orders her racoon-eyed son to get a box of chocolates they keep in a special place. I say, 'No, no, I am full.' But the family collectively insist I take a couple. Then the mother fetches a large keyring from the next room and insists I take it, and then two strings of prayer beads.

'Which one do you want?' asks Ziyyad.

'No more, no more!' I insist. 'I don't have room in my luggage,' and I accept what seems to be the less expensive of the two.

'Why don't you take the other one?' Ziyyad asks.

'No, please, I like this one,' I lie.

It is 11.00. I stand up, again. It has been raining heavily and the rain has just let up. 'I really have to go, pack to leave and all, it was all wonderful, the food the best I have had in Aleppo, really superb.'

They all stand. I take the hand of Ziyyad's brother in mine and kiss him on the cheek, thrice, the elaborate three-peat, and I take hold of his father's hand, intending to shake it, when Ziyyad says, in English, 'Kiss Daddy, kiss Daddy!' The whole family giggles and I am standing there, holding his father's hand, looking into his eyes, hesitating. Time seems to slow down.

The younger brother chimes in, 'Kiss Daddy, kiss Daddy.' So I reach over and kiss daddy, and he cradles my head in his free hand and kisses me, the three-peat.

I put my shoes on and leave with Ziyyad. We ignore the moment just passed, the Oedipal dynamic of desire, the boys wanting to see me in an embrace with their father, the father passive, excited, expectant. What of that embrace? They want me, from America, from the West, to kiss daddy, to comfort daddy, to console him in his distress at failing the family, at being underemployed, at having squandered their futures by investing years of savings in a hapless British swindle.

And the voice of the West? The family hear nothing, despite its siren calls and their monetary investment. Silence. Not even a reply! No, they are not going to the West, not as a family.

Or, perhaps there is a possibility. I appear. There is hope for you, Daddy. He is not with the Mukhabarat. Don't leave, stay a little longer, whatever it takes.

I leave then, but I keep in touch with Ziyyad, and spend much time with him on each subsequent visit to Aleppo. In between, he sends me 'Dear Sir' emails, initially missives culled from English prose that say nothing precise about his own situation except for an unmentionable and amorphous desire.

'If you live to be a hundred, I want to live to be a hundred minus one day, so I never have to live without you.'

And: 'Life is too deep for words, so don't try to describe it, just live it.

—C. S. Lewis.'

And: 'He who takes his life for granted is a pencil without an eraser.

—C. S. Lewis.'

I reply that I enjoy the wisdom of the sayings, but I want to hear in his own words what and how he is doing—and, by the way, he should quit calling me 'Sir'.

He writes back, 'Dear Sir, how do u do? u ask me not to call you "Sir" any more, while i call some idiotic nut at the university "Sir." they dont deserve to be called "Sir" and "maam" but u truly do. So Sir, what can one get the Nobel prize for literature?'

The next time I visit, I give him a Graduate Record Exam test book to study how to obtain admission to an American graduate programme. He promises to study hard after completing his exams at the University of Aleppo. I promise to visit again in six months. He writes, 'I will be on fire till december. i wanna be out of this Schmuckville very soon, after all, this is a livin hell. So sir, what do u recommend i do in the time i have till i join u in america?'

I explain that it is unlikely he could get into Princeton, but there are other good universities where he could begin advanced study. One step at a time. I realize he is projecting all these hopes on to me, and I fear being another promise unfulfilled, a failed father, another 'British swindle'.

He writes, 'hi sir i am sorry for not writing for long but i have been a mess i have been on meds and sedations after the results of our exams had come through. i did things i am not proud of when i was all angry and almost lost it (smashed a window, broke a couple of electrical fans…). it was a real mess. the psycho bitch from hell flunked me in american lit and i assure u it was the best course i ever studied and another hateful woman flunked me in 2 other courses (comp lit 1 and 2). These two women have been on to me for a while. yes i am not praying too much and i am working on the GRE for a while now, even math, but the GRE is really hard all of it. and sir make no mistake about it i will never forget you.'

I ask him why he doesn't enquire about what he did wrong. He laughs and says that is impossible. The grades are final, and there are no comments available.

Several months go by. He is recovering, slowly: 'i am not having any pleasure in this hellhole it is like in jail and i am dying to be bailed out of here more than soon. so i did what they call the makeup tests and i am waiting and i was thinking of writing to you after the results come through.

'big hug sir thank u for caring.'

This time, his test results are positive, he informs me, and he resumes studying for the American university admissions tests.

I tell him I am giving some talks on Syria.

'Are you writing about me?' he asks.

'Should I?' I ask in return.

He encourages me to write about him.

'Use anything,' he replies. ☐

GOD AND ME
Richard Mabey

Hardy called it 'dimmity', the moment when the certain shapes of the world dissolve. In the emptiness of the Wessex marshlands, against the twilit mass of Glastonbury Tor, the air begins to quiver, to fill with dark scribblings. More than a million starlings are homing in on this ancestral swamp for their nightly communion. They stream in from every direction, joining, breaking ranks, floating free, like some black aurora. Suddenly, they become plasmic. They are one immense organism, pulsating like a single cell. They swing up to the sky and then skim the reeds in folds and falls of black. They fill out great parabolas and helixes, with a symmetry you do not expect from living things. Then, birds again, they fall into the reeds.

It is experiences like this that are supposed to fill us godless folk with intimations of the spiritual. A glimpse of the universal geometry that lies behind the chaos of life, of the workings of a group consciousness outside anything we can imagine—surely this must bring on feelings of immanence, a sense of some order beyond the surface of things. The trouble is, I know these birds away from their dusk rites. They are a long way from being aerial ectoplasm. They're urchins, opportunists, prodigious mimics. Mozart had a pet starling, which famously learned a theme from his G Major Piano Concerto, but jumped it forward a couple of centuries by changing the G natural to a G sharp. And, like all living creatures, they're victims, too. I once saw, too close for comfort, a starling being dismembered by a sparrowhawk. Its beak was wide open, not to utter a G sharp or even a scream, but because it was being slowly squeezed to death. No moral context for these birds, no more blame on the hawk for being what it is than on the starling for being weaker and slower and so very edible. No sacrifice of the self for some higher significance—unless joining the great chain of dependence is itself a kind of sacrament.

It's always been like this for me with spirituality. I catch a whiff of the numinous, and it turns visceral in a moment, part of the digestive process. The first time was when I was a teenager. I fell into a state of thraldom to the hill above our house. It wasn't a particularly special hill, just a chalk swell that looked out over a wooded valley and a thin winterbourne that, according to local legend, was a woe-water, which flowed only in time of trouble. But I thought it was the most achingly beautiful prospect I had ever seen. It haunted me with some not quite graspable meaning, like the image of the mountain in *Close Encounters of the Third Kind*. It was an unsettling feeling, edgy, indefinable, a mixture of exquisite pleasure and butterfly discomfort. At times it turned into an actual physical sensation that made the backs of my legs clench, as if I was peering down from a great height. I experienced the same ethereal feelings singing medieval carols with the school choir in the lamplit porches of the big houses at the edge of our town, and then at the ritual reading of Chapter 13 of St Paul's Epistle to the Corinthians at the end of term: 'When I was a child I spake as a child...but when I became a man, I put away childish things.' I hadn't the slightest interest in the religious content of these ancient texts, but they seemed like a bridge across time, a fleeting glimpse of something inexpressibly bigger than the shackling routines of school, perhaps a first intimation of the continuity of life. If any of these blurrily romantic feelings had depths beyond that, I guess they were in Deep England, which was beginning to cast its dubious aura over me.

Then about ten years later, something different. I was trying to navigate my way through the last stages of a long anxiety attack, to get through the 'glass wall' such states erect between you and reality. I was suddenly struck by a piercing moment of heightened perception, as if a lens had been clamped over my eye. I was convinced I could pick out the minute physical details of the world nearly a quarter of a mile away: individual bricks, the ears of a man, the discrete eddies in a plume of smoke. Of course, I'd simply become aware of part of the sensory processing that I did unselfconsciously every second of my life. But it seemed, in that moment of hypersensitivity, to be some inexplicable, supernatural gift. It looked as if 'the beyond', for me, was always going to be just a few hundred yards away.

But the eye ought to have made me pause. For the religiously inclined it's not only the mirror of the soul but a kind of portal to the mysteries beyond evolution. For decades it was thought to be the blind spot in Darwin's theory. How, even over thousands of millions of years, could any living structure of such extraordinary complexity have been developed by chance mutations? How could it all, the light-sensitive iris, the nerve-transmitters in the retina, the lens, the lids, the tears...how could it all be *coordinated* as well? Anne Stevenson's poem about a new baby ponders the origins of 'the distinct eyelashes and sharp crescent/fingernails... Imagine the /infinitesimal capillaries, the flawless connections/of the lungs, the invisible neural filaments...' She calls the poem 'The Spirit is too Blunt an Instrument'. And God perhaps too exact a watchmaker. What is clear from the increasingly remarkable revelations about the intricacy of the living world is that Intelligent Design is a logical impossibility. It's not that God isn't clever enough, but that life isn't that kind of process. The Reverend Paley's celebrated vision of the living world as an exquisitely engineered watch is as inappropriate as seeing Creation as a symphony unfolding from a written score. What it *is* like is a vast piece of musical improvisation, unpredictable, free-form, exuberantly bodged, yet melding exquisitely with what already exists. And, of course, like all such music, quite without meaning, just gloriously itself.

Isn't this something to have faith in? The *stuff* of life, the astonishing, resilient, surreal inventiveness of it all? The extravagant iridescence in the wings of butterflies. The minute convolutions of Henle's loop in the human kidney, 'like the meanders in a creek'. The song of the Albert's lyrebird, which takes it six years to learn and segues the phrasing of every other bird in the Queensland bush. At times the gratuitousness of creation, its sheer wild playfulness, can only understood only as a kind of unscripted comedy.

Long before I knew much about the fantastic domestic arrangements that are the norm for life in the tropics, I learned about the transactions of Britain's rarest butterfly, the large blue. Its larvae feed for a while on wild thyme, and start producing honey on their abdomens. They also produce a pheromone that mimics the scent of ant grubs. The adult ants gather up the butterfly larvae, take them off to their nests and look after them as if they were their own offspring—drinking their honey in return. All the while the larvae are singing to the ants, echoing the rhythmic noises of the grubs... Wouldn't it have been simpler, Annie Dillard enquires in her rodeo-ride of God in *Pilgrim at Tinker Creek*,

> just to rough in a slab of chemicals, a green acre of goo?... The lone ping into being of the first hydrogen atom ex nihilo, was so unthinkable, violently radical, that surely it ought to have been enough. But look what happens. You open the door and all heaven and hell break loose.

Wouldn't it have been easier, for that matter, to have nothing at all, no lone hydrogen atom, no first cause? The fact that there is anything is the one impenetrable mystery. Once there was, the eventual emergence of the planet's grand comedy of manners was pretty well inevitable.

Once in an interview, trying to sidestep the queries about spirituality that are always beamed at those who confess a more than scientific fascination with nature, I suggested that I could be described as a 'transcendental materialist'. It wasn't a very creditable answer, and I should have had the guts to call myself a straightforward materialist. But beyond the posing, I was trying to say that, for me, the physicality of the living world—its veracity, its anciently involved intelligence, its wit, its refusal to be pinned down—transcends itself, not into the realm of the supernatural, but into that of the hyper-real. The true Transcendentalists in nineteenth-century America believed almost the exact opposite of this, arguing, anthropocentrically, that the material world was a product of some mystical, ideal force. 'Nature is the incarnation of thought,' wrote Ralph Waldo Emerson, their guru. 'The world is mind precipitated'. Emerson's friend Thoreau called himself a Transcendentalist, but was altogether more grounded. His epic climb up into the desolate wilderness of Mount Katahdin is the seminal statement about the absolute authority of the physical: 'Talk of mysteries! Think of our life in nature—daily to be shown matter, to come into contact with it—rocks, trees, wind on our cheeks! The *solid* earth! The *actual* world! The *common sense*! *Contact! Contact!*' In *Walden*, less frenziedly, Thoreau writes about measuring the depth of his pond. It's a passage which is both literal and metaphorical, about reality and responsibility: 'The greatest depth was exactly one hundred and two feet; to which may be added the five feet which it has risen since, making one hundred and seven. This is a remarkable depth for so small an area; yet not an inch of it can be spared by the imagination… While men believe in the infinite some ponds will be thought to be bottomless.' The imagination, he is suggesting, needs detail and finitude, not abstraction, for its full flowering.

My one bottomless pond is the mystery of self-consciousness, a phenomenon which I suspect is no more open to 'explanation' than the fact that something came to exist. Pondering it when I was young was another vertiginous experience. If the sense of self was a product of the processes of the brain, could there be another 'me', somewhere else, where the immense possibilities of the universe had thrown up an identical physical being? And if I couldn't be a self in two places at once, could I be so in two different times? Might brain chemistry be the answer to reincarnation?

Thankfully I grew out of tormenting myself with unanswerable questions, but the self remains the chink in the materialist's armour. And on a very few occasions I've had the feeling, which I suppose is the one thing common to all so-called spiritual experiences, that its boundaries are relaxing a little. One May night especially, listening to nightingales in Suffolk, was something close to a moment of communion. The setting was narcotic. A full moon, mounds of cow parsley glowing like suspended balls of mist, the fen arching like a lustrous whaleback across the whole span of the southern horizon. The nightingale was a shaman, experienced, rhetorical, insistent. I sank into its charms, a willing initiate. A shooting star arced over the bush in which it was singing. As I edged closer, its song seemed to become solid, to be doing synaesthetic things with the light. I was aware that my peripheral vision was closing down, and that I had no sense of where I was in space. And then, for just a few seconds, the bird was in my head, and it was me who was singing.

Conventionally, one is supposed to feel awe and humility at moments like this. Not a bit of it. Awe would seem to me an appropriate emotion for God, viewing the exuberance of the living world from a distance. But not for a creature caught up in it. I was part of the home team, on the winning side, fist in the air, cheering in solidarity. Nor did I feel that my self had shrunk, or grown insignificant, but rather that bird and landscape and I were at that moment part of a larger being.

It's telling how often music is the agency for such experiences, and a metaphor for what they mean. The great American biologist Lewis Thomas wrote often of the sensory communications which keep the planet working harmoniously, of signals 'informing tissues in the vegetation of the Alps about the state of eels in the Sargasso Sea'. He once imagined what it might be like if we could hear the planet's 'grand canonical ensemble', if we could make out vibrations of a million locusts in migration, the descants of whales, the timpani of gorilla breasts, termite heads, drumfish bladders. The combined sound might be a sacred oratorio that would lift us off our feet. □

THE MUMMERY BOOK

A Parable Of The Divine True Love, Told By Means
Of A Self-Illuminated Illustration Of The Totality Of Mind

By

ADI DA SAMRAJ

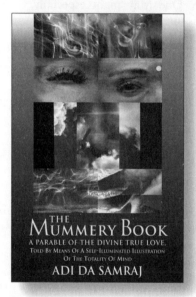

288 pages
Hardcover $29.95
ISBN: 1-57097-175-7

Paperback $19.95
ISBN: 1-57097-176-5

**A "prose opera" that shatters
the conventional limits of
language and raises literary
portrayal to radical levels
of consciousness.**

If Dylan Thomas and Buddha
shared a soul, *The Mummery Book*
is what I would expect from such
a joining.

—**ROBERT BOLDMAN**
The Alchemy of Love

Adi Da makes words crackle and
swoon, pound and console with an
endless suggestiveness guided by
a desire to open up the reader's
heart and imagination to the
possibility of transformation. . . .
The Mummery Book is an absolutely
unique literary occasion.

—**PHILIP KUBERSKI, PhD**
Wake Forest University

GRANTA

CRUISING
Kamran Nazeer

Glasgow

'Is it all right to smoke in this car?'

'Aye, brand new. Jump in, man, jump in.'

Cakes (Jaffer; popular brand of baked goods: Jaffa Cakes; ergo Cakes) pulled his seat forward, Chiffon (Kashif; non-Asians' mispronunciation: Kasheef; ergo Chiffon) climbed into the back seat and I got us cruising again, out of the car park of the Nautical College, a street away from Glasgow's Central Mosque. We were in a Mercedes E220 CDi with tan leather interior and nineteen-inch alloys. On coming into the mosque, before shedding his shoes, Chiffon had told his dad he needed to wash and then snuck out the other door. We were all supposed to be reading *tarawih* prayers; it was the third day of Ramadan and we were already skiving.

Chicago

'Is it halal to smoke in this car?'

'It's all halal, bro. Get in.'

Veer (Tanveer; for a few weeks after he'd been to Pakistan: Tanned Veer; ergo Veer) jumped in and Huguenot (Maqsood; infamous lie: 'I'm a Hugo Boss model'; ergo Hugo Not, or Huguenot) smoothed the car back into traffic. It was a Porsche Cayenne S with bull bars and chrome plates on the air inlets. We were on the northern bounds of Chicago. We were aiming for the sweet shop three blocks along. The snow had shifted to a powder theme and it looked like the same heap was blowing one way across the road and then back again. As Veer lit his cigarette, Huguenot and I reached back to grasp cigarettes too. He and I had just eaten chicken curry and rice with our hands off takeaway plates. He was Bengali and, a couple of years ago, had seemed to pick manual dining as his Bengali cultural motif. We didn't really want cigarettes but we wanted the car at least to smell of something else. Huguenot had to be very careful though. His next-door neighbour had spoken to his mother about finding a *thubba* of butts in her garden—all thrown there by Huguenot from his second-storey bedroom window. Before he left the car in the garage at the end of the evening, he'd have to douse it with the new bottle of Emporio Armani Night he'd bought earlier and put in the glove compartment.

I hadn't seen Veer in six years but my sister had told me that his parents were looking for a match for him. I turned the stereo down.

'Salaam, *bheyya*,' I said, twisting my arm around behind my seat so he could shake it. 'You engaged yet?'

'Why?' said Veer. 'You fuckers planning on taking me to a strip club?'

'Something I heard...' Huguenot and I grinned, and Huguenot said, 'Nyup.'

'Uh-huh?'

'You're asking she wear a *hijab*?' I said.

My sister was pissed at him. She and Veer used to be friends when Veer's family lived in Glasgow. She didn't expect it of him. She'd directed me to bring it up frequently.

'Fuck, so you been briefed, yeah? She's dinghying all my calls.' I smiled to hear Veer say 'dinghying'. It was Glasgow patter, meaningless, its origin mysterious, and it was still with him though he'd grown four inches and twenty-five pounds since he'd left there. 'Your wonderful, superb, superlative sister,' Veer added, in case, I suppose, his irritation at my sister had impugned my honour.

'Are you going to wear the *hijab* too?' I asked, swivelling in my seat so I could see him.

'Look, bro,' he said, putting his hand on my shoulder, 'I've fucked around, okay. I've fucked around a lot. I won't lie to you guys. You guys know it. But getting married is like a new start, you know? It's like a new life. I just need someone I can trust. I can't get married to someone who's lived like me. That isn't going to work—you know?'

'But it's okay that you've fucked around?'

'I have, bro, and I can't change that. I'm not five times daily, you know? I'm not holy. But I need to trust the girl that I marry and maybe she'll change me. Maybe she will. Who knows? That's what I'm saying, bro. That's all I'm saying.'

Huguenot had parked up. 'That's all he's saying,' I said.

'Yeah, right,' said Huguenot, and turned the stereo back up.

We sat in the car with our elbows on the window sills, gazing out at the street for a couple of minutes, and then scrambled over into the sweet shop.

Glasgow

At the cafe where we docked after slipping away from the mosque we got removed to the outdoor patio. There was a poetry reading inside and me, Cakes and Chiffon kept interjecting, 'Waah, waah'—which is how the audience demonstrates its appreciation at a Punjabi poetry reading. We'd never been to a Punjabi poetry reading but these echoes of our grandparents kept us laughing while the poetry got worse; but then some of the poets got cross and spoke to the staff. They didn't want to ask us to leave (Cakes and Chiffon were regulars; Cakes had brought back five hubble-bubbles for the owners to dispense when he was last in Cairo) and so the outdoor patio worked for everyone.

There had been no place like this in Glasgow when I lived there. It was down a slope from the university and served Arab food and dispensed flavoured tobacco in tall hubble-bubbles. Cakes, Chiffon, Danny (Mudassar; abbreviation: Mud, which quickly becomes Muddy and then Waters; ergo Danube or Danny) and Rothschild (Mehmood; grandmother's pet name for him: Moodi, which rhymes with Yehudi, which is Punjabi for Jew; ergo Rothschild), and all of their friends, were now in there all the time. For all of Ramadan, it was staying open until 2 a.m. every Friday and midnight otherwise. The waitress even asked us how many *tarawih* we'd read before arriving when she took our orders. Chiffon kept checking his watch. We needed to get him back to the mosque for 10.15 p.m., which was when *tarawih* prayers ended. That way, both he and his father could respectably adhere to the fiction that he'd been in the mosque throughout. Danny was supposed to be coming to join us but he had a new girlfriend, so he wasn't expected. Evening prayers were a convenient alibi for many things.

Seven, eight years ago, much more often than not, we'd have gone to the mosque. We'd have done so almost every night, at least during Ramadan. Any prayers you complete during Ramadan are supposed to count seventy times over, some scholars say more. When we were in university together, we even spent a season on the committee of the Muslim Students' Association. We circulated a fake newsletter for the Dundee University Muslim Brothers' and Sisters' Association, or DUMBSA. There was an article on 'Male Hijab Week', a note on a campaign to raise funds to buy our Afghan brothers a combat helicopter (this was funny in 1995 or, at least, it was possible to joke about it) and a mock interview with a Muslim scholar under the headline 'Sheikh the Room'. We were dismissed after that stunt, though without due process. The other committee members just stopped telling us when the meetings were. The same waitress had also asked us earlier about how hard it was to fast and, after we'd passed the mouthpiece of the pipe around, we got back to this. 'I get headaches,' said Chiffon. He was training to be a lawyer and was in the phase of his training contract where the firm made him work the longest hours. 'I don't get hungry, I just can't concentrate because of my head. Plus it's that I've been up at sunrise, at 5 a.m., and you don't get to sleep properly after that.' Chiffon had started drinking a glass of water every day. This was prohibited. The fast was broken if you ate or drank anything at all between first light and sunset, if you smoked, even if you received an injection. Nevertheless, he could explain it to himself and now to us.

'It'd be all right if all of Ramadan was holidays,' said Cakes. He ran an Asian foods store. It was impossible for him not to fast. His customers would be horrified, even the kind of customers that he was trying to draw. He believed that Asian food stores needed to become like modern supermarkets: don't put out the crates in which the vegetables came packed, have a display; serve the meat from behind a proper glass counter, have it all cut beforehand, don't do it on a wooden slab in bloody overalls in front of the customer, tossing curls of fat into the big white bin by your side. Maybe older people could tell when they were getting a good cut of meat, when the butcher was preparing it well or, alternatively, when the butcher was taking advantage, but younger people couldn't and they didn't want to learn; they wanted their meat fresh, so do have it out, but then weigh it and pack it quickly, put a barcode on it and place it in their shopping basket.

'It isn't even that in Muslim countries,' I said.

'So maybe that's it,' said Cakes, leaning in. 'It used to be a month of holidays, when it started out, but it isn't that way any more—but you still have to fast like it is a month of holidays.'

We all paused. We looked about ourselves. If you made us watch a tape of this, we'd snicker nervously. Chiffon went first: 'If I didn't live at home, I wouldn't fast.' Released by his statement, we all began nodding. Cakes accidentally kicked the table as he crossed his legs over the other way. I didn't live at home. I still fasted eight years after moving.

'It's not just that,' I said. 'It's a really difficult taboo to break. It's like trying to touch your eye. You know that you can do it, you know that you can do it without harming yourself, but you're still not able.'

'O-eh, Salaam, Mussulmen,' declared Rothschild, arriving late—this meant he'd stayed at the mosque to read the first eight. It was perfectly fine to read eight. Lots of people only read eight rather than twenty. It's told that the Prophet Muhammad sometimes only read eight. Even Cakes, Chiffon and I were reading eight a year ago. It was more complicated not to read any: you had to come back at the end so it didn't look like you weren't there at all. But, if you read eight, then you could leave, go wherever. As Rothschild shook our hands in turn, I realized that what had begun as delinquency—truancy from the mosque, practical jokes like the newsletter—was, for a whole group of us, tacking out into scepticism. Now we couldn't take the easier option, now it was enfeebling to pray, hypocritical. I also realized that now Rothschild had got in, with the *mehk* of mosque incense on his clothes, we were going to change the agenda. He knew we weren't in the mosque. He smoked too, and hid the fact from his parents. But the conversation we were having was difficult, we'd all almost had to spit on our palms and shake hands before we could start it. Rothschild wouldn't understand. So we talked about cars instead and Rothschild's new one: a brown BMW 645 Ci.

Chicago

As soon as the snow stopped, we hummed open the windows of the jeep. There was a Bollywood track playing on the stereo. Huguenot was driving us down through the city to UIC, the University of Indians and Chinese (also known as the University of Illinois at Chicago). The cold was etching itself on to the skin on the back of my hands and on my cheeks but my feet were toasty from the car's heating system. We weren't talking, just looking out the windows with the music turned up loud. At a set of traffic lights, Veer held his cigarettes out to a passing homeless guy. When he stepped forward, Veer looked in the pack and saw that there were only three left; he handed it over.

'God bless you,' he said to the man in a heavy Indian accent.

We drove around the UIC campus for half an hour. There were a couple of parties breaking up, or maybe just bars closing.

'*Haiyy*, I used to date her,' exclaimed Veer. We all looked. She was tall, dressed in a poncho. She looked like the kind of girl who might quit her job suddenly after seeing a photograph of a beautiful village in Sicily. I remembered her. I'd seen a photograph of them together. She was sitting on a rock high up, it was a hillside, and Veer was standing underneath in a pose to make it look like he was holding her up on one hand. Veer slipped down in his seat and Huguenot held the horn down for three full seconds. She came over.

'Hey, you,' she said to Veer. I looked over at Huguenot and we both guessed the same from her manner: *she'd* dumped him. Veer didn't reply. She came to my window instead. 'Hi, I'm Melanie,' she said to me, offering her hand. I shook it as she noticed Huguenot.

'Maqsood! How are you?'

'Right as rain,' he replied, and they both laughed.

'Tanveer,' she tried again, though standing by my window and without turning to him.

'Tanveer, will you answer my emails please?'

'I don't speak English not very much,' he said in a mock Indian accent. 'Please not be disturbing my good fellows, these my friends.'

He expected Huguenot and me to start laughing. Huguenot shook his head instead. I turned in my seat. 'Stop being such a dick.'

Melanie got called back over by a friend. She shook her head gently and began to ease away. 'Nice to meet you,' she said.

'*Enchanté*,' said Maqsood, waving at her from somewhere around my face. He started up the car and we set off.

'Fuck both of you,' muttered Veer from the back seat.

'I am so sorry, Sir, I am not of your understanding,' said Huguenot.

Later, as we headed for the John Hancock Center in the centre of town, I tried to make peace with Veer. When he was fifteen, he was able to identify the make and model of any car from its wing mirrors, even from seeing just its rear lights. Now he ran one of his father's car dealerships. When he lived in Glasgow, sometimes we had spent entire weekends test-driving cars from garages all across central Scotland, taking care not to hit the same salesman more than once in any period of six months.

'Do you remember the A77?' I said.

'Fuck, bro,' he replied, after a pause. 'I was just thinking about that.'

The A77 links Paisley, south of Glasgow—where Veer's family used to live—to Kilmarnock, in Ayrshire. There was a McDonald's restaurant along it, the closest one to Veer's house, and it stayed open twenty-four hours a day. On Eid day, the end of Ramadan, Veer's mother invited all of his friends around late at night once everyone had finished sitting with their own families. Veer's father was away in Bahrain at the time and I think she liked the company. She sat with us for a while and fed us for longer. Then it was about 3 a.m. and we were hungry again.

Veer, Cakes and I went to buy Filets-O-Fish. It was the only *halal* item on the menu and there were twelve of us to feed, so we phoned in an order for thirty Filets. The restaurant staff were used to getting these calls from Veer's house and said to give them thirty minutes. Veer had a new car, bought for him for Eid (BMW 318i with body-coloured bumpers). As we walked out the door, Veer handed me the keys. I'm a fast driver now; I was a fast driver then. Veer wanted me to show him how fast his car could be driven. So I used the limits of the lanes to find the slickest routes through corners, I revved the engine until its sinuses opened up, but then, on the A77, making a bend, the car's tyres lost their grip on a slab of black ice and the car started to spin. I knew that it wasn't possible to stop the spin and so I waited. We all did. The stereo still played. No one breathed. The car went round and round then hit the barrier by the roadside and the airbags popped open. The cabin filled with the gassy honk from the canisters that release the airbags and with our adrenalin-soaked carbon dioxide as we finally exhaled. We climbed out of the car and remained calm until, up on the verge, we turned round. The car looked as though it had been sliced and someone had tried to stick it back together, like a working model of how tectonic plates move and cause earthquakes.

We all started murmuring prayers, all the prayers we knew. I held Veer and apologized over and over. Before we'd done anything, called anyone, another car pulled up on the hard shoulder and the driver came running towards us. Veer was closest and the man pretty much leapt into the air and down on to him. He held him in an embrace for a very long time. Drawing back, in sobs, he told us that he had only an hour ago received news of another accident, that he was driving to the hospital, the hospital where a friend of his had just been declared dead. Seeing another crash, he'd feared the worst, feared that he was somehow on the trail of death that night. Then he reached into his coat pocket and pulled out a small bottle of whisky. He offered it to us and, without hesitation, though none of us were drinkers, we each took a long slug. The man seemed to know what to do that night and we followed his lead. We passed the bottle round till it was empty. Then we rang the police (who didn't breathalyze us, thank goodness).

It was the first time any of us had taken a drink. The police drove us back to Veer's house, where by this time our relatives had gathered. There were prayers and benedictions. My mother read four *surahs* from the Qur'an and blew on me, transferring the blessing. I thought about the taste of the whisky, its heat in my throat.

As Veer and I finished recalling the A77, a story that Huguenot hadn't heard before, he rubbed his forehead thoughtfully. He'd slowed his car right down and it was snowing again. We all watched an old couple walk past us, her arm through his. 'I know a place that'll serve us,' he said finally. It was 2 a.m.

'So you are taking me to a strip club?' said Veer from the back seat.

'Nyup,' said Huguenot.

'No, no, Mr Tanveer,' I said, taking the Indian accent for the first time that night. 'We are most duty-bound to give you a new start in your life.'

Glasgow

We made it back to the mosque just in time. I got out of the car and greeted Chiffon's dad. I hadn't seen him on this trip.

'You didn't stay for the talk afterwards?' he asked.

'We were sitting in the car, just talking, Uncle,' I replied carefully, managing not to lie, not quite.

'You take him, if you like,' said Chiffon's dad, nodding towards his son. '*Beita*, give me the car keys. You come with your friends.'

Chiffon stepped out, shook his dad's hand salaam and handed them over. Cakes came out too and shook hands. As Chiffon's dad headed off, we got back in the car, an Audi A6 2.4 SE, black with visible red brake discs.

'He looks well,' I said. Chiffon's dad had undergone a heart bypass operation six months ago.

'He is well,' said Chiffon. 'Which is why he shouldn't be smoking fags. Still—he'll only have two on the drive home, tops.'

Cakes and I smiled. Uncle's purpose in sending Chiffon back with us became clear.

'What did your grandfather used to call him?' asked Cakes.

'Taxi-wallah,' I said.

'Your dad drove a taxi?' Cakes said, turning round to see Chiffon.

'No, no. There was a bunch of them walking one night. Early days, this is—'64 or something. Kami's grandfather, my dad and some other guys were talking about what cars they were going to buy when they made their money in this country. My dad didn't know anything about cars and so, when it came to his turn, he pointed to the first big car he saw and said, "That one," and, right—it was a taxi. A black cab. The name stuck: *taxi-wallah*. It's so weird. I was flying to Pak two years ago, when my grandmother died, and I was sitting on the plane next to this guy who turns out to be from the same town as us and he's trying to work out who my dad is, whether he knows him. And I tell him my dad's name. No connection. I say "taxi-wallah" and immediately he lights up: oh, oh. He knows my dad. Knows him by that name. Never met my dad. Knows him by that name.'

'Let's follow him,' said Cakes.

'*Yaar*, let him have his cigarette in peace,' I said, and set us back on the way to the cafe where the poetry reading, thankfully, was over.

Chicago

We had one drink each at the bar. And a shot each of Emporio Armani Night. Huguenot sprayed it around his car as well after we dropped off Veer. I was staying the night at Huguenot's house and, as we stepped through the front door, his mum was up. She'd just read her *tahajjud* prayers, the non-obligatory middle of the night prayers. She gave us both a hug and a shake of her head. She asked about my mother and made us both read a few lines from the Qur'an aloud with her. Then, satisfied, she asked us if we wanted anything to eat. The question was a formality. I was staying with her, she hadn't fed me anything yet and I was leaving at 6 a.m. without a proper breakfast the next morning.

Over samosas and pakoras and three different kinds of green chilli chutney, she spoke to us about politics.

'Sometimes I'd like to go up to that Bush and just shoot him myself,' she declared.

'Ummi,' despaired Maqsood.

'Afghanistan, fine. No problem. Iraq, okay—difficult, difficult, difficult—but fine. Why only Muslims, though? Why not Israel? Why not stop Russia killing Chechens?'

'America should invade Russia?' I said. 'Auntie, come on. Be serious.' Maqsood kept his head down, a grin on. He wasn't having this argument, not tonight.

'Oh, Kami. I don't know. It just doesn't feel right to me.'

'Who did you vote for, Mum?' said Maqsood, sliding in.

'You joke your mother like this?' she asked me, tapping her son's head affectionately.

'I hope so,' I replied, and then holding up a samosa, I added: 'She also gives me indigestion, just like you.'

For this, I got a tap on the head too.

She left after she'd tidied away the fryer, kissed us both goodnight. Huguenot and I sat up until we'd finished all the food. There was a lot of it. We paused a couple of times, then smiled at one another and resumed. We talked without thinking, without trying to create angles, without a plan. Finally, we went upstairs and slept, away, for a couple of hours, from both our worlds. □

GOD AND ME
Andrew Martin

I go to Church about once a fortnight. Whereas Catholics are supposed to attend Mass every week, I'm not sure what frequency is required by my lot—the Church of England—although I'm confident that the standard must be laxer. When I started writing this article I decided to try and find it out but, this being the Church of England, the press officer I called didn't know for certain. 'There is some kind of prescription for attendance,' he said, racking his brains, 'but I'm not sure what it is. You're definitely supposed to go on Easter Sunday but... I'll get back to you.'

So far, he hasn't done. But he did send me some figures suggesting that church attendance is not declining as you might expect but is in fact rising slightly. These figures are complicated but I take their real meaning to be that church attendance is not quite as bad as it might be given that hardly anybody goes to church any more. Certainly, I always go alone.

I normally go to Evening Prayer at my local church in north London, a service usually attended by about thirty. But I might nip into one anywhere. If I'm staying in the country, I'll find out the service times at the nearest church, perhaps doing so on a Saturday evening while en route to the nearest pub. If the notice says, EIGHT A.M. COMMUNION ON THE FOURTH SUNDAY IN THE MONTH (these churches are pretty sparsely manned, so that's typical) and I work out that the next day is the fourth Sunday, then I'm delighted. I'm correspondingly depressed if eight o'clock the following morning finds me standing bereft and alone in some frosty graveyard, having figured out that what I'd thought was the fourth Sunday of the month was in fact the fifth in a veritable month of Sundays.

Do I believe in God? At the moment, I would say that depends what you mean by 'believe' and what you mean by 'God', but you can be sure there will be no such sophistry from me if I have advance warning of my own death. Right now, I regard myself as taking a leap of faith, like Kierkegaard (easy to write 'like Kierkegaard' in that casual way; I have read a couple of summaries of his opinions, rather than any of his actual works). The leap takes the form of walking through a church door, and it's a bigger leap for me than some.

My father was, and is, vociferously atheistic. If, as a boy growing up in York, I heard him answering a knock on the door with a brisk 'bugger off' I knew it was the Jehovah's Witnesses who'd called. He

213

listened to everything on Radio Four except *The Morning Service*. As a boy, I must have heard hundreds of times the continuity announcer saying: 'And now, *The Morning Service*. Today's broadcast comes from the church of...' followed by the resonant click of the off switch.

Yet I always liked going into churches, especially York Minster, which I'd visit almost every Saturday afternoon, just sitting in a pew, wearing my denim jacket while dangling a plastic bag containing some newly bought new wave LP between my knees. I enjoyed the beauty of the surroundings (as testified to by the hundreds of foreign tourists milling all around); the airiness of the place; the lack of pressure. Nobody expected me to be there; nobody I knew was likely to see me there.

I would not attend the services, which can be a particularly intimidating matter in a cathedral, where you have to weave between the tourists while pursuing signs that bathetically culminate in some insignificant side chapel where half a dozen harassed-looking people sit waiting with their prayer books. Spiritually, this is the engine house of the whole enterprise, but it certainly doesn't look it.

No, I'd just sit there watching the clerics bustling about, listening to someone playing the organ out of sight. Often the organist was only practising, doodling even though there might be a thousand sightseers in the church, but the more desultory the playing the more I liked it. All in all, it was a bit like being on a train. You weren't doing anything, but you were getting somewhere just by sitting still— in the sense of thinking things over; holding a conversation with either God or your better self.

I began going regularly to my local church ten years ago, in my early thirties. I did so in order to get my children into the nearby Church of England primary school. Everyone plays the same game around here. The local church knows it's a game, and the parents know that the church knows. You and your young children must attend the cacophonous Family Service at mid-morning on a Sunday. The children are not expected to endure the sermon; when that comes around you take them into a side building where a crèche is run in tandem with the Sunday school. If your children's names appear a sufficient number of times over a couple of years on the register for either crèche or Sunday school then they're in, which is a real 'result', as they say in north London, since the school is as good as most private prep schools, for which you'd be paying ten grand a year. You can then go safely back to ignoring the church that facilitated it all, and buttoning your lip if your child should bring home a religious scene for colouring in.

But when I saw that I would actually have to go to church, I embraced the fact, having always had a taste for it, and I attended classes leading to confirmation. I cannot remember much about this process, except that it was conducted by a curate who struck me as very intelligent, and who read more novels than I, which seemed to signify psychological generosity. My father attended the confirmation service, and I had one very uneasy moment when the vicar said, 'We now say a prayer', and I caught sight of Dad dutifully scuffling about for his kneeler.

He's far too much of a gent to have complained, but I suppose he thinks I'm nuts. As I stumble over the responses in church (I am not quite regular enough for them to be ingrained) I sometimes think so, too. There are moments of great embarrassment. I might start trying to sing the wrong hymn, until someone leans across from the pew behind to correct me; and, this being a church, there's no possibility of them hissing, 'It's this one, you bloody idiot,' a constraint that heightens the tension still further.

A part of me still thinks of church as a place for goody-goodies in cloyingly patterned sweaters, and the consequent embarrassment has led me into transgression. Once, emerging from my local church after Evening Prayer, I walked over to the nearby pub, where I sat reading first the parish magazine (collected from the church), before moving on to the main section of the *Observer*. Looking up, I saw a man I'd been at university with: a tough, sceptical man. As he walked across with hand outstretched, I found myself furtively slipping the parish magazine beneath the *Observer*. This is Peter disowning Jesus all over again; it is *exactly* what you're not supposed to do.

I am still insecure enough about my churchgoing to take comfort from discovering that some particularly rigorous, astringent celebrity is a practising Christian: the ferocious racing driver Ayrton Senna; the sepulchral and eternally voguish singer Nick Cave. I remember reading the last chapter of John Updike's autobiography, *Self-Consciousness*, in real suspense. He discusses religion objectively until at a certain point thrillingly declaring, 'I decided to believe it.'

What do I get from churchgoing? To put the case for organized worship at its lowest: you can always get a seat in church. It might be argued that the presence I sense is perilously akin to an absence, but I like the vastness of a church in relation to the (usual) size of the congregation. It's a very anachronistic and welcome discrepancy in our over-crowded age. I also enjoy the civility of the people. I would put the chances of your sitting next to an irritating person in church at practically nil. And then there is the licensed quiet. 'We now keep a moment's silence.' Those words having been pronounced, my mind will veer about between local trivialities for a while: 'I thought that man in front had a full head of hair, but it turns out he's balding at the back.' 'Is that woman in the corner giggling or crying?' But I will eventually get down to formulating some proper resolutions: try to be kinder to X; don't get so worried about Y; it's not necessary to reply to Z's email but that's exactly why you should do it.

There is generally some moment that moves me. I might get a feeling of harmony and tranquillity from the language of the Book of Common Prayer, which I prefer to the modernized, Common Worship liturgy. Or it might be during the singing of a hymn, although the catchy, melodic ones that I remember from school assembly—'For All the Saints', for example, with its belting tune by Ralph Vaughan Williams—seem forever on the page next to the one I am actually being required to sing.

Above all, a coherent church service is concentrated moral instruction. What strikes me about the Gospels is the apparently monomaniacal concern with morality far above such matters as family loyalty or mere kindness. When Jesus encounters the paralysed man lowered towards him on a mat, he doesn't say, 'How are you today?' or even, 'Hello,' but, 'Your sins are forgiven.' The man is not thereby cured of his physical condition; this happens only later, and almost as an afterthought, the lesson as I understand it being the priority of morality over mere miracles.

The point is that, in the cosy, Betjemanesque guise of a Church of England service, comes a very radical message—not that it isn't beginning to dissolve the moment I step out of the door. But the afterglow lasts for a few hours at least and if you want a favour from me then wait outside the church door of a Sunday evening. I once stepped out to see a man stranded beside a broken-down car on

Highgate West Hill. Here was such a perfect opportunity that for a second it crossed my mind that he might have been a stooge planted by the vicar to test my progress. Anyway, I pushed that car almost single-handedly to the top of the hill.

Later in the week you'll have to look harder for any signs of my having been 'stirred up to godliness', as the prayer book puts it. A *lot* harder, and come the following Sunday my wife will most likely be urging, 'Look, Andrew, will you *please* go to church again?' Paradoxically, the course of treatment will only be said to have worked when she no longer has to do that. □

GOD AND ME
Lucretia Stewart

Three years ago I was raped. A man broke into my flat in Camden in the middle of the night, woke me up by punching me in the face, menaced me with my own carving knife, tied me up, raped me and then threatened to burn me alive. Against overwhelming odds, I escaped. Afterwards I found myself saying over and over again, 'Thank you, God, for saving me.' I never once thought, 'Why did You let this happen to me?'

I realize how lucky I was to have that response, not to be bitter, but to be grateful. Bizarrely, I am even grateful that I was raped because it forced me to deal with reality, to evaluate my life and to realize what was important and what was not. If I hadn't been raped and if I hadn't believed in God and therefore reacted to the rape as I did, I wouldn't have the life I now have. I probably wouldn't have had the courage to leave London, even though I had been unhappy and dissatisfied there for a long time. Sometimes it takes something terrible to make you act. God does move in mysterious ways and it takes time to make sense of His plan.

It's almost impossible to describe how it feels to believe in God. There really aren't words elevated enough to explain it. You don't want to say that it's a safety net, though this is part of it. But to be a good Christian demands a very difficult response to life—forgiveness, magnanimity, humility, generosity, tolerance. I don't possess all those virtues by any means. I am aware that I am very intolerant and I pray for greater patience. I believe that, to avoid total selfishness and self-centeredness, particularly if you live alone, it is important to have a spiritual dimension to one's life and a belief in the Christian God is mine.

As I get older, I find myself more prone to despair. It becomes more and more difficult to be optimistic (though in the year after I was raped, I felt more hopeful than for many years, because I was alive). I have always tried to be a realist. I don't want to base my happiness on something false, yet I hate feeling hopeless. God, believing in God, helps. I sometimes think that I believe in God because life would be just too terrifying if I didn't. A priest once suggested that I use the mantra, 'Christ, walk with me,' as an antidote to despair. That usually works. And one day on the radio I heard someone quote these lines, 'My ending is despair/Unless I be relieved by prayer,' and they resonated.

I have believed in God all my life and I go to church regularly. This, I am convinced, is a direct consequence of the way that I was educated, which gave me a certain outlook on life, which enabled me to put what happened to me into perspective. Two weeks after the rape, I rang the Margaret Pyke Centre in Goodge Street to make an appointment for Aids and other tests. I was told that that there were no appointments for a month. 'But I've been raped,' I said. The woman on the phone told me that she had been raped, too—as an eight-year-old girl in Sri Lanka. My ordeal seemed insignificant by comparison.

The rapist stole the crucifix that I always wore round my neck and the first thing I did when I got to Naxos, where I now live, was to buy another one. I never take it off. I don't exactly believe that it protects me, but I do believe that it is a symbol of God's love and protection.

I don't know how people who are brought in a secular environment ever decide to believe in God. If religion hadn't played such a large part in my childhood, I doubt that I would have been able to turn to God as an adult. Rationally the whole thing is so improbable that you need to accept it as a child to believe it as an adult. There was never a moment when God suddenly spoke to me and I believed. If that had happened, it might have had the opposite effect, given that I tend to be cynical and sceptical. But I seem always to have believed. It's a part of me. I don't have a mental picture of God—either as an old man with a long beard or as anything else—and it doesn't seem to matter, though trying to articulate what I mean by God is the most difficult thing that I have ever done. Christ is different. Because of the Gospels, it is easy to form a picture of Him. Yet it tends to be to God the Father that I turn in times of trouble.

I have also never distinguished between God and religion, that is between the Christian God and Christianity. The two have always been indivisible—you can't have God without His Church. The one is the visible manifestation of the other. It's lucky for me that I like church; it's no hardship to go every Sunday. In Naxos where mass is celebrated in a mixture of Greek and Latin in the small, white marble, twelfth-century cathedral, I rarely understand more than a few words of the sermon. Usually part of the pleasure of organized religion is familiarity with the ritual; the beloved hymns and so on. Here everything is totally unfamiliar, particularly because the Catholic Church follows the same calendar as the Orthodox Church, celebrating Easter later than the rest of Christian Europe. This forces me, perhaps, to think about what it actually means, even on the most basic level. After two years of going every Sunday, I still have to concentrate to understand the language of the liturgy and only recently can I read it in Greek without difficulty. I enjoy it all the same, perhaps all the more, though I know that religion is not supposed to be about pleasure.

A year after I was raped, I was asked to appear on a daytime television chat show about rape. I think it was *Kilroy*, though no longer presented by Kilroy. It soon became clear that I was coping better than the other 'victims'. 'But you must think about it all the time,' insisted the presenter. 'No, I don't,' I said truthfully, 'I have other things to think about.' I like to think that my education, specifically my religious education, played a part in my ability to put what had happened to me into perspective. Being raped didn't make me religious, it didn't make me believe in God, but it had the effect of bringing home to me that I do believe and that fundamental belief, which underscores everything in my life, made it possible for me to cope. □

GRANTA

JESUS WHO?

Alison Smith

'Christ taken up into a high mountain' by James Tissot

In July 1984 my brother Roy died in a car accident. He was eighteen. It was raining when he left for work that morning. A half-mile from our house an oncoming car spun out of control on the wet road and collided with my brother's car. Both drivers died.

In the days after the accident, our house filled with adults—friends of my parents, distant cousins, the parish priest, a half-dozen nuns. Until Sister Pat got the prayer circle going in the living room, they wandered through the rooms of our house looking for coffee and passing round boxes of Kleenex. I was fifteen that summer, old enough to understand death, but I could not believe that Roy was really gone. I walked to the end of the driveway several times that first afternoon, and looked up the road, waiting for his car to take the turn at the top of the hill and head toward home. He didn't show up.

The yard soon overflowed with neighbours and I discovered that the only place I could be alone was the upstairs bathroom. I sat on the hamper in the shadowed room, my foot wedged against the door, and called Jesus' name. Jesus appeared. He sat across from me, on the edge of the tub. The hem of his robe was tattered and dusty, and he looked winded, as if he had just walked up a steep hill. But I didn't mind. I was happy to see him. He pushed his hair out of his eyes, tucked it behind his ears and looked at me. 'Yes?' he said.

It wasn't the first time that I had seen Jesus. The first time happened when I was five. I was in the backyard, in the sandbox. My brother had been called into the house; he had a phone call from Bob. Roy was a solitary child. He had a limited social circle. Besides me, Bob, who lived across the street, was my brother's only friend. When he was not with me, he was either alone or with Bob. I was terribly jealous of Bob.

I was waiting for my brother to get off the phone so that we could get back to building a castle. Three mounds of sand stood in front of me, that's as far as we'd got before the phone rang. Roy was the mastermind behind all of our building projects and I didn't dare touch the mounds in his absence. It was a sunny day; the needles on evergreens that grew along the back fence shimmered in the afternoon light. I heard a voice behind me.

'Knock, knock.'

I turned around. 'Roy?'

'Knock, knock.'

I stood up and looked over the fence. The neighbour's yard was empty and silent. I sat back down in the sand. 'Who is it?' A soft-eyed, bearded man in a shapeless white shift stepped out from behind an evergreen. I recognized him right away. He looked exactly like the character in my illustrated children's Bible.

'Jesus.' I said. 'Aren't you supposed to be at church?' I was not allowed to talk to strange men, but Jesus was not a stranger. He was a friend of my father's. My father had spoken often about his relationship with Jesus Christ.

'Knock, knock,' Jesus said.

I blinked at him.

'Come on. Humour an old man.'

'You're not that old.'

'Knock, knock.'

I looked down at the three mounds of sand, looked behind me at the back door to the house. Roy was nowhere to be seen. 'Who's there?' I said.

'Aardvark.'

'Aardvark who?'

'Aardvark a million miles for one of your smiles.' He grinned and sat down on the edge of the sandbox. His pale feet crossed, the grass pricked his ankles.

'What are you doing here?' I asked.

'I came to see you.'

'Why?'

'You are a child of God.'

'No. You're the child of God. I'm the child of my mom and dad.'

I didn't want to be the child of God. Jesus was and I saw what it had done to him: his father was God, his mother was human, he was stuck in the middle, he didn't seem to fit in anywhere, and then they killed him for it.

'Okay,' he said. 'Have it your way.' He leaned over and placed a hand on the first mound of sand. 'What are you making?'

'Don't touch that,' I said.

He pulled his hand away.

'My brother and I are making a castle and I don't want to mess it up.'

The screen door slammed. I twisted my head around and watched

Roy walk towards the sandbox. When I turned back to Jesus, he was gone.

The next day, Roy went into the woods at the end of our street to collect lichen moss. He used it as groundcover on his model train set. He usually took me with him on these collection trips, but that morning he took Bob. They left just after breakfast. I watched them go. Roy walked down the road, Bob beside him, a paper shopping bag folded up and tucked under his arm.

Later that morning, I was sitting in the backyard alone and looking at the castle we had built the day before, when Jesus came walking across the lawn, a grin on his face. I waved. 'Hi, Jesus.'

He retrieved a baseball from behind the maple stump next to the garden and tossed it to me. It fell short. 'I've got a good one for you today,' he said as I ran after the ball.

'Knock, knock.'

'Who's there?'

'Centipede.'

'Centipede who?'

'Centipede on the Christmas tree.'

I stood up and held the ball in my hand. 'You shouldn't make fun of Santa.'

Jesus shrugged. He looked into the sandbox at the castle.

'He brings presents,' I said.

I tossed the ball to him. He missed it. His reflexes were so slow that he didn't move till the ball was well past him. I had never seen such a bad fielder. But I didn't say anything because, when he did finally reach for the ball, I saw the hole in the centre of his hand where they had driven the nail through. His hand looked like a doughnut. Dried blood still collected around the wound. I wondered why he didn't wash it off.

From the Bible stories my father had told me, I knew that Jesus had a serious guilt complex. He'd taken on the sins of the entire world and I had always felt sorry for him. And now here he was, wandering the suburban backyards of upstate New York, telling children knock-knock jokes. He looked lonely. I figured that a lot of people only talked to him because his father was God.

'Do you want to be my friend?' I asked. 'Is that why you're here?'

'Sure!' he said, a little too brightly. 'I have lots of friends. You could be one of them.'

I crossed my arms in front of my chest. 'Where are they?'

He looked around the yard. 'Everywhere.'

I sat down in the sandbox. 'I see.' I squinted up at him. 'Do you want to come in my sandbox?'

He stepped over the edge and stood next to the three-towered castle. The morning light filtering through the holes in his hands, his pale, bloody feet planted deep in the sand.

'Knock, knock,' he said.

I smiled. 'Who's there?'

Over the next few years, I saw a lot of Jesus. He waited for me on the front stoop in the morning and walked me to the school bus. At night, when I was restless, he sat at the end of my bed until I fell asleep. He showed up during particularly trying spelling tests at Saint Thomas More Elementary. I learned that Jesus preferred grape Bubblicious to strawberry (just like me), that he was a terrible speller, that he preferred Bread to the Beatles and that he cried when ET flew away on the bicycle. When we played ball, I was very patient with Jesus. Every time he missed a throw, I ran after the ball and retrieved it for him. And, no matter how much time he spent with me, no matter how many surprising things I learned about him, I kept our friendship a secret. I figured he would want it that way. I never even told Roy.

But my father figured it out. He saw me talking to the empty air in the backyard, gingerly tossing a ball and then running after it, and he knew. I could tell my father was impressed. In our insular Catholic world, Jesus Christ was still a big celebrity and I was his best and possibly only friend. Whenever my father mentioned my connection with Jesus, he did so quietly, on the sly, so that Roy and Mom did not hear. He knew how important it was to protect Jesus' privacy and I respected him for knowing that.

One day, while we were out in the backyard sprinkling plant food on his prize roses, he said, 'Why don't you ask Jesus for that baseball mitt? You know he loves you best of all.' He smiled and patted my shoulder. I was stunned. I stood back and watched him shake the powdered food over the roses. Clearly, my father understood things only up to a point. He had no real grasp on how to be friends with the man whose father was God. You don't just go around asking him for things, especially things you know your father is already getting you for your birthday. If you ask Jesus for things then you just look like any other star-struck, needy fan. I was disappointed in him. But I didn't want to offend my father. After all, he was the only one who had figured out that I was friends with Jesus. So I smiled appreciatively, as if he had just said something really smart.

The next day, I mentioned the conversation to Jesus. I wanted him to know that I knew other people asked him for stuff but that I was above that.

'Dad wants me to ask you for a baseball glove,' I said, 'but don't worry about it. I know he's buying me one for my birthday.'

Jesus didn't say anything, but he looked relieved. I offered him a piece of grape Bubblicious. He accepted.

'Knock, knock,' he said.

'Who's there?'

'Ammonia.'

'Ammonia who?'

'Ammonia a bird in a gilded cage.'

By the summer of 1984 I'd known Jesus for over ten years and I had never asked him for something I really needed. But that afternoon in the bathroom I was desperate. I sat on the hamper and watched Jesus. Perched on the edge of the tub across from me, his hands folded in his lap, he looked small and pale. His skin was so white that he almost blended into the white tile behind him. But this frail, fragile man was well connected. His father had the power to bring Roy back.

'Where is Roy?' I asked Jesus. 'When are you going to let him come back?' I was too shy to say upfront that I wanted my brother home right away, but we both knew what I was getting at.

Jesus did not answer my question. He would not even look at me. He stood up, wavering for a moment on the tile floor. He seemed nervous—his fingers played with the cuffs on his sleeves. I waited for him to answer me, but he did not. Instead he turned around and walked away. I watched the back of his head and the long hair where it fell over his shoulders and across his robe. I realized that, in all those years, I had never seen his back before.

I sat on the hamper and waited. I imagined Jesus going off to consult some divine ledger in which he could look Roy up. He'd scan the pages, a pencil in his mouth, his finger running down the column of tiny print. He'd find Roy's name, his birth date and the date of his preordained death. He'd stop there, his finger on the death date, remove the pencil from his mouth, erase '1984' and write in '2044'. It was easy: just change three numbers and Roy would be back. After ten years of tossing the ball and running after it for him, laughing at every one of his tired jokes, it didn't seem too much to ask.

I waited. The minutes ticked by. The sun wound its way across the sky. Outside the door, I heard my father weeping on the stairs, the women chanting Hail Marys in the living room, the clatter of dishes in the kitchen. But inside the bathroom, there was just silence. It had never been this quiet before. I felt a panic rise in my throat. I swallowed, pushing it back down.

Perhaps Jesus had been waylaid. There was some delay at the divine records office. Or perhaps he was with my father. My father was taking the news of the accident pretty badly, so it would not have surprised me if Jesus had gone to sit with him. I left the bathroom and went looking for him. But my father was alone, sitting on the third step of the stairs, an untouched cup of tea beside him.

Downstairs, Sister Pat cornered me in the front hall. She leaned in and said, 'He's with God now.' I nodded. I squeezed her hand. I said, 'I know.' She walked away. But I didn't know if she was referring to Roy or Jesus. Who was with God? I looked through the living room, the kitchen, the back hall, the basement—no Jesus. I ran out to the yard, to the very back, past the swing set. I looked in the garage, in the fort. He was gone.

I used to tell people that I lost my faith the day my brother died. I would tell them that as a child I heard Christ's voice and that it was beautiful, but one day I realized that God was a fraud. And I stopped. I turned my back on faith. But now I don't think that's true. I never rejected Christ. He rejected me. □

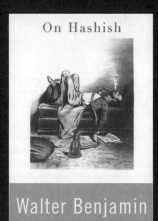

GOD AND ME
Nell Freudenberger

When I was seven, I sat down to draw God. God wore a pirate shirt, purple harem pants and a red fez. He sat in cross-legged meditation, the toes of his spangled slippers pointing up. I had a sense that Lord of Hosts would wear His hair as Dorothy Hamill wore hers (and as I wore mine) and so I gave God a bowl cut.

Nothing I drew, however, could match the illustrations in the *D'Aulaires' Book of Greek Myths*: Pan chasing Syrinx; Tithonus withering into a grasshopper; Cadmus's fierce warriors sprouting from dragon's teeth sown in the soil of Thebes. I got that book for my seventh birthday, and it was a treasured possession by the time we moved from New York City to Los Angeles later that year. My father, who had been a director of stage plays, was going to try his luck as a television writer.

Soon after arriving on the west coast, my parents began looking for a church. They tried Westwood Presbyterian, but the music was a disappointment. At St. Augustine's-by-the-sea, the sanctuary was Fifties modern, a style my mother found particularly uninspiring. The day after we'd attended our first service there, Father Phil rang our doorbell to find out how we'd enjoyed worshipping with him, a gesture that smacked of desperation. My parents must've thought of church simply as a way to integrate ourselves into a new community, but I noticed that we hadn't needed religion in New York. Church, I thought: a flighty, Californian thing.

Finally we found All Saints, an Episcopal congregation in Beverly Hills, only a ten-minute drive from our house. The building was Spanish colonial, with a red-tiled roof and whitewashed, vaulted ceilings. It boasted ornate wooden pulpits and a professional choir. As an additional enticement, chocolate doughnuts were available after the service.

My parents were sold, but I remained sceptical. Why would you call a church after 'all saints' instead of selecting one particular patron? The fact that they hadn't been able to choose did not bode well: they were as indecisive as my parents! It occurred to me that I couldn't in good conscience go to a Christian church. I accepted that the Titans had unseated Uranus, and that Metis had toppled Cronus by way of a magic herb, but I didn't see how this invisible Christian God had overcome mighty Zeus. Our God had impregnated one, very inexperienced Nazarethian girl, while Zeus had metamorphosed from bull to thundercloud to swan, sowing his seed from Thrace to Crete. I decided that my heart belonged to the Olympic pantheon: in short, I was a pagan.

When I confessed to my mother, she was not as dismayed as I had hoped. 'There's nothing wrong with that,' she told me. 'You can believe in both—or neither. We just want you to have the experience.' You could not believe in *both*, I wanted to tell her—unless you wanted to be struck by a thunderbolt, turned into a stone, or give birth to a monster who feasted on human flesh. But none of those things happened to my mother, and I was forced to accept the deeply unsatisfying conclusion of the D'Aulaires' book: *Everything must come to an end, and so did the rule of Zeus and the other Olympian gods. All that is left of their glory on earth are broken temples and noble statues.*

All Saints' greatest asset was its young priest, Matthew Finch, who bore a striking resemblance to the actor Peter Gallagher. His personal charisma was matched by his power at the pulpit: his sermons were funny, and they often focused on his personal failures. Like Zeus and Ares, Hera and Athena, Matthew Finch got jealous. He envied his neighbours and coveted their possessions. He got angry, he told us, and overreacted. Then he regretted it and got depressed. The more he talked about his flaws, the more self-deprecating his jokes, the more people liked him. He was worldly, modern, ambivalent: he was one of us.

I preferred church to Sunday School. There was something dismal about the small, blue room with its child-sized table and chairs. I had no problem paying attention in school, where my efforts were rewarded with consistent praise, but although Sunday School simulated the conditions of the classroom, it was clear to everyone that it didn't count. There were no grades; it was the weekend; and 'class' was taught by a parent who volunteered. The room's only decoration was a picture of Jesus in a plexiglass frame, opening his arms to His children, the sun setting in glorious Technicolor behind him. Jesus had soft, cinnamon-coloured hair, which he wore in shoulder length waves, like Willie Nelson. I looked elsewhere for salvation.

I didn't last long in the children's choir (standards were predictably high) but the acolyte programme almost won me over. Dressed in white robes, we carried tall candles in gilded sconces, a bronze cross, or, on especially holy days, a bejewelled censer that swung on a silver chain, trailing aromatic, grey smoke. When I carried the censer I was the sibyl of Delphi, dreaming and murmuring prophecies on the slopes of Mount Parnassus.

Everything must come to an end, however, and anyone who wanted to be confirmed was required to return to ecclesiastical education. Confirmation classes consisted of the memorization of biblical verses, which appealed to me. I had a good head for languages: my best subject was French, and the Bible seemed to me a similar kind of euphonious nonsense. I could look at the verses we were supposed to learn in the morning while I ate my cereal, or even in the car on the way to church, and by the time I got to class I was line perfect. By that afternoon, of course, the verses were gone.

I was disappointed to learn that the actual confirmation wouldn't include any kind of public performance. There was at least a prize at the end of the class for the student who had accumulated the most verses, and I triumphed in the face of a discouraging lack of competition. Of course, I hadn't memorized those verses for a prize. (I had memorized them in order to defeat the other children). Still, I couldn't help being disappointed by the contents of the irregular, foil-wrapped package: a plastic Christmas elf wearing overalls and a peaked cap, seated, inexplicably, on a fortune cookie. A fortune trailed from the ornament on a tired white ribbon: CHRIST IS BORN.

By the time I was in high school, we had stopped going to All Saints on a regular basis. Now on Sundays I focused my attention on the real family religion: academic success. My father hoped I might go to Harvard, his alma mater; I hoped I could manage that and maintain a social life at the same time. Because an all-girls school was challenging in that respect, the students paid an inordinate amount of attention to the romances of our teachers. In particular there was a very gentle young math teacher, Ms Keppler, who was engaged to be married. To my great surprise, we learned one day that her intended was our handsome, blue-eyed pastor, Matthew Finch.

I went away to Harvard and studied literature, as my father had. My parents remained connected to our school, if not to our church: my father served on the board, and my mother volunteered. That was how I heard, only a few years later, that Mrs Finch had become Ms Keppler again. According to the rumours, the math teacher was divorcing our minister because he had been beating her.

233

I remember the power of Matthew Finch's sermons: how he was able to make the case for a contemporary kind of faith in a way that was inspiring to the congregation of a Beverly Hills church, at the end of the twentieth century, just a few blocks from the consumer paradise of Rodeo Drive. There was also the music. When I hear baroque music being sung, I always wonder if it sounded different in the throats of the eighteenth-century choirs: does singing those notes require the sort of faith that moved the composers to write them? In the same way, I can't help wondering whether our pastor's empathy for the failings of his parishioners could have come from his own experience of sin—and if so, was it worth it?

Redemption is the Christian model, but it's hard to accept. We want our God to be perfect, which is why we don't like to draw him a human face. Perhaps the truly devout can dispense with pictures and music and architecture; the Greeks, in any case, could not. In one of my favourite illustrations, Apollo gives chase on human legs while Daphne's feet grow roots, her waist hardens to a narrow trunk, and her fingertips sprout dark green leaves. Only her face remains in the bark: a nymph's face, terrified. The god of music is left angry and bewildered, his arms thrown open, so it's hard to know if he would like to hold or slap her. ☐

GRANTA

ST LUCY'S HOME FOR GIRLS RAISED BY WOLVES

Karen Russell

Stage 1: The initial period is one in which everything is new, exciting, and interesting for your students. It is fun for your students to explore their new environment.
—from The Jesuit Handbook on Lycanthropic Culture Shock

At first, our pack was all hair and snarl and floor-thumping joy. We forgot the barked cautions of our mothers and fathers, all the promises we'd made to be civilized and ladylike, couth and kempt. We tore through the austere rooms, overturning dresser drawers, pawing through the neat piles of the Stage 3 girls' starched underwear, smashing light bulbs with our bare fists. Things felt less foreign in the dark. The dim bedroom was windowless and odourless. We remedied this by spraying exuberant yellow streams all over the bunks. We jumped from bunk to bunk, spraying. We nosed each other midair, our bodies buckling in kinetic laughter. The nuns watched us from the corner of the bedroom, their tiny faces pinched with displeasure.

'*Ay Caramba,*' Sister Maria de la Guardia sighed. '*Que barbaridad!*' She made the Sign of the Cross. Sister Maria came to St Lucy's from a Half-Way House in Copacabana. In Copacabana, the girls are fat and languid and eat pink slivers of guava right out of your hand. Even at Stage 1, their pelts are silky, sun-bleached to near invisibility. Our pack was hirsute and sinewy and mostly brunette. We had terrible posture. We went knuckling along the wooden floor on the calloused pads of our fists, baring row after row of tiny, wood-rotted teeth. Sister Josephine sucked in her breath. She removed a yellow wheel of floss from under her robes, looping it like a miniature lasso.

'The girls at our facility are *backwoods*,' Sister Josephine whispered to Sister Maria de la Guardia with a beatific smile. 'You must be patient with them.' I clamped down on her ankle, straining to close my jaws around the woolly XXL sock. Sister Josephine tasted like sweat and freckles. She smelled easy to kill.

We'd arrived at St Lucy's that morning, part of a pack fifteen-strong. We were accompanied by a mousy, nervous-smelling social worker; the baby-faced deacon; Bartholomew the blue wolfhound; and four burly woodsmen. The deacon handed out some stale cupcakes and said a quick prayer. Then he led us through the woods. We ran past the wild apiary, past the felled oaks, until we could see the white steeple of St Lucy's rising out of the forest. We stopped short at the edge of a muddy lake. Then the deacon took our brothers. Bartholomew helped him to herd the boys up the ramp of a small ferry. We girls ran along the shore, tearing at our new jumpers in a plaid agitation. Our brothers stood on the deck, looking small and confused.

Our mothers and fathers were werewolves. They lived an outsider's existence in caves at the edge of the forest, threatened by frost and pitchforks. They had been ostracized by the local farmers for eating their silled fruit pies and terrorizing the heifers. They had ostracized the local wolves by having sometimes-thumbs, and regrets, and human children. (Their condition skips a generation.) Our pack grew up in a green purgatory. We couldn't keep up with the purebred wolves, but we never stopped crawling. We spoke a slab-tongued pidgin in the cave, inflected with frequent howls. Our parents wanted something better for us; they wanted us to get braces, use towels, be fully bilingual. When the nuns showed up, our parents couldn't refuse their offer. The nuns, they said, would make us naturalized citizens of human society. We would go to St Lucy's to study a better culture. We didn't know at the time that our parents were sending us away for good. Neither did they.

That first afternoon, the nuns gave us free rein of the grounds. Everything was new, exciting and interesting. A low granite wall surrounded St Lucy's, the blue woods humming for miles behind it. There was a stone fountain full of delectable birds. There was a statue of St Lucy. Her marble skin was colder than our mother's nose, her pupilless eyes rolled heavenward. Doomed squirrels gambolled around her stony toes. Our diminished pack threw back our heads in a celebratory howl—an exultant and terrible noise, even without a chorus of wolf-brothers in the background. There were holes everywhere!

We supplemented these holes by digging some of their own. We interred sticks, and our itchy new jumpers, and the bones of the friendly, unfortunate squirrels. Our noses ached beneath an invisible assault. Everything was smudged with a human odour: baking bread, petrol, the nun's faint woman-smell sweating out beneath a dark perfume of tallow and incense. We smelled one another, too, with the same astounded fascination. Our own scent had become foreign in this strange place.

We had just sprawled out in the sun for an afternoon nap, yawning into the warm dirt, when the nuns reappeared. They conferred in the shadow of the juniper tree, whispering and pointing. Then they started towards us. The oldest sister had spent the past hour twitching in her sleep, dreaming of fatty and infirm elk. (The pack used to dream the same dreams back then, as naturally as we drank the same water and slept on the same red scree.) When our oldest sister saw the nuns approaching, she instinctively bristled. It was an improvised bristle, given her new, human limitations. She took clumps of her scraggly, nut-brown hair and held it straight out from her head.

Sister Maria gave her a brave smile.

'And what is your name?' she asked.

The oldest sister howled something awful and inarticulable, a distillate of hurt and panic, half-forgotten hunts and eclipsed moons. Sister Maria nodded and scribbled on a yellow legal pad. She slapped on a nametag: HELLO, MY NAME IS_____! 'Jeanette it is.'

The rest of the pack ran in a loose, uncertain circle, torn between our instinct to help her and our new fear. We sensed some subtler danger afoot, written in a language we didn't understand.

Our littlest sister had the quickest reflexes. She used her hands to flatten her ears to the side of her head. She backed towards the far corner of the garden, snarling in the most menacing register that an eight-year-old wolf-girl can muster. Then she ran. It took them two hours to pin her down and tag her: HELLO, MY NAME IS MIRABELLA!

'Stage 1,' Sister Maria sighed, taking careful aim with her tranquillizer dart. 'It can be a little over-stimulating.'

> Stage 2: After a time, your students realize that they must work to adjust to the new culture. This work may be stressful and students may experience a strong sense of dislocation. They may miss certain foods. They may spend a lot of time daydreaming during this period. Many students feel isolated, irritated, bewildered, depressed, or generally uncomfortable.

Those were the days when we dreamed of rivers and meat. The full moon nights were the worst! Worse than cold toilet seats and boiled tomatoes, worse than trying to will our tongues to curl around our false new names. We would snarl at one another for no reason. I remember how disorienting it was to look down and see two square-toed shoes instead of my own four feet. Keep your mouth shut, I repeated during our walking drills, staring straight ahead. Keep your shoes on your feet. Mouth shut, shoes on feet. Do not chew on your new penny loafers. Do not. I stumbled around in a daze, my mouth black with shoe polish. The whole pack was irritated, bewildered, depressed. We were all uncomfortable, and between languages. We had never wanted to run away so badly in our lives; but who did we have to run back to? Only the curled black grimace of the mother. Only the father, holding his tawny head between his paws. Could we betray our parents by going back to them? After they'd given us the choicest part of the woodchuck, loved us at our hairless worst, nosed us across the ice floes and abandoned us at the Half-Way House for our own betterment?

Physically, we were all easily capable of clearing the low stone walls. Sister Josephine left the wooden gates wide open. They unslatted the windows at night, so that long fingers of moonlight beckoned us from the woods. But we knew we couldn't return to the woods; not till we were civilized, not if we didn't want to break the mother's heart. It all felt like a sly, human taunt.

It was impossible to make the blank, chilly bedroom feel like home. In the beginning, we drank gallons of bathwater as part of a collaborative effort to mark our territory. We puddled up the yellow carpet of old newspapers. But later, when we returned to the bedroom, we were dismayed to find all trace of the pack musk had vanished. Someone was coming in and erasing us. We sprayed and sprayed every morning; and every night, we returned to the same ammonium eradication. We couldn't make our scent stick here; it made us feel invisible. Eventually we gave up. Still, the pack seemed to be adjusting on the same timetable. The advanced girls could already alternate between two speeds, 'slouch' and 'amble'. Almost everybody was fully bipedal.

Almost.

The pack was worried about Mirabella.

Mirabella would rip foamy chunks out of the church pews and replace them with ham bones and girl dander. She loved to roam the grounds wagging her invisible tail. (We all had a hard time giving that up. When we got excited, we would fall to the ground and start pumping our backsides. Back in those days we could pump at rabbity velocities. *Que horror!* Sister Maria frowned, looking more than a little jealous.) We'd give her scolding pinches. 'Mirabella,' we hissed, imitating the nuns. 'No.' Mirabella cocked her ears at us, hurt and confused.

Still, some things remained the same. The main commandment of wolf life is Know Your Place, and that translated perfectly. Being around other humans had awakened a slavish-dog affection in us. An abasing, belly-to-the-ground desire to please. As soon as we realized that someone higher up in the food chain was watching us, we wanted only to be pleasing in their sight. Mouth shut, I repeated, shoes on feet. But if Mirabella had this latent instinct, the nuns couldn't figure out how to activate it. She'd go bounding around, gleefully spraying on their gilded statue of St Lucy, mad-scratching at the virulent fleas that survived all of their powders and baths. At Sister Maria's tearful insistence, she'd stand upright for roll call, her knobby, oddly muscled legs quivering from the effort. Then she'd collapse right back to the ground with an ecstatic oomph! She was still loping around on all fours (which the nuns had taught us to see looked unnatural and ridiculous—we could barely believe it now, the shame of it, that we used to locomote like that!), her fists blue-white from the strain. As if she were holding a secret tight to the ground. Sister Maria de la Guardia would sigh every time she saw her. *'Caramba!'* She'd sit down with Mirabella and prise her fingers apart. 'You see?' she'd say softly, again and again. 'What are you holding on to? Nothing, little one. Nothing.'

Then she would sing out the standard chorus, 'Why can't you be more like your sister Jeanette?'

The pack hated Jeanette. She was the most successful of us, the one furthest removed from her origins. Her real name was GWARR! but she wouldn't respond to this any more. Jeanette spiffed her penny loafers until her very shoes seemed to gloat. (Linguists have since traced the colloquial origins of 'goody two-shoes' back to our facilities.) She could even growl out a demonic-sounding precursor to 'Pleased to meet you.' She'd delicately extend her former paws to visitors, wearing white kid gloves.

'Our little wolf, disguised in sheep's clothing!' Sister Ignatius liked to joke with the visiting deacons, and Jeanette would surprise everyone by laughing along with them, a harsh, inhuman, barking sound. Her hearing was still twig-snap sharp. Jeanette was the first among us to apologize; to drink apple juice out of a sippy cup; to quit eyeballing the cleric's jugular in a disconcerting fashion. She curled her lips back into a cousin of a smile as the travelling barber cut her pelt into bangs. Then she swept her coarse black curls under the rug. When we entered a room, our nostrils flared beneath the new odours: onion and bleach, candle wax, the turnipy smell of unwashed bodies. Not Jeanette. Jeanette smiled and pretended like she couldn't smell a thing.

I was one of the good girls. Not great and not terrible, solidly middle-of-the-pack. But I had an ear for languages, and I could read before I could adequately wash myself. I probably could have vied with Jeanette for the number one spot; but I'd seen what happened if you gave in to your natural aptitudes. This wasn't like the woods, where you had to be your fastest and your strongest and your bravest self. Different sorts of calculations were required to survive at the Home.

The pack hated Jeanette, but we hated Mirabella more. We began to avoid her, but sometimes she'd surprise us, curled up beneath the beds or gnawing on a scapula in the garden. It was scary to be ambushed by your sister. I'd bristle and growl, the way that I'd begun to snarl at my own reflection as if it were a stranger.

'Whatever will become of Mirabella?' we asked, gulping back our own fear. We'd heard rumours about former wolf-girls who never adapted to their new culture. It was assumed that they were returned to our native country, the vanishing woods. We liked to speculate about this before bedtime, scaring ourselves with stories of catastrophic bliss. It was the disgrace, the failure that we all guiltily hoped for in our hard beds. Twitching with the shadow question: '*Whatever will become of me?*'

We spent a lot of time daydreaming during this period. Even Jeanette. Sometimes I'd see her looking out at the woods in a vacant way. If you interrupted her in the midst of one of these reveries, she would lunge at you with an elder-sister ferocity, momentarily forgetting her human catechism. We liked her better then, startled back into being foamy old Jeanette.

In school, they showed us the St Francis of Assisi slide-show, again and again. Then the nuns would give us bags of bread. They never announced these things as a test; it was only much later that I realized that we were under constant examination. 'Go feed the ducks,' they urged us. 'Go practise compassion for all God's creatures.' *Don't pair me with Mirabella*, I prayed, *anybody but Mirabella*. 'Claudette,' Sister Josephine beamed, 'why don't you and Mirabella take some pumpernickel down to the ducks?'

'Ohhkaaythankyou,' I said. (It took me a long time to say anything; first I had to translate it in my head from the Wolf.) It wasn't fair. They knew Mirabella couldn't make breadballs yet. She couldn't even undo the twist tie of the bag. She was sure to eat the birds; Mirabella didn't even try to curb her desire to kill things—and then who would get blamed for the dark spots of duck blood on our Peter Pan collars? Who would get penalized with negative Skill Points? Exactly.

As soon as we were beyond the wooden gates, I snatched the bread away from Mirabella and ran off to the duck pond on my own. Mirabella gave chase, nipping at my heels. She thought it was a game. 'Stop it,' I growled. I ran faster, but it was Stage 2 and I was still unsteady on my two feet. I fell sideways into a leaf pile, and then all I could see was my sister's blurry form, bounding towards me. In a moment, she was on top of me, barking the old word for tug-of-war. When she tried to steal the bread out of my hands, I whirled around and snarled at her, pushing my ears back from my head. I bit her shoulder, once, twice, the only language she would respond to. I used my new motor skills. I threw dirt, I threw stones. 'Get away!' I screamed, long after she had made a cringing retreat into the shadows of the purple saplings. 'Get away, get away!'

Much later, they found Mirabella wading in the shallows of a distant river, trying to strangle a mallard with her rosary beads. I was at the lake; I'd been sitting there for hours. Hunched in the long cattails, my yellow eyes flashing, shoving ragged hunks of bread into my mouth.

I don't know what they did to Mirabella. Me they separated from my sisters. They made me watch another slide-show. This one showed images of former wolf-girls, the ones who had failed to be rehabilitated. Long-haired, sad-eyed women, limping after their former wolf packs in white tennis shoes and pleated culottes. A wolf-girl bank teller, her make-up smeared in oily rainbows, eating a raw steak on the deposit slips while her colleagues looked on in disgust. Our parents. The final slide was a bolded sentence in St Lucy's prim script:

DO YOU WANT TO END UP SHUNNED BY BOTH SPECIES?

After that, I spent less time with Mirabella. One night she came to me, holding her hand out. She was covered with splinters, keening a high, whining noise through her nostrils. Of course I understood what she wanted; I wasn't that far removed from our language (even though I was reading at a fifth-grade level, halfway into Jack London's *The Son of the Wolf*.)

'Lick your own wounds,' I said, not unkindly. It was what the nuns had instructed us to say; wound-licking was not something you did in polite company. Etiquette was so confounding in this country. Still, looking at Mirabella—her fists balled together like small, white porcupines, her brows knitted in animal confusion—I felt a throb of compassion. How can people live like they do? I wondered. Then I congratulated myself. This was a Stage 3 thought.

> Stage 3: It is common that students who start living in a new and different culture come to a point where they reject the host culture and withdraw into themselves. During this period, they make generalizations about the host culture and wonder how the people can live like they do. Your students may feel that their own culture's lifestyle and customs are far superior to those of the host country.

The nuns were worried about Mirabella, too. To correct a failing, you must first be aware of it as a failing. And there was Mirabella, shucking her plaid jumper in full view of the visiting cardinal. Mirabella, battling a racoon under the dinner table while the rest of us took dainty bites of peas and borscht. Mirabella, doing belly-flops into compost.

'You have to pull your weight around here,' we overheard Sister Josephine saying one night. We paused below the vestry window and peered inside.

'Does Mirabella try to earn Skill Points by shelling walnuts and polishing Saint-in-the-Box? No. Does Mirabella even know how to say the word walnut? Has she learned how to say anything besides a sinful "HraaaHA!" as she commits frottage against the organ pipes? No.'

There was a long silence.

'Something must be done,' Sister Ignatius said firmly. The other nuns nodded, a sea of thin, colourless lips and kettle-black brows.

'Something must be done,' they intoned. That ominously passive construction; a something so awful that nobody wanted to assume responsibility for it.

I could have warned her. If we were back home, and Mirabella had come under attack by territorial beavers or snow-blind bears, I would have warned her. But the truth is that by Stage 3 I wanted her gone. Mirabella's inability to adapt was taking a visible toll. Her teeth were ground down to nubbins; her hair was falling out. She hated the spongy, long-dead foods we were served, and it showed— her ribs were poking through her uniform. Her bright eyes had dulled to a sour whisky-colour. But you couldn't show Mirabella the slightest kindness any more—she'd never leave you alone! You'd have to sit across from her at meals, shoving her away as she begged for your scraps. I slept fitfully during that period, unable to forget that Mirabella was living under my bed, gnawing on my loafers.

It was during Stage 3 that we met our first purebred girls. These were girls raised in captivity, volunteers from St Lucy's School for Girls. The apple-cheeked fourth-grade class came to tutor us in playing. They had long golden braids or short, severe bobs. They had frilly-duvet names like Felicity and Beulah; and pert, bunny noses; and terrified smiles. We grinned back at them with genuine ferocity. It made us nervous to meet new humans. There were so many things that we could do wrong! And the rules here were different depending on which humans we were with: dancing or no dancing, checkers-playing or no checkers-playing, pumping or no pumping.

The purebred girls played checkers with us.

'These girl-girls sure is dumb,' my sister Lavash panted to me between games. 'I win it again! Five to none.'

She was right. The purebred girls were making mistakes on purpose, in order to give us an advantage. 'King me,' I growled, out of turn. 'I SAY KING ME!' and Felicity meekly complied. Beulah pretended not to mind when we got frustrated with the oblique, fussy movement from square to square and shredded the board to ribbons. I felt sorry for them. I wondered what it would be like to be bred in captivity, and always homesick for a dimly sensed forest, the trees you've never seen.

Jeanette was learning how to dance. On Holy Thursday, she mastered a rudimentary form of the Charleston. *'Brava!'* the nuns clapped. *'Brava!'*

Every Friday, the girls who had learned how to ride a bicycle celebrated by going on chaperoned trips into town. The purebred girls sold 700 rolls of gift-wrap paper and used the proceeds to buy us a yellow fleet of bicycles-built-for-two. We'd ride the bicycles uphill, a sanctioned pumping, a grim-faced nun pedalling behind each one of us. 'Congratulations!' the nuns would huff. 'Being human is like riding this bicycle. Once you've learned how, you'll never forget.' Mirabella would run after the bicycles, growling out our old names. Hwraa! Gwarr! Trrrrrr! We pedalled faster.

At this point, we'd had six weeks of lessons, and still nobody could do the Sausalito but Jeanette. The nuns decided we needed an inducement to dance. They announced that we would celebrate our successful rehabilitations with a Debutante Ball. There would be brothers, ferried over from the Home for Man-Boys Raised by Wolves. There would be a photographer from the *Gazette Sophisticate*. There would be a three-piece jazz band from West Toowoomba, and root beer in tiny plastic cups. The brothers! We'd almost forgotten about them. Our invisible tails went limp. I should have been excited; instead I felt a low mad anger at the nuns. They knew we weren't ready to dance with the brothers; we weren't even ready to talk to them. Things had been so much simpler in the woods. That night I waited until my sisters were asleep. Then I slunk into the closet and practised the Sausalito two-step in secret, a private mass of twitch and foam. Mouth shut-shoes on feet! Mouth shut-shoes on feet! Mouthshutmouthshut...

One night I came back early from the closet and stumbled on Jeanette. She was sitting in a patch of moonlight on the window sill, reading from one of her library books. (She was the first of us to sign for her library card, too.) Her cheeks looked dewy.

'Why you cry?' I asked her, instinctively reaching over to lick Jeanette's cheek and catching myself in the nick of time.

Jeanette blew her nose into a nearby curtain. (Even her mistakes annoyed us—they were always so well intentioned.) She sniffled and pointed to a line in her book: 'The lakewater was reinventing the forest and the white moon above it, and wolves lapped up the cold reflection of the sky.' But none of the pack besides me could read yet; and I wasn't ready to claim a common language with Jeanette.

The following day, Jeanette golfed. The nuns set up a miniature put-put course in the garden. Sister Maria dug four sandtraps and got

Clyde the grounds-keeper to make a windmill out of a lawnmower engine. The eighteenth hole was what they called a 'doozy', a minuscule crack in St Lucy's marble dress. Jeanette got a hole-in-one.

On Sundays, the pretending felt almost as natural as nature. The chapel was our favourite place. Long before we could understand what the priest was saying, the music instructed us in how to feel. The choir director, aggressively perfumed Mrs Valuchi, gold necklaces like pineapple rings around her neck—taught us more than the nuns ever did. She showed us how to pattern the old hunger into arias. Clouds moved behind the frosted oculus of the nave, glass shadows that reminded me of my mother. The mother, I'd think, struggling to conjure up a picture. A black shadow, running behind the watery screen of pines.

We sang at the chapel annexed to the Half-Way House every morning. We understood that this was the human's moon, the place for howling beyond purpose. Not for mating, not for hunting, not for fighting, not for anything but the sound itself. And we'd howl along with the choir, hurling every pitted thing within us at the stained glass. 'Sotto voce,' the nuns would frown. But you could tell that they were pleased.

Stage 4: As a more thorough understanding of the host culture is acquired, your students will begin to feel more comfortable in their new environment. Your students feel more at home and their self-confidence grows. Everything begins to make sense.

'Hey, Claudette,' Jeanette growled to me on the day before the ball. 'Have you noticed that everything's beginning to make sense?'

Before I could answer, Mirabella sprang out of the hall closet and snapped through Jeanette's homework binder. Pages and pages of words swirled around the stone corridor, like dead leaves off trees.

'What about you, Mirabella?' Jeanette asked politely, stooping to pick up her erasers. She was the only one of us who would still talk to Mirabella; she was high enough in the rankings that she could afford to talk to the scruggliest wolf-girl. 'Has everything begun to make more sense, Mirabella?'

Mirabella let out a whimper. She scratched at us and scratched at us, raking her nails along our shins, so hard that she drew blood. Then she rolled belly-up on the cold stone floor, squirming on a bed of spelling-bee worksheets. Above us, small pearls of light dotted the high, tinted window.

Jeanette frowned. 'You are a late bloomer, Mirabella! Usually, everything's begun to make more sense by Month Twelve at the latest.' I noticed that she stumbled on the word *bloomer*. HraaaHA! Jeanette could never fully shake our accent. She'd talk like that her whole life, I thought with a gloomy satisfaction, each word winced out like an apology for itself.

'Claudette, help me,' she yelped. Mirabella had closed her jaws around Jeanette's bald ankle and was dragging her towards the closet. 'Please. Help me to mop up Mirabella's mess.'

I ignored her and continued down the hall. I only had four more hours to perfect the Sausalito. I was worried only about myself. By that stage, I was no longer certain of how the pack felt about anything.

At seven o'clock on the dot, Sister Ignatius blew her whistle and frogmarched us into the ball. The nuns had transformed the rectory into a very scary place. Purple and silver balloons started popping all around us. Black streamers swooped down from the eaves and got stuck in our hair like bats. A full yellow moon smirked outside the window. We were greeted by blasts of a saxophone, and fizzy pink drinks, and the brothers.

The brothers didn't smell like our brothers any more. They smelled like pomade and cold, sterile sweat. They looked like little boys. Someone had washed behind their ears and made them wear suspendered dungarees. Kyle used to be a blustery alpha male, BTWWWR!, chewing through rattlesnakes, spooking badgers, snatching a live trout out of a grizzly's mouth. He stood by the punch bowl, looking pained and out of place.

'My stars!' I growled. 'What lovely weather we've been having!'

'Yeees,' Kyle growled back. 'It is beginning to look a lot like Christmas.' All around the room, boys and girls raised by wolves were having the same conversation. Actually, it had been an unseasonably warm and brown winter, and just that morning a freak hailstorm had sent Sister Josephina to an early grave. But we had only gotten up to Unit 7: Party Dialogue; we hadn't yet learned the vocabulary for Unit 12: How to Tactfully Acknowledge Disaster. Instead, we wore pink party hats and sucked olives on little sticks, inured to our own strangeness.

The Sisters swept our hair back into high, bouffant hairstyles. This made us look more girlish and less inclined to eat people, the way that squirrels are saved from looking like rodents by their poofy tails. I was wearing a white organdie dress with orange polka dots. Jeanette was wearing a mauve organdie dress with blue polka dots. Linette was wearing a red organdie dress with white polka dots. Mirabella was in a dark corner, wearing a muzzle. Her party culottes were duct-taped to her knees. The nuns had tied little bows on the muzzle to make it more festive. Even so, the jazz band from West Toowoomba kept glancing nervously her way.

'You smell astoooounding!' Kyle was saying, accidentally stretching the diphthong into a howl and then blushing. 'I mean…'

'Yes, I know what it is that you mean,' I snapped. (That's probably a little narrative embellishment on my part; it must have been months before I could really 'snap' out words.) I didn't smell astounding. I had rubbed a pumpkin muffin all over my body earlier that morning to mask my natural, feral scent. Now I smelled like a purebred girl, easy to kill. I narrowed my eyes at Kyle and flattened my ears, something I hadn't done for months. Kyle looked panicked, trying to remember the words that would make me act like a girl again. I felt hot, oily tears squeezing out of the red corners of my eyes. Shoesonfeet! I barked at myself. I tried again. 'My! What lovely weather…'

The jazz band struck up a tune.

'The time has come to do the Sausalito,' Sister Maria announced, beaming into the microphone, 'Every sister grab a brother!' She switched on Clyde's industrial flashlight, struggling beneath its weight, and aimed the beam in the centre of the room.

Uh-oh. I tried to skulk off into Mirabella's corner, but Kyle pushed me into the spotlight. 'No,' I moaned through my teeth, 'noooooo.' All of a sudden the only thing my body could remember how to do was pump and pump. In a flash of white-hot light, my months at St Lucy's had vanished, and I was just a terrified animal again. As if of their own accord, my feet started to wiggle out of my shoes. *Mouth shut*, I gasped, staring down at my naked toes, *mouthshutmouthshut*.

'Ahem. The time has come,' Sister Maria coughed, 'to do the

Sausalito.' She paused. 'The Sausalito,' she added helpfully, 'does not in any way resemble the thing that you are doing.'

Beads of sweat stood out on my forehead. I could feel my jaws gaping open, my tongue lolling out of the left side of my mouth. What were the steps? I looked frantically for Jeanette; she would help me, she would tell me what to do.

Jeanette was sitting in the corner, sipping punch through a long straw and watching me with uninterest. I locked eyes with her, pleading with the mute intensity that I had used to beg her for weasel bones in the forest. 'What are the steps?' I mouthed. 'The steps!'

'The steps?' Then Jeanette gave me a wide, true wolf smile. For an instant, she looked just like our mother. 'Not for you,' she mouthed back.

I threw my head back, a howl clawing its way up my throat. I was about to lose all my Skill Points, I was about to fail my Adaptive Dancing test. But before the air could burst from my lungs, the wind got knocked out of me. *Oomph!* I fell to the ground, my skirt falling softly over my head. Mirabella had intercepted my eye-cry for help. She'd chewed through her restraints and tackled me from behind, barking at unseen cougars, trying to shield me with her tiny body. '*Caramba!*' Sister Maria squealed, dropping the flashlight. The music ground to a halt. And I have never loved someone so much, before or since, as I loved my littlest sister at that moment. I wanted to roll over and lick her ears, I wanted to kill a dozen spotted fawns and let her eat first.

But everybody was watching; everybody was waiting to see what I would do. 'I wasn't talking to you,' I grunted from underneath her. 'I didn't want your help. Now you have ruined the Sausalito! You have ruined the ball!' I said more loudly, hoping the nuns would hear how much my enunciation had improved.

'You have ruined it!' my sisters panted, circling around us, eager to close ranks. 'Mirabella has ruined it!' Every girl was wild-eyed and itching under her polka dots, punch froth dribbling down her chin. The pack had been waiting for this moment for some time. 'Mirabella cannot adapt! Back to the woods, back to the woods!'

The band from West Toowoomba had quietly packed their instruments into black suitcases and were sneaking out the back. The boys had fled back towards the lake, bow ties spinning, snapping suspenders in their haste. Mirabella was still snarling in the centre of it all, trying to figure out where the danger was so that she could defend me against it. The nuns exchanged glances.

In the morning, Mirabella was gone. We checked under all the beds. I pretended to be surprised. I'd known she would have to be expelled the minute I felt her weight on my back. Clyde had come and told me this in secret after the ball, 'So you can say yer goodbyes.' I didn't want to face Mirabella. Instead, I packed a tin lunch pail for her: two jelly sandwiches on saltine crackers, a chloroformed squirrel, a gilt-edged placard of St Bolio. I left it for her with Sister Ignatius, with a little note: *Best wishes!* I told myself I'd done everything I could.

'Hooray!' the pack crowed. 'Something has been done!'

We raced outside into the bright sunlight, knowing full well that our sister had been turned loose, that we'd never find her. A low roar rippled through us and surged up and up, disappearing into the trees. I listened for an answering howl from Mirabella, heart-thumping— what if she heard us and came back? But there was nothing.

We graduated from St Lucy's shortly thereafter. As far as I can recollect, that was our last communal howl.

Stage 5: At this point your students are able to interact effectively in the new cultural environment. They find it easy to move between the two cultures.

One Sunday, near the end of my time at St Lucy's, the Sisters give me a special pass to go visit the parents. The woodsman had to accompany me; I couldn't remember how to find the way back on my own. I wore my best dress and brought along some prosciutto and dill pickles in a picnic basket. We crunched through the fall leaves in silence, and every step made me sadder. 'I'll wait out here,' the woodsman said, leaning on a blue elm and lighting a cigarette.

The cave looked so much smaller than I remembered it. I had to duck my head to enter. Everybody was eating when I walked in. They all looked up from the bull moose at the same time, my aunts and uncles, my sloe-eyed, lolling cousins, the parents. My uncle dropped a thigh bone from his mouth. My littlest brother, a cross-eyed wolf-boy who has since been successfully rehabilitated and is now a dour,

Karen Russell

balding children's book author, started whining in terror. My mother recoiled from me, as if I were a stranger. TRRR? She sniffed me for a long moment. Then she sank her teeth into my ankle, looking proud and sad. After all the tail-wagging and perfunctory barking had died down, the parents sat back on their hind legs. They stared up at me expectantly, panting in the cool grey envelope of the cave, waiting for a display of what I had learned.

'So,' I said, telling my first human lie. 'I'm home.'   □

GOD AND ME
Simon Gray

It happened in Montreal, when I was about seven years old, I'd
think—so let's say Montreal 1943, either spring or fall, because I
was wearing the appropriate clothes for weather that was neither
hot nor cold: short grey trousers, fresh new shirt, short socks and
light shoes, shoes I could run and jump in, shoes I could climb trees
in, nevertheless proper and respectable shoes. But what was I doing,
out and about in Montreal respectably dressed, on my own? Unless
it was a Sunday, and I wasn't where I was meant to be, which would
have been Sunday school, though I may have been on my way there,
or on my way back. It was very unusual to be without my brother
Nigel on an official occasion, such as Sunday school. Our
grandparents who, with our Aunt Gert, were looking after us for the
duration of the war, tended to send us about as a pair, presumably
on the understanding, entirely mistaken, that we would look after
each other. We are far more protective of each other, now that we
are elderly, than we ever were as children. Anyway, I clearly remember
being without Nigel and on my own and dressed as I've described
above, on a sunny afternoon in Montreal, climbing the highest tree,
a fir tree, in our neighbourhood. It was in a small park, more a scrap
of common land, with the back yards of houses around it, and a path
into it from Vendome Avenue, where we lived—No. 4047, Vendome
Avenue. I don't remember any other tree there, only this giant. The
intention of climbing it had grown out of my intense love of Batman's
sidekick, Robin, the Boy Wonder, who was often perched on a high
place, from which he would leap, with the assistance of ropes and
small machines, pulleys and so forth, concealed about his person—
but where about his person? He was covered from neck to toe by his
Boy Wonder costume, it was a sort of body stocking and tight briefs,
on his feet ankle-length bootees, and the cape and mask of course,
where could he possibly have kept his ropes and pulleys? Unless they
sprang out of his belt, which, now I think about it, was rather thick
and possibly contained Batman-designed devices—but that's not the
point, the point is the image I had of myself as the Boy Wonder,
scaling high, and posing there before rising even higher and then
descending rapidly on to the back of a gangster, or mobster, or mad
genius—then POW! WHAM! So forth.

As I've said, it was a very high tree, at least to me as I was then,
and I believe that it would be a high tree to me as I am now, in fact

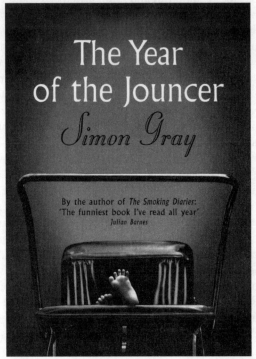

impossibly high if I were to contemplate climbing it. It took me quite a time to get to near the top, and then much longer to get on to the last horizontal branch—there were a few branches that stuck straight up, which offered no purchase—but the last branch was large and firm-looking, with a lot of foliage at the tip that shaped itself into a cup, perfect for sitting in, and swaying in, as I looked down into the empty backyards. I remember the silence from the backyards, and how they made a pattern of rectangles and squares when surveyed from a great height, and I can still feel in today's sixty-nine-year-old body how I swayed there, quivering with pride and fear, and then the cup opened, and dropped me down, and down and down. I fell upright, like a soldier, my arms clamped to my sides, fell through the branches which flicked and scraped at me like fingers, on and on and down and down, I seemed to fall for ever, at great speed, and apart from the rustling and snapping noises from the tree, quite silently. It was like a dream, at the end of which was death, I supposed. The last few branches clutched at me, pushed me from one to the other as if deliberately, and then I was at the bottom of the tree, with a few cuts and scratches, and almost no clothes, just tatters of trousers and shreds of my shirt and patches of socks—and immediately a sense, that I'd never had before in my life, and have never had since, of exaltation.

The earthbound feelings, of relief, shock, bewilderment, followed fairly swiftly and were swiftly followed in turn by mundane and panicky thoughts, that I had to get home in this semi-naked state, had to conceal these rags, because what would Gert say when she saw what I'd done to them? and I'd have to change into proper clothes that were like the ones I'd just lost—I know I did get home without being seen, did manage to change, but I don't remember further than that, though I expect Gert eventually found the rags, and I must have offered an explanation.

There have been other near misses in my life—for instance, in a cinema in Halifax, Nova Scotia, I moved my seat for no reason apart from a sense of uneasiness—a feeling, actually, that I was being watched—seconds before a large lump of concrete fell from the ceiling and landed in the seat I'd just left, and destroyed it. And then when I was teaching English to trainee caterers in Clermont-Ferrand—walking home very late, I stepped off the pavement to pick up something that was glistening in the gutter just as a large black car, a Citroën I expect, rushed noiselessly out of the dark, along the pavement and would certainly have run me over if I'd still been where I'd been a second before, instead of busy in the gutter. A few years later, again late at night, drunk and lost, I laid myself down on a low wall in a field outside Agrigento and fell asleep, and discovered when I woke up that on the other side of the wall was a sheer drop into a quarry— After each of these occasions I saw myself as amazingly lucky, as I would have been counted amazingly unlucky if I'd been killed—'he died in a ridiculous accident—fell off a wall into a quarry while he was asleep, my dear!—crushed by a lump of concrete in a cinema, of all places!—run over on a pavement in Clermont-Ferrand, French drivers!' I was certainly relieved and grateful to have survived, but I didn't feel as I felt when I landed at the foot of the tree, scratched and almost naked and exalted by something alien, mysterious and kindly that was the tree itself, or something within the tree, that was my fate and my God...

Sometimes, when I used to think about it, it would occur to me that perhaps I was saved, being saved, on those other occasions too, that really the same mysterious and kindly force had diverted my eye to the gutter, raised me from my seat in the cinema, kept me steady in my sleep on the wall, it was just that I'd grown up and become too educated to allow God's breath on my skin.

But when I think about it now, at this end of my life, it occurs to me that if indeed I've been saved so often, it might be for an altogether ghastlier and more appropriate end than falling through a tree or off a wall, crushed in a cinema or on a pavement, that really I'm in a novel that somebody is still writing, or at least is still writing as I write this.   □